$\mathcal{B}c$

Rethinking democracy

Rethinking democracy

Freedom and social cooperation in politics, economy, and society

CAROL C. GOULD

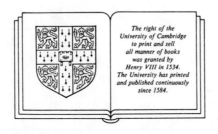

The right of the
University of Cambridge
to print and sell
all manner of books
was granted by
Henry VIII in 1534.
The University has printed
and published continuously
since 1584.

CAMBRIDGE UNIVERSITY PRESS

CAMBRIDGE

NEW YORK   NEW ROCHELLE   MELBOURNE   SYDNEY

Published by the Press Syndicate of the University of Cambridge
The Pitt Building, Trumpington Street, Cambridge CB2 1RP
32 East 57th Street, New York, NY 10022, USA
10 Stamford Road, Oakleigh, Melbourne 3166, Australia

©Cambridge University Press 1988

First published 1988

Printed in the United States of America

Library of Congress Cataloging-in-Publication Data
Gould, Carol C.
Rethinking democracy.
Bibliography: p.
Includes index.
1. Democracy.   2. Liberty.   3. Political
participation.   I. Title.
JC423 G67   1988   321.8   87–24254

British Library Cataloguing in Publication Data
Gould, Carol C.
Rethinking democracy : freedom and social
cooperation in politics, economy, and society.
1. Democracy
I. Title
321.8'01   JC423

ISBN 0 521 35048 4

For M.W.W.

Contents

Contents

Acknowledgments

I would like to thank the Rockefeller Foundation for its support of my research on this book, which began in 1978–9 when I held a Humanities Fellowship. I would also like to express my thanks to Stevens Institute of Technology for a research leave in 1986–7, during which time I made final revisions of the manuscript.

The development of my ideas was aided by criticisms and comments from many colleagues, on the occasions on which I presented various earlier versions of chapters of the manuscript, including the meetings of the American Philosophical Association, Eastern Division (1980), the Metaphysical Society of America (1979 and 1983), the Society for Philosophy and Public Affairs, New York Chapter (1981 and 1982), the Northeastern Political Science Association (1985), the Ninth Plenary Congress of the American Section of the Society for Philosophy of Law and Social Philosophy (1982), the World Congress of Philosophy of Law and Social Philosophy (1979), the Seventeenth World Congress of Philosophy (1983), the Tenth Interamerican Congress of Philosophy (1981), the Conference on Socialism and Democracy (University of Lund, 1980), the Inter-University Centre of Postgraduate Studies (Dubrovnik, 1979 and 1981), the Conference on Foundations of Science and Ethics (Dubrovnik, 1981); and invited talks at Loyola University of Chicago (1982), Balliol College, Oxford (1981), the Institute of Philosophy and the Institute for Systems Theory, USSR Academy of Sciences (1986), the Van Leer Jerusalem Institute (1987), and at the Universities of Vienna (1981), Stockholm (1982), Uppsala (1982), Turku (1982), and Frankfurt (1982). I would like to express my appreciation to my colleagues at these various meetings for their thoughtful comments.

An earlier version of Chapter 4 was published in *Economic Justice: Private Rights and Public Responsibilities*, edited by Kenneth Kipnis and Diana T. Meyers, Totowa, NJ: Rowman and Allanheld, 1985;

Acknowledgments

and of Chapter 6 in *The Journal of Philosophy*, Vol. LXXVII, no. 11 (November 1980). A part of Chapter 9 was published as "Socialism and Democracy" in *Praxis International*, Vol. I, no. 1 (April 1981).

Among many other colleagues who have helped me to formulate and refine the ideas in this book, I would like especially to thank Professors Virginia Held, Robert Paul Wolff, David Schweickart, Sidney Morgenbesser, Mihailo Marković, Carl Wellman, Mitchell Aboulafia, John Girling, and the late Richard Martin. I am also grateful to Jonathan Sinclair-Wilson, my original editor at Cambridge University Press, for his help in seeing the manuscript through, and to the current editor, Terence Moore, for his assistance in the final stages of publication.

Finally, I would like to express deep thanks to my husband Marx Wartofsky, to whom this book is dedicated, for his incisive criticisms and very helpful suggestions, and for his enthusiastic support.

Introduction

DEMOCRACY ON NEW FOUNDATIONS

This book proposes a fundamental rethinking of the theory of democracy. It presents the philosophical foundations of a theory that argues that democratic decision-making not only should apply to politics but should be extended to economic and social life as well. I offer a normative argument for the right of participation in decision-making in all of these domains. The book therefore speaks to such contemporary developments as workers' self-management and participation in economic decision-making, the worldwide movement for greater political democracy, as well as the issue of the democratization of decision-making in social and cultural institutions.

The book's concern, however, is principally philosophical. Thus it starts from a reconstruction of the ethical foundations of democracy, in which I redefine the traditional concepts of freedom and equality. I develop an argument concerning the preeminent value of the freedom of individuals and their equal right to the conditions of self-development. I make a case for the conception of positive freedom, interpreted in a new way, as central to an adequate theory of democracy. A principal concern of the argument here is to show how the apparently conflicting values of individual liberty, on the one hand, and of social cooperation and social equality, on the other, are in fact compatible. On the basis of these arguments, I conclude that democratic participation in decision-making is a requirement as much in social and economic contexts as in political ones.

A further philosophical focus of the work is the analysis of the ontological foundations of democracy, that is, of the nature of individuals as agents and of their social relations, as well as of the nature of society and of institutions as constituted entities. The book also reformulates the fundamental political conceptions of property, authority, economic justice, and human rights. On the basis of these various philosophical considerations, I go on to propose concrete forms of social and economic institutions that would serve to realize the philosophical principles. Thus the book addresses such issues as the forms of workers' self-management, democratic control of technology, and democracy in international relations.

One of the important concerns in this connection is to establish the normative and theoretical foundations for workers' self-management. Such self-management is, in general, understood as either the workers' participation in or control of the decision-making of the firms in which they work. The central questions that arise here are, first, whether workers can be said to have rights to such participation and control; and if so, what grounds there are for such rights. Or instead, is the argument concerning workers' self-management simply a pragmatic or empirical question of the relative efficiency (or inefficiency) of this form with respect to other forms of management or control in the economy? Second, if there are rights to workers' self-management, what exactly are these rights *to?* Do workers simply have a right to some input into managerial decisions that are ultimately made by others (that is, to what has been called "worker participation"); or do they have a more extensive right to make managerial decisions themselves, either directly or through a right to appoint and recall managers (what has been called "worker control")? Third, what is the locus of such decision-making? Is it at the level of the immediate or smallest work unit or shop committee, or is it at the level of the firm? Or again, is such decision-making properly located at the level of workers' representation in industrywide or national economic policy-making and planning? In this book, I will address these questions and argue for a particular view of workers' self-management in the broader context of the democratic theory that I develop here and will consider a model of such workers' self-management in the context of a market economy with certain planning functions.

The premise of this book is that there is a need for a new theory of democracy and for a rethinking of its philosophical foundations. This need derives, in the first instance, from the inadequacies of the traditional democratic theory of liberal individualism which, despite the strength of its emphasis on individual liberty, fails to take sufficiently into account the requirements of social cooperation and social equality. However, the alternative theories – socialist or holist – which emphasize such social cooperation and equality are also problematic in that they tend to subordinate individual rights to the needs of the community or to the welfare of society as a whole. These two countervailing political philosophies, which dominate contemporary thought, thus present a stark choice between what appear to be the irreconcilable values of individuality and sociality. But are these two values in fact incompatible? Or, on the contrary, can they be integrated in a consistent political theory? One of the central claims of this book, as I indicated earlier, is that they are in fact compatible and that it is through the extension of democracy that these values can be most fully realized.

A new theory of democracy would thus preserve the values of individual liberty and of equality and social cooperation represented in the prevailing alternatives, but would eliminate those features of these views which make them unacceptable. Such a new theory cannot, however, be a cleaned-up version of the old theories, which simply combines their virtues and eliminates their vices. It would have to stand on new foundations and establish its own coherence. To this end, the primary values of freedom and equality have to be rethought.

The intentions of this book are therefore constructive and not primarily critical. The attempt is to provide normative foundations and to give philosophical arguments for this new conception of democracy. However, in the section that follows, as well as elsewhere in the book, it will be useful to consider critically, even if briefly, those alternative views that provide the background for the development of my own theses.

LIBERAL INDIVIDUALISM VERSUS SOCIALISM: A PRELIMINARY CRITIQUE OF ALTERNATIVE POLITICAL PHILOSOPHIES

The first of these views, liberal individualism, starts from the premise of individual liberty as the principal value to be protected by government. It also holds that the right to private property is to be secured by the state against interference. This view has in the main been developed as a theory of political democracy, in which equal civil liberties and political rights are assured by the state. All other activities, including the economic, the social, and the personal, are regarded as private rather than public matters and therefore outside the sphere of political decision (except insofar as the government protects such private activities from interference).[1]

This liberal individualist view has been criticized on two major counts: first, for its conception of human beings as asocial, egoistic individuals whose fundamental motivation in acting is the satisfaction of their own interests. It has been argued that this view therefore cannot account for social cooperation or common interests among individuals, except perhaps as aggregations of individual self-interest and therefore as purely instrumental in satisfying such interests. Thus, the argument continues, liberal individualism fails to capture the social nature of much human activity or indeed even serves to legitimate antisocial and selfish modes of behavior, which are unacceptable on moral grounds.[2] Second, this theory has been criticized, especially by socialist critics, for countenancing and justifying extreme inequalities in economic and social life by protecting the right to the unlimited accumulation of private property regardless of its social con-

4

sequences. It has been argued that such social and economic inequalities tend to undermine the political equality at the basis of democracy because of the inordinate political power that great concentrations of wealth are able to exercise. On the basis of these two criticisms, it is further objected that liberal individualism in this form necessarily counterposes individual liberty to social welfare and that it subordinates the latter to the former. That is, because of its exclusive emphasis on the values of individual liberty and initiative, it disregards the well-being of society as a whole, and especially of its neediest members.

Against such criticisms, however, the liberal individualist has argued that neither economic equality nor social cooperation can be legislated, since to enforce them would be incompatible with individual freedom of choice. Rather, they must be left to voluntary decision and the free market. Further, it has been argued in defense of this individualism that the welfare of society, and even the well-being of its neediest members, is best served by the pursuit of individual self-interest and by the efficiency of a free market that reflects the unrestricted liberty and initiative of individuals rather than by the constraints on this liberty that a welfare state would impose. The critics' response to this defense in turn has been either to argue that the free market is a myth in that the market economy is manipulated by the most powerful economic interests in their own favor, or to argue that the free market is itself instrumental in leading to and exacerbating economic inequalities. In either case, it is argued that such economic inequalities undercut political equality and thus the very equal liberties and rights of individuals that liberal individualism proposes as its primary value.

My own criticism of liberal individualism as it is developed in this book has a somewhat different focus from these classical criticisms. It deals principally with the concept of negative freedom, or freedom from external constraint or interference, which underlies the liberal individualist theory of democracy. I show how such negative freedom, while it is a necessary condition for the development of full or concrete freedom, is insufficient in itself and needs to be supplemented or enlarged by a conception of positive freedom, as freedom of self-development.

Socialist theory, which developed in part in response to what were perceived as the failings of liberal individualism, emphasized the values of social and economic equality and social cooperation. It saw social and economic inequality and exploitation as arising from the institutions of private property and capitalist competition, for which liberal individualism was held to provide the ideological support. The socialist critique argued that the liberal individualist values of liberty and political democracy remain empty or merely formal if the material means of well-being are lacking or are so inequitably distributed that some individuals are totally dependent on others for their livelihood. Further, in contrast with the liberal individualist conception of individual self-interest as the principal motive of action, socialist theory emphasizes the centrality of social or collective interest – whether as class interest or as human solidarity – as a motive for action. Thus, socialist theory proposes social and economic equality and social cooperation as norms for the good society. It is therefore not principally a theory of political democracy, as liberal individualism tends to be, but it bears on the development of the conception of democracy, both in its critique and in the alternative it poses.

With respect to the question of how to implement the norms of equality and social cooperation, socialist theory has had several interpretations. The dominant one, which has also served to guide the practice of most actually existing socialist societies, posits the need for a strong and centralized state power and for centralized planning of the economy. Such political control of the economy and of planning is seen as necessary for the development of production to meet the needs for material well-being and for the development of a system of distribution that will satisfy the norm of equality. The furtherance of social cooperation is seen as stemming from increasingly collectivized forms of work, while the state

6

itself is seen as the representation or expression of the social whole or the collective interest.

The main problem with these interpretations of socialist theory and with the attendant practices, as critics have pointed out, is that they have condoned and led to authoritarian state power and the repression of individual liberty and political democracy. In theoretical terms, this has meant the subordination of individual rights to the requirements of social and economic equality and social cooperation. Individual freedom, in this context, has often been regarded either as "petty bourgeois individualism" – a luxury for some to satisfy their needs without regard for the social and economic unfreedom of the majority – or, in any richer sense of freedom, as something that would have to wait for its realization until after the achievement of equality. Further inadequacies of this socialist view that reveal themselves in practice are, first, that it fails to live up to its own theoretical norm of social and economic equality and instead leads to new forms of social and economic hierarchy and stratification. These consist in the large discrepancies with respect to social status and economic power and privilege between those in authority and those not. Second, the central planning and command economies characteristic of these societies have been inefficient in the very project of increasing production to provide the conditions for well-being and in meeting the goal of equalizing distribution.

It may seem from this account that the problems with socialist theory arise only with respect to the implementation of its norms and the interpretations to which this has given rise. However, there are inadequacies that may be noted in the basic theoretical structure itself, though even here, one must be careful to distinguish the work of Karl Marx himself from the interpretations and extensions of it in the most prevalent forms of socialist theory.[3] In such socialist theory, there is a tendency to counterpose sociality and individuality, and to posit the primacy of the social whole over individuals. Such holism, as I will argue later, leads to the disregard of individual differences and of the requirements of individual liberty, and in practice serves to legitimate the overarching authority of the state over its citizens. Finally, the theory has often tended to be reductionistic in the interpretation of all social phenomena as, in the last instance, economic in their determination. This economistic tendency has led to the denigration of other dimensions of social life and in particular of political freedom and democracy.

Both liberal individualist and socialist theories have been revised in response to the criticisms made of them, as well as in response to historical changes in social, political, and economic practices. Such theoretical developments as the pluralist approaches of Schumpeter or of Dahl, the contractarianism of Rawls, and the libertarianism of Nozick may all be regarded as in some sense modifications or revisions of liberal individualism. Similarly, traditional socialist theories have been considerably revised in such approaches as that of democratic socialism (e.g., in the work of the Yugoslav *Praxis* group), or that of the theory of communicative action of Jürgen Habermas. And some political theorists have explicitly attempted to mediate between the values of the alternative traditions of liberal individualism and socialism. Here, one may mention the theories of democracy of C.B. Macpherson and Carole Pateman.

These recent theories will be critically discussed at various points in subsequent chapters, in the course of developing my own proposal for a new democratic theory. However, it may be useful to note these theories here and to suggest briefly the ways in which they fail to resolve the original tension between individual freedom, on the one hand, and equality and social cooperation, on the other.

Pluralist theories, such as those of Schumpeter or Dahl,[4] generally make the claim to being value-free descriptions or empirically based accounts of how actual democracies function in fact, rather than as they have been ideally or normatively proposed. Pluralism differs from classical liberal individualism in taking politics as an arena of the conflicting interests of groups in a society, rather than of the representation of the choices of individuals, each of whom pursues his or her separate interests. Democracy is seen as a functional system in which an equilibrium among conflicting groups is established by means of the mechanism of periodic elections. This electoral procedure is understood as a competition among elites for political power which is achieved by gaining the support of various groups or coalitions of such groups, rather than as an expression of the popular will. This view eschews any notion of a common good as anything more than a political myth. It may be noted parenthetically that Dahl in a later work has himself assessed the problems and defects in pluralist democracy[5] and has also presented a sympathetic account of workers' self-management in a recent book.[6]

Pluralist theories may be criticized on several points relevant to my argument: First, this approach not only leaves untouched the inequalities outside the political sphere (as does liberal individualism generally), but it introduces these inequalities ("realistically," to be sure) as systemic features of the competition for political power among conflicting groups. It may be claimed that in such competition, in which elites need the support of diverse groups for political power, these elites would be responsive to the needs of socially and economically disadvantaged groups whose support they seek. However, those groups that have access to wealth or economic power have a clear advantage in influencing the electoral process and political decision-making by their access to, and use of, the media, lobbying, etc., which require great outlays of money in contemporary political contexts. Second, in regarding democracy as a method by which elites compete for political power, this view denigrates representation and participation in politics as at best instrumentalities for the election of elites and at worst as a threat to social stability. Of course, pluralist theory, as noted, claims to be merely descriptive and value-free and hence realistic in its account of actual democracies. But, as a number of critics have pointed out, such descriptivism serves, in effect, to justify the status quo by redefining democracy in these terms and making competition among elites for political power appear acceptable as a fact of life or, indeed, as the best possible alternative.[7]

A third criticism of this pluralist approach is that it fails to give an adequate account of sociality or cooperation, for its characterization of groups takes them to be no more than temporary aggregates of individuals bound only by their individual self-interest, which they pursue instrumentally through the group. In thus reducing social cooperation to the vector-sum of individual self-interests, pluralism, as I will argue, does not resolve the antithesis between individuality and sociality.

John Rawls's contractarian theory addresses the claim not only of political liberty but also of economic equality within the context of a theory of distributive justice.[8] His theory, like pluralism, may be seen as a contemporary revision of liberal individualism, but one that takes as a major value the amelioration of social and economic inequalities. In this respect, one may characterize it as welfare liberalism. Like liberal individualism, Rawls's theory posits equal basic liberties, including civil liberties and political rights, in his first principle of justice. In this sense, it implies a theory of political democracy. Again, in the tradition of classical liberal individualism, Rawls uses the procedural model of a contract, based on equal rationality, to establish his principles of justice. However, Rawls goes beyond the limits of traditional liberal individualism to address the problems of social and economic inequality as questions of justice. He proposes as a second principle of justice the requirement of fair equality of opportunity and what he calls the difference principle according to which inequalities in the distribution of social and economic goods are justified only if such inequalities work to the benefit of the least advantaged. He claims that the application of such a principle would result in a tendency to equality and that it is compatible with either capitalism or market socialism. Another contrast with the traditional liberal individualist view and its conception of society as the domain of the pursuit of individual self-interest is Rawls's view that there are genuinely common or shared aims among individuals and that this gives rise to "social union." This conception, together with his emphasis on reciprocity, marks Rawls's concern with the theme of social cooperation in this theory.

Yet for all of Rawls's concern with social and economic equality and social cooperation, I will argue later that he does not give an adequate account of these values or of how they are integrated with individual liberty. For example, as several critics have noted, Rawls does not recognize how certain social and economic inequalities undermine the equal liberty which he takes to be preeminent.[9] Moreover, he doesn't see that the principle of equal liberty, with its requirement of democracy, ought to apply to social and economic life, as well as to the political domain to which he restricts it. Further, it may be seen that Rawls's "difference principle" is compatible with economic exploitation and possibly also with social domination (as a number of critics have also argued). In these ways, I will argue, Rawls's theory fails to give an adequate account the integral relation between political liberty and social welfare.

Another point on which I will criticize Rawls's view is his exclusive concern with distributive justice and his lack of any theory of entitlement. By contrast, I will propose a conception of equality and justice in the production process, and will consider what theory of entitlement and of property is compatible with justice. Finally, though Rawls's remarks about social union as an account of social cooperation and of common purpose are suggestive in taking his account beyond individualism, they are not developed very far, and more important, this conception is extrinsic to the basic principles of his theory, which I will argue remain individualist. Likewise, though Rawls recognizes the importance of reciprocity, it will be seen that his account of it remains limited to a relatively asocial conception of returning benefit for benefit done, or "tit for tat."

Another contemporary version of liberal individualism is not, like Rawls's, an attempt to revise it so as to include considerations of welfare and equality but rather is an attempt to return to original principles of individualism. This is

11

the theory of Robert Nozick,[10] which we might characterize as libertarian fundamentalism. He argues against the revisions of liberal individualism (such as that of Rawls), which posit what Nozick calls "end-state principles"–for example, equality or welfare. On Nozick's view, such an approach tends to justify intervention by the state in order to achieve these ends and this necessarily interferes with the liberty of individuals.

According to Nozick, individuals have rights that express the inviolability and separateness of persons and serve as moral constraints on the actions of other individuals and on the policies of a state. The theory proposes a conception of justice as entitlement, in which one has a right to whatever one has acquired justly or has received justly from another, that is, by free gift or voluntary exchange.

Unlike Rawls, Nozick emphasizes production as well as distribution and he appears to suggest that individual productive activity and free exchange is the basis for just distribution. As might be expected from Nozick's individualist orientation, he sees social cooperation (in the economy, at least) as a matter of voluntary individual transfers or exchanges, in which each individual acts as a "miniature firm." One may say that Nozick takes free market exchange as the model of social interaction in this context. Finally, although Nozick argues for individual choice and voluntary association as a basis for the state, he does not develop his theory as a theory of democracy in any explicit way. Rather, he makes a distinction between the minimal state as a framework that protects individual liberties, and the various communities within it whose members ought to be free to arrange whatever social order or way of life they agree upon, presumably including undemocratic ones.

While Nozick is correct in suggesting that there ought to be a relation between entitlement and productive activity, I will argue that he is wrong to base this entitlement exclusively on individual acts of appropriation. Instead, I will propose that in addition to individual rights of entitlement, there is also what we may call social entitlement, based on social labor.

Further, since Nozick reduces sociality and cooperation to sequential individual one-on-one exchanges or relations, his view may also be criticized, as traditional liberal individualism has been, for failing to recognize the distinctive nature of common activity and of joint interests, which are characteristic of much of social, political, and economic life.

Finally, rejecting the view that there is exploitation in a free market economy, Nozick argues that in such a free market there is voluntary and uncoerced exchange between workers and employers, which meets the criteria of justice in transfer. In my criticism of this view, I will show that Nozick's argument fails to meet his own criterion of just transfer. Moreover, Nozick's acceptance of even extreme social and economic inequalities in the name of preserving individual liberties (in the practices of just acquisition and transfer) will be seen to be based on a too narrow conception of individual freedom and one that ignores the liberty of those whose actions are severely constrained by their economic dependence and inequality. Thus I will argue that Nozick's view, far from resolving the tension between liberty and equality, or between the individual and the social, reverts instead to a position that either ignores or explains away these tensions, or sees them as the acceptable consequences of the proper regard for liberty as the primary value.

Socialist theory, like liberal individualism, has also been revised in view of what were taken to be theoretical and practical defects in the prevailing formulations and their applications. One major revision of this sort, which is especially relevant to democratic theory, is what may be broadly characterized as democratic socialism. In general, this set of approaches combines a commitment to socialism with an emphasis on political democracy. Democratic socialism has arisen as a response to authoritarian or totalitarian forms – especially Stalinism – that developed in actually existing socialist societies. It has also been a critical response to the economic and social failures of central planning and bureaucracy, and to the economic and social hierarchies of wealth and power that have arisen in these societies in conflict with their stated ideal of social equality. With respect to theory, democratic socialism has proposed alternatives to those received interpretations of socialism that holistically subordinate the individual to the social whole and that subordinate political democracy and individual liberties to the requirements of economic development and social cooperation. Such democratic socialist approaches remain socialist in retaining the notion of social, rather than private, ownership and control of the means of production. In this context, they stress the original socialist idea that those who produce should be in control of production and that there should be no privileged hierarchies of wealth or political power in society.

Democratic socialism is not a unitary approach, but represents a variety of theoretical and political movements. Its forms range from the indigenous democratic reform movements within existing socialist societies (e.g., Solidarity in Poland, or others that argue against central bureaucracies and for workers' self-management and the protection of individual liberties and political rights); through Western European socialism, which combines programs for public ownership or control of certain basic parts of the economy with a strong commitment to political democracy; to U.S. democratic socialism, which includes such directions as those stemming from the New Left for participatory democracy in political, economic, and social life, and those that emphasize workers' self-management and economic democracy; or again, those that propose a greater role for government in regulating the economy and planning in the public interest. Not to be included here as forms of democratic socialism would be movements or theories (e.g., social democracy) that are principally aimed at welfare-oriented reforms within a capitalist framework.

Perhaps the most clearly articulated theoretical formulation of democratic socialism, though one which is distinctive in some important respects, is that provided by the political philosophers of the *Praxis* group in Yugoslavia.[11] It may be useful to consider briefly a few elements of their approach to see whether they resolve the conflict of values between individual freedom and social equality and cooperation, which is of concern here.

The central characteristic of the theory of the *Praxis* philosophers is its critique of authoritarian and bureaucratic forms of socialist practice, which it sees as standing in direct contradiction to the Marxist conception of the human being as, in their words, a "free, creative being of praxis." By this they mean that human beings creatively transform not only the world of objects but also themselves and their social relations. Human beings are thus also essentially social beings. With Marx, the *Praxis* philosophers see alienated forms of activity as inhibiting this creative potential. The overcoming of such alienation is understood to require not only social ownership of the means of production and the end of class exploitation, but also full democratic participation in all aspects of political, social, and economic life. The *Praxis* philosophers see the persistence of such alienation both in capitalist forms of society and in the authoritarian, bureaucratic, and undemocratic forms of existing socialist societies. The solution that they see as the way of realizing socialist democracy in the economy is workers' self-management, in which all those who take part in a productive enterprise participate in making decisions concerning it, for example, in fixing wages, setting prices, determining the process of production, and in electing managers.[12] In addition, the theory proposes such self-management, decentralized where feasible, as a model for democratic decision-making in all other domains.

Although the democratic socialism of the *Praxis* philosophers does emphasize the importance of participation in democratic decision-making as a condition for extending social cooperation and equality while preserving individual freedom, there are several respects in which they fail to resolve the tension between these values. First, while they acknowledge the function of representational forms of democracy and specifically the parliamentary forms, they tend to see the parliamentary form itself as by its nature embodying domination, inasmuch as it is an institutional form of the state. The state, on this view, necessarily functions to maintain the existing social order, including whatever inequalities it contains.[13] In place of such parliamentary political forms, they propose what they call organs of self-management.[14] However, I think that their view here fails to recognize the importance of such representational forms of political democracy, however formal they may be. Provided that such forms are not rendered ineffectual by gross inequalities of real power outside the political sphere or by manipulation within the political sphere, they would seem to afford a necessary means of political participation through representation with respect to all those general public functions for which the state remains indispensable. Similarly, while the *Praxis* theorists recognize the importance of civil liberties as protections of individual freedom, they tend to regard them as merely negative freedoms characteristic of bourgeois societies and, though important, as in some sense less important than the freedom of self-management or self-determination. Here again, I would regard these civil liberties or negative freedoms as indispensable and as integral to any further conception of freedom as, for example, self-management or self-development.

Two further criticisms that I will make of the *Praxis* philosophers in subsequent chapters concern, first, their proposal to integrate social, economic, and political decision-making within some multicameral political body; and second, their interpretation of social property as property "belonging to society as a whole." I will argue that both of these views tend toward an increase in the power of the state, contrary to the values that the *Praxis* philosophers themselves have voiced.

The foregoing criticisms suggest that despite their concern with democracy and the free individual, the *Praxis* theorists do not yet give sufficient attention to the protection of individual rights and liberties and of representational forms of political democracy, nor do they convincingly show how social cooperation and economic equality can be increased without a correlative increase in state power.

Jürgen Habermas presents one of the most widely discussed alternatives in the revision of socialist theory; however one that is only problematically related to democratic socialism as it has been considered thus far. For Habermas's theory is neither a theory of democracy nor a theory of socialism. It is instead centrally a theory of social interaction and, more specifically, of what he calls communicative action, namely, that form of discursive practice that aims at common understanding and agreement.[15] The ideal norm that is implied in such communicative action is, according to Habermas, "the ideal speech situation," or "undistorted communication," in which participants would be free and equal in their dialogue roles and in which they would arrive at a rational consensus. This counterfactual norm serves as the basis of critique of those forms of social interaction that represent "systematically distorted communication," that is, those that are characterized by social domination, reification, authoritarianism, etc. In this sense, Habermas's critical social theory is a continuation or development of the neo-Marxist critique of alienation of the social theorists of the Frankfurt School (e.g., Horkheimer, Adorno, and Marcuse).

Habermas's views constitute a revision of socialist theory and, in particular, of what he takes to be its "positivistic" or purely instrumental emphasis on production and the correlative subordination of the social and reflectively critical dimensions of human activity. In keeping with democratic socialism, Habermas's theory suggests a critique of authoritarian and bureaucratic forms of state power and of social domination, whether in presently existing capitalist or socialist societies. It also proposes grounds for the development of greater social cooperation and equality that would not require state power for their implementation. These grounds consist in the norms of reciprocity or mutual recognition, equality, and the aim of consensus, which Habermas sees as implicit in the very structure of communication or discourse itself.

However, while Habermas might seem to be suggesting an ideal of democracy in his conception of the "ideal speech situation," it is not in fact put forth as a model of political decision-making or organization. Rather, it remains an abstract norm without concrete institutional interpretation. Thus Habermas makes no particular contribution to democratic theory or to any explicit democratization of socialist theory. Further, he seems to reject proposals for participatory democracy and for self-management in the economy, regarding them as unfeasible and undesirable in the present complex forms of society.[16] Moreover, the abstractness of Habermas's discussion of the norms of sociality and equality and of the ideal speech situation leaves it entirely unclear how these norms could even be approximated to in practice.

A more serious criticism of Habermas's social theory is that it does not give sufficient regard to individual liberty. As I will argue later, Habermas's proposal of consensus as the aim of communication puts too exclusive an emphasis on agreement, and insufficient emphasis on the recognition and appreciation of individual differences. Further, the focus on consensus may itself create pressures for conformity and the denigration of dissent as something necessarily to be overcome. In these ways, Habermas's theory does not, in my judgment, reconcile the values of social cooperation and equality, on the one hand, and individual liberty and democracy, on the other.

Finally, in this review of contemporary revisions of liberal individualist and socialist theories, we turn to the views of C.B. Macpherson[17] and Carole Pateman.[18] Both of these may be seen as attempts to draw upon a combination of liberal and socialist sources in order to develop a viable democratic theory.

In important respects, Macpherson's essays in democratic theory have influenced my own views. There are also similarities that derive from common sources in social and political thought. Thus, Macpherson proposes what he calls "developmental power" or the ability to use or develop the individual's capacities as the central aim of a democratic society. There is some similarity between this view and my own conception of self-development, which I take to be the meaning of full or positive freedom, and which serves as the central normative conception of the theory of democracy that I propose in this book. So too, Macpherson emphasizes the importance of "access to the means of labor," that is, to the material conditions of productive activity, as a requirement for the development of individuals' capacities; he also speaks, more generally, of the desirability of providing for the "equal effective right [of the individual] to live as fully humanly as he may wish."[19] This bears some similarity to the principle of equal positive freedom, which I will argue for in this book, namely, the principle of *prima facie* equal rights to the conditions of self-development.

However, my differences from Macpherson's views are significant. Among them I may note that he has an essentialist view of these human capacities which individuals ought to develop as an expression of their freedom – namely, that these capacities are specifiable as characteristics of human nature in general. By contrast, I will argue for an open-ended conception of human nature and human capacities in which these are themselves seen as the results of human choices and actions. Again, though Macpherson introduces the notion of "developmental power" as the ability to exercise human capacities, he does not give any positive account of what such development would mean or of its systematic relation to the conception of free choice, as I do. Instead, his account of development remains largely negative: Developmental liberty is defined by and measured by the absence of impediments to the ability to exercise one's capacities. Further, Macpherson's approach remains too narrowly individualist in its ontology (despite his telling critique of "possessive individualism"), without a complementary conception of social agency and of the social conditions for the development of human powers. I will propose instead an ontology of social individuals, that is, of individuals in social relations as the fundamental account of society.

Macpherson's argument for equal rights, moreover, seems to me to lack an adequate philosophical grounding and indeed sometimes even appears to be merely situational – as simply what the modern 20th-century world demands. Although he offers a critique of exploitation which seems to rest on some notion of the violation of equal rights, and although he talks about an "equal effective right" of development, nonetheless his argument finally devolves upon a conception of "maximizing the net aggregate of developmental powers" as the guiding social value. Such an approach undercuts any substantive notion of equal rights as a requirement of justice and instead opts for a utilitarian approach that works with an aggregative notion of the social good. More generally, despite his major contribution to the development of contemporary democratic theory, Macpherson does not offer a systematic construction of such a theory, in which normative criticisms and proposals for social change are clearly related to a set of sufficiently elaborated and coherent basic principles. Further, in the course of my discussion later in this book, I will have occasion to consider critically Macpherson's account of property and his failure to draw an adequate distinction between negative and positive freedom. Here, however, it will suffice to remark finally on Macpherson's conception of the need for increased democratic participation in decision-making, an issue that is also of central concern in the present work. For Macpherson, such increased participation principally takes the form of an increase in political participation; and insofar as he speaks of participation in economic decision-making, he means mainly participation in political decisions about economic life. That is, he advocates increased political–democratic control over the economy. He does not, however, elaborate the idea of direct participation by workers in decision-making concerning their workplaces or firms. That is, there is little consideration of questions of workers' self-management or worker control, issues that are central to my own argument for the extension of democracy to the sphere of economic life.

By contrast to Macpherson's view, Carole Pateman proposes direct or participatory forms of democracy in economic life, and specifically workers' self-management, as well as such direct democracy in political life. Pateman develops this view on the basis of a reading of historical sources in democratic theory, in particular, Rousseau and J.S. Mill. Like them, she also emphasizes the politically educative role of participation, that is, that people become competent at self-governance or self-management through actual participation in decision-making. Pateman argues for participation on the grounds of freedom and equality, as the right of each to control his or her own life. She argues that the liberal ideals of freedom and consent, when taken in their full sense, entail a different organization of political life than that of merely formal democracy or of representational forms of decision-making. In these respects, the view I present is similar to Pateman's. However, as noted, her views are largely suggested as an interpretation of historical sources or as criticisms of alternative views in contemporary democratic theory. She does not develop a systematic approach to the normative foundations of participation, as I propose to do in this book. Further, while Pateman does offer a social conception of the individual, seeing the individual in the context of relations of mutuality with others, this account of sociality remains at the level of face-to-face relations among individuals and does not extend to a consideration of social institutions or the conditions under which sociality can develop. More problematic still, Pateman counterposes participation as direct democracy on the Rousseauian model to any representational forms, and ends with a completely participatory and antirepresentational system, based on what she characterizes as voluntarism and self-assumed obligations. This amounts to a sort of anarchist theory, which seems to reject any representational forms as incipiently statist and to extol the virtues of smallness and spontaneous association. However engaging such an ideal of complete direct democracy may be, it seems to me to be incompatible with large-scale and complex societies. I will propose instead a system of democracy that has both participatory and representative features.

It is interesting to note that most of the theoretical alternatives in political philosophy that I have just reviewed have counterparts in existing social and political practices, though most often in mixed or degenerate forms. Thus liberal individualism, primarily in its pluralist revision, is exemplified by many of the Western democracies in various ways. At the same time, many of these democracies also exhibit to various degrees features of welfare capitalism, which call to mind the Rawlsian emphasis on overcoming gross social and economic inequalities and on supplementing individual liberty with considerations of social welfare. Against the movements for social welfare, there have developed in recent years countermovements that argue for a return to pure free market principles. These correlate in some measure with Nozick's liberal fundamentalism, though they cannot be said to share his emphasis on libertarianism or anarchism. Similarly, socialist theory, principally in its statist interpretations, has had its practical expression in various forms of actually existing socialism, for example, in the Soviet Union and Eastern Europe. Democratic socialist theory, which combines an emphasis on political democracy with an emphasis on social and economic equality, is difficult to identify with any existing societies though, as noted earlier, it characterizes a number of significant social and political movements.

More important for our purposes is the development of those practices in political and economic life that may be characterized as participatory democracy and as workers' self-management. In addition to the rather atypical traditional form of direct or participatory political democracy of the New England Town Meeting sort, there are also contemporary examples of participatory decision-making in such small-scale or lower-level contexts as community organizations (e.g., block or tenant associations), union organizations (e.g., shop-floor or rank-and-file committees), and voluntary associations (e.g., self-help associations or food coops). On a larger scale, the political referendum has been regarded as an instance of participatory decision-making. The Israeli Kibbutz has also often been cited as a participatory form of social, economic, and political life.

Workers have come to take part in decision-making in the workplace in a number of ways in recent years. Minimally, in what has often been called worker participation, "quality of life" circles have been instituted in some workplaces, in which joint committees of workers and management make decisions concerning improvement of working conditions and production procedures, quality control, and work organization. Additionally, in some enterprises, there are also higher-level labor–management committees in which representatives of the workers participate with management in some limited aspects of the decision-making concerning production, safety, and welfare in the firm. Another development has been the spread of worker ownership, though this remains a relatively minor phenomenon in capitalist economies. Such worker ownership does not necessarily imply worker control. It ranges from Employee Stock Ownership Plans (in which the workers are allocated a certain portion of the firm's stock, which is placed in trust for them), to direct purchase by workers in the market of common stocks of the firms by which they are employed (where they are not necessarily the exclusive owners of common stock), to complete and exclusive ownership by the workers of the firm. This latter case would most often imply not only worker ownership but also worker control of the firm. Self-management or worker control, properly speaking, is the strongest and also the least common of these forms of worker participation in economic decision-making in the workplace. Such self-management connotes the determination by the workers of managerial decisions or the workers' power to elect or appoint and recall managers. Self-management in this sense may be conjoined with worker ownership of the firm; or it may be linked with public, or social, or state ownership of enterprises. Perhaps the most widely developed case of workers' self-management is that of Yugoslavia where it constitutes a major portion of the economy. But there are many other important examples, such as that of Mondragon in Spain, as well as specific firms in the United States and Western Europe. There has also been a growing interest in some limited forms of workers' self-management in the Soviet Union and in some Eastern European countries, as well as in China.

In addition to these developments of participatory democracy and of workers' self-management, there has been a worldwide upsurge in the demand for traditional forms of political democracy and for the democratization of social life. With the end of colonial rule in many Third World countries, there have been movements for autonomous democratic governments, as well as struggles to overthrow homegrown authoritarian or totalitarian regimes. So too, there have been growing demands for political democratization in various East European socialist countries. Movements for the democratization of social life have come to prominence in the United States and Western Europe, especially since the sixties, centered on issues of social equality (e.g., sexual and racial) and equal opportunity, and such issues as patients' rights, consumers' rights, and other aspects of participation in social decision-making.

All of these burgeoning practical demands for the democratization of political, social, and economic life express the need for the articulation of an adequate theory that would provide the normative argument for the extension of democracy in these contexts. An adequate theory of this sort is as yet lacking. Though the theory of political democracy, as such, has been fairly well developed historically, a comparable theoretical grounding for the extension of democracy – for example, as workers' self-management or as participatory democracy in the contexts of social and political decision-making – has not yet been offered. Moreover, as I suggested earlier, such a theory would have to show how the values of social equality and cooperation could be made compatible with the value of individual freedom, and how such equality and cooperation could be achieved without an increase in state power or centralized authority. But as we have seen, the major alternative political theories have been unable to show how the apparent conflict between these values can be resolved. It is the aim of this book to develop the framework for such a resolution and to provide the philosophical foundations for an adequate theory of democracy.

Introduction

In this book I argue that when the concepts of freedom and equality are properly understood, what follows from them is the requirement for the extension of democracy beyond the political sphere to social and economic life; and that in all of these spheres, the form of decision-making should be participatory to the extent feasible, and representative otherwise. Therefore, on my view, an adequate treatment of the concepts of freedom and equality in political philosophy demands a theory of democracy in which these concepts can be elaborated and in the practice of which these values can come to be realized. Further, in such a theory of democracy, the apparently conflicting values of individual freedom, on the one hand, and equality and social cooperation, on the other, can be seen to be compatible. For I will argue in this book that individual freedom is to be understood not only as a capacity for free choice but also as an activity of self-development. As will be seen, this entails the equality of all individuals insofar as they are all equally agents. It also entails that social cooperation is a necessary condition for individual self-development. This does not imply, however, that the reality of social conflict or of antagonistic differences among individuals is ignored or imagined away. Rather, the view provides for those modes of participation in decision-making in which such conflict can be mediated or resolved. More fundamentally, the distributional principles to be developed here are intended to confront problems that lead to such conflicts and to eliminate some of the traditional grounds for social conflicts, for example, in the economic sphere. The view I will propose entails further that access to material conditions for well-being is a necessary condition for self-development. I will argue that the equality of individuals extends to *prima facie* equal rights to the conditions (social and material) for their self-development (that is, what I will call equal positive freedom). On this basis I will propose that there follows an equal right to participate in those decisions that concern the common activities which are among the conditions for self-development. These areas of joint decision-making will therefore include not only the political domain, as has been argued in traditional democratic theory, but also the domains of social and economic life. Equal freedom, understood as an equal right to self-development, therefore requires the right of democratic participation in all these contexts. Thus it will be seen that freedom understood as self-development requires equality and social cooperation in the senses suggested above. Conversely, social cooperation among equals requires their individual freedom as agents, since otherwise it would be a form of domination or coercion of some by others.

Thus on the theory to be presented in this work, the values of individual freedom and equality and social cooperation turn out not only to be compatible but also to require each other for their realization. Moreover, the compatibility of these values can be realized in social practice only by the extension of democracy, since it is in this form that the individual's freedom or right to self-determination is exercised jointly and equally with others in common or social activities. The argument for the extension of democracy to be developed in this work is thus founded on a theory of freedom. In this theory, which provides the ethical or normative framework for the analysis, the requirements for social cooperation and the extension of democracy are derived from the conception of freedom, on a certain interpretation. It will also be seen that such an approach therefore rules out the increase of state power or of centralized authority as justifiable means for effecting social or economic equality or an increase in social cooperation, since this would inhibit the rights of individuals to self-determination as well as their rights to maximally participate in decision-making concerning their joint or social activities.

I also present an ontological framework for the theory of democracy – that is, an analysis of the nature of individuals and of social reality – which proposes to overcome the traditional antithesis between the individual and society and which in turn undergirds the argument for the compatibility of individual freedom and social equality. This approach, which I have called social ontology, will be used to explain how the requirement for the extension of democracy follows from the nature of individuals as agents and as social beings.

The approach in this book is therefore to develop a theory of democracy in terms of an ethical and ontological framework. This approach may be characterized as quasi-foundationalist, in the sense that it seeks to ground its arguments on the fundamental value of freedom and on the nature of human beings and of their sociality, but eschews an essentialist interpretation of these foundations, taking them instead as constituted by the choices and the social and historical actions of individuals. Such an approach thus contrasts with the alternative approaches in political philosophy, which tend either to be foundationalist in an essentialist way (e.g., to take human beings to have a fixed and innate essence or nature) or to be antifoundationalist in a relativist way, and thus put in question the possibility of any normative and critical standpoint.

These foundational considerations are taken up in the first part of this book. I then go on to develop the theory of democracy further in terms of central concepts in political philosophy and show how these concepts are systematically transformed in relation to the basic framework presented earlier. Thus I consider in some detail the concepts of equal rights, economic justice, property, human rights, and authority. In the discussion of authority, for example, it is shown how, on such a reconstruction, the concept of political authority can be made compatible with an extended conception of democratic participation.

In the last four chapters of the book, the theoretical framework and conceptual analysis of the earlier sections are brought to bear upon some significant contexts of application. First, and perhaps central, is the construction of a social and economic model of the extension of democracy and of workers' self-management. Subsequent chapters deal with the problem of the democratic control of technology and of technological development, and the question of what constitutes a democratic personality (by contrast to an authoritarian one), able to participate effectively in democratic decision-making. In the last chapter, I consider how democratic principles can be interpreted across national boundaries in the context of international relations.

Finally, there are several methodological qualifications that need to be made concerning the aims and the scope of this book. First, it is not the intention here to produce a work in general ethics, that is, a general theory of right conduct or of the good, which would apply to all and any human actions. Rather, my concern is to elucidate fundamental values and principles that ought to guide our social and political institutions and practices. That is, the book is intended as a work in social and political philosophy. It might well be that the ethical considerations discussed here have a bearing beyond the questions that this book addresses, but it is only with social ethics or with the relevance of these values and principles to social, political, and economic life that I will be concerned in this work.

Second, the book is not intended as a treatise on or as a critique of political democracy itself. It may follow from the common acceptation of the term *democracy* that a book on democratic theory would be expected to focus primarily on the political sphere, but as I have indicated, the main focus here is on the justification of democracy as a normative requirement not only for political life but for economic and social life as well. Nonetheless, considerations of political democracy enter integrally here in many ways with respect to such questions as the role of civil liberties and political rights and their relation to economic rights, the requirement for more participatory forms of decision-making in politics, the relation between political authority and participatory or representational forms of decision-making and the issue of political obligation, and the question of moral principles in international relations.

Third, this work is not a study in empirical social science, but rather in normative social and political philosophy. That is, it is principally concerned with what ought to be and not with the description or analysis of existing institutions. However, this is not to say that empirical findings with respect to social, economic, or political behavior, or empirical analyses of the actual functioning of social institutions, are irrelevant to the principles discussed here. It is to say that the normative principles are not derived as empirical generalizations from observed behavior or simply as an uncritical reflection of prevailing norms, but rather are constructed on the basis of a critical reflection upon the fundamental character of human agency and the possibilities of human development, which, as I shall argue, already have normative import. Thus, these principles provide criteria for what ought to be, in a sense compatible with what can be.

Fourth, the book does not give a detailed analysis of the systematic economic issues which arise in the context of the implementation of workers' self-management and of economic democracy more generally. Such an analysis is beyond the scope of the present work, the focus of which is instead principally on philosophical issues.[20] I do, nonetheless, present a model of workers' self-management in a market economy that suggests, in outline, how the principles may be applied in a concrete economic context.

Fifth, the work is not utopian. That is, it does not propose either specific institutional forms that are hopelessly ideal or normative principles that are unrealizable in practice. Though I do propose a model, this is intended as a guide or direction for practice and not as a blueprint for the future or as a prescription of necessary institutional structures of a particular sort. Moreover, the main focus in this book is not on devising institutional forms but on getting the principles straight. These principles are also not be be understood as simply abstract or a priori normative ideals. Rather I would hold that they are grounded in actual and recognizable features of human agency and sociality; and further, that they constitute a theory for a range of presently emerging practices. Thus I would claim that these principles are in fact realizable and I discuss a range of practical applications of them in institutional contexts. Having said all this, there is yet one sense in which the work may be characterized as utopian. That is the sense in which theoretical ideals are not to be taken as reflections of contemporary institutions and practices, but rather as transcending them and thus as providing a critical normative basis for evaluating and improving them.

Chapter 1

Freedom, reciprocity, and democracy

Traditional theories of democracy – the classical theories of 18th- and 19th-century liberalism – have proven to be inadequate to the demands for greater freedom and equality in the twentieth century. Despite the abiding virtues that these theories retain, there is a need for a new and enlarged conception of democracy and for the articulation of its philosophical foundations. Traditional theories have viewed the democratic form of governance as the condition for human freedom, where this freedom is conceived principally in terms of the liberty of individuals to do as they choose without external constraint. A fundamental principle here is equal liberty under the law, which entails equal civil liberties and political rights. Democracy is accordingly interpreted as that form of political rule in which this freedom is maximized and in which those constraints that are required for social order are self-imposed, in that they are determined by a process of mutual consent.

Such traditional theories have recently come under criticism for their limited conception of freedom as absence of constraint and for their restriction of democracy to the political sphere. Against these traditional views, some recent social and political theorists have argued that there is a need to go beyond political and juridical equality to equality in social and economic rights or benefits. This is also sometimes coupled with a requirement for greater participation in all contexts of decision-making, including the economy. Thus, such recent critics have proposed egalitarian and radical democratic principles as the normative foundation for the further democratization of social life. To one degree or another, views of this sort are expressed in recent work by such theorists as C.B. Macpherson, Carole Pateman, Steven Lukes, Mihailo Marković, David Schweickart, Lawrence Crocker, and Kai Nielsen.[1]

Though I agree with the general thrust of these recent views, there remains a need to develop a systematic conceptual framework for the redefinition and extension of democracy, that is, for a new democratic theory. Whereas traditional liberal democratic theories have elaborated their basic concepts in great depth and have constructed coherent normative systems to support their views, there is as yet no comparable development of the philosophical and ethical foundations of a new theory of democracy or of the basic philosophical concepts of freedom and equality.

In this chapter, I will present an argument for an interpretation of the concepts of freedom and equality which differs from the traditional conceptions in fundamental ways. This will provide a normative foundation for the claim that democracy ought to be extended beyond the political sphere to social and economic life. Specifically, I propose four theses here: First, that the concept of freedom has to be understood more broadly than it is in traditional theories of democracy. Whereas in these theories freedom is understood as the absence of external constraint or as free choice, I argue that it should be interpreted as the activity of self-development, requiring not only the absence of external constraint but also the availability of social and material conditions necessary for the achievement of purposes or plans. Second, the concept of equality likewise needs to be extended beyond its interpretation in liberal democratic theory as political and legal equality to equality in social and economic life as well. In particular, the normative principle I will propose is that of *prima facie* equal rights to the conditions for self-development. Third, fundamental modes of social relations—namely, reciprocity and joint or common activity—not only serve as conditions for freedom understood as self-development but also have implications for the form and scope of democratic decision-making. The recognition of the importance of these forms of sociality also distinguishes this new democratic theory from traditional liberal individualist theories of democracy. Fourth, from the three earlier theses, it will be seen to follow that democratic forms of decision-making, which involve equal rights of participation, are relevant not only to political contexts but should be extended to social and economic contexts as well, and where feasible the form of such decision-making should be participatory.

There are several philosophical problems that arise concerning these theses and which will need to be addressed. A major one concerns the justification for my first claim that a broader conception of freedom is required, which, while retaining the traditional conceptions of individual choice and freedom from external constraint, goes beyond them and sees access to social and economic conditions as a requirement for self-determination or self-development. Are there good philosophical grounds for such an extension of the concept of freedom or does such a claim confuse freedom with the conditions for its exercise (a criticism that Isaiah Berlin makes against such a view[2])? Another problem concerns the claim that everyone ought to have *prima facie* equal rights to the social and economic conditions required for their development. Why should one suppose that there is an equal claim to these conditions rather than that they should be distributed differentially in accordance with varying individual desert or capacities? Further, from the statement that it is desirable or valuable for everyone to have such conditions available to them for their self-development, it is not clear how it would follow that they have a *right* to these conditions, much less an equal right to them. The transition from *values* to *rights* would seem to be no less problematic than the transition from *is* to *ought*. In addition, if there were an equalization of social and economic conditions, this would appear to conflict with the freedom of those individuals whose needs or capacities require a greater portion of such conditions than do others and thus would appear to constrain the freedom of such individuals to develop fully.

With respect to the proposed emphasis on reciprocal forms of social relations as a condition for self-development, the question arises as to whether such reciprocity in fact goes beyond the merely instrumental relation of tit for tat. Such an instrumental model of reciprocity could be accommodated by the principle of enlightened self-interest or rational egoism characteristic of traditional liberal theory and thus could not be said to constitute an alternative approach within democratic theory. Further, does the emphasis on sociality as common activity and joint decision-making in social and economic life lead to a denigration of individual freedom and initiative by virtue of the holism and collectivism which this would seem to entail? Finally, there is the structural question of whether the broader conception of democracy proposed here needs to be systematically derived from the new conceptions of freedom and equality, or whether democracy is rather an autonomous value that needs no further normative grounds; or indeed, whether democratic theory ought to be without foundations altogether and instead a matter of social agreement, consensus, or mere political preference at a given time.

In this chapter, I will set out the ethical framework for the new conception of democracy that I propose and will address some of these questions (reserving the discussion of the others to later chapters.) The present chapter is divided into four parts. The first deals with the proposed redefinition of freedom as self-development, particularly as it applies to the actions of individuals. The second part centers on equality and the justification of the principle of *prima facie* equal rights to the conditions of self-development. The third considers the social relations of reciprocity and of common activity as a basis for some of the subsequent arguments concerning democratic decision-making. The final section deals with the extension of democracy to more participatory forms in social, economic, and political life on the basis of the values of freedom and equality.

THE NORM OF SELF-DEVELOPMENT AND
THE CONCEPT OF POSITIVE FREEDOM

On the whole, traditional political theory has taken freedom to mean the absence of external constraints. Thus for example Thomas Hobbes writes, "Liberty, or freedom, signifieth, properly, the absence of opposition; by opposition, I mean external impediments of motion."[3] With respect to a person, liberty "consisteth in this, that he finds no stop, in doing what he has the will, desire or inclination to do."[4] A similar contemporary view is expressed by Isaiah Berlin who writes, "I am normally said to be free to the degree to which no man or body of men interferes with my activity. Political liberty in this sense is simply the area within which a man can act unobstructed by others."[5] Or again, Benn and Peters suggest that "In general, when we say that a person is free, we mean that, if a person *wants* to do something, he will not be impeded by some kind of constraint or limitation."[6]

Although this view captures an important aspect of what we understand by freedom, it leaves out two essential features of the concept: First, while it addresses the requirement that agents not be externally constrained in exercising their choices, it ignores the complementary requirement that the means necessary for realizing these choices be available to them. I will argue that the social and material means for realizing purposes, or what I shall call the enabling conditions of action, are essential to freedom. Second, in its account of free choice, this view takes as its focus individual or isolated actions and leaves out of consideration the development over time of the agent or person through these actions and the realization of long-term purposes or plans. I will argue that an adequate conception of freedom must relate the account of the exercise of free choice or the agent's actions to such a process

35

of self-development. I will later specify the particular sense in which I use the term self-development. As will be seen, it differs sharply from either essentialist views of self-realization such as Aristotle's or from radical individualist conceptions of self-actualization or self-fulfillment.

The distinctions I propose here may be analyzed in terms of the distinction between negative and positive freedom which has been discussed in recent political theory.[7] The traditional view of freedom as freedom from external constraints may be understood as what has been called negative freedom or "freedom from." On analysis, such a view presupposes free choice as an abstract capacity which may be distinguished from the actual exercise of that capacity in making specific choices under given conditions. Thus if a person A chooses some particular course of action c, we presuppose that A is capable of making choices in general and that A could instead have chosen some alternative course of action c^1. In this context, negative freedom signifies that there is no external constraint on A's doing c if A so desires or wills. But negative freedom is not identical with the ability to make choices, for someone could freely make a choice to do c and yet be prevented by external impediments from carrying it out in action. Thus this negative freedom has been characterized principally in terms of the absence of constraints or limitations on one's action, rather than the agent's incapacity to act or the unavailability of material means to carry out the desired action. Further, negative freedom has for the most part been understood in terms of freedom from constraints imposed by other persons rather than in terms of external impediments of a natural sort. Negative liberty has accordingly been understood as applying primarily to contexts of political freedom, where it connotes the freedom of individuals from interference or control by the state, or protection by the state of individuals from interference or harm by others.

In his classic discussion in "Two Concepts of Liberty," Isaiah Berlin introduces a sharp distinction between this form of freedom and positive freedom as the "freedom which consists in being one's own master" or of being "the instrument of my own, not of other men's, acts of will."[8] Berlin argues that this conception of positive freedom has led to the notion that "being one's own master" is identical with knowing what is best to do or what is rationally or ideally necessary. This is then associated with the idea of a higher self whose task it is to control or discipline the lower or irrational self or the "passions." According to Berlin, this higher or "real" self is then identified with "something wider than the individual . . . as a 'social whole' of which the individual is an element or aspect . . . ; this entity is then identified as being the 'true' self which, by imposing its collective, or 'organic', single will upon its recalcitrant 'members', achieves its own, and therefore their 'higher' freedom."[9] Once a state is seen as embodying such a higher rationality, this is taken to justify coercing others for their own sake, since this is supposedly getting them to do what they would choose for themselves if they were fully rational.

On these grounds, Berlin rejects the notion of positive liberty as leading to totalitarian or coercive regimes and opts instead for negative liberty as what democratic states should be concerned with. I will consider this particular criticism of the concept of positive freedom later. Here I want to focus on the inadequacy of defining freedom as narrowly as Berlin does in terms of negative liberty alone. For, as I will argue, this view leaves out of account the positive conditions necessary for the realization of one's choices. Such conditions go beyond the mere absence of external constraint imposed by other people on one's actions.

One may be free of external constraint by others and yet not be free to realize one's chosen purposes because the necessary conditions or means are not available. Thus for example, although I am free to make the choice to travel to China, without the money to pay for the trip I am lacking one of the conditions necessary to act on my choice. Thus my freedom remains merely formal. Concrete freedom requires not only the absence of external constraint but also the availability of the objective conditions that are necessary if choices are to be effected. Such conditions may be characterized as *enabling* conditions or positive conditions for action as distinct from the *constraining* conditions, the absence of which defines negative freedom. Thus, for example, although there may be no legal or discriminatory barriers to prevent someone from entering a given profession or trade, one cannot make such a choice effectively if there are no jobs available. Thus the availability of jobs is an enabling condition for making one's choice effective or for realizing one's purposes, even in the absence of interference by others in one's choice. The presence of such enabling or positive conditions is an essential constituent of what I am characterizing here as positive freedom in the distinctive sense in which I am using it here.

Some commentators on Berlin's discussion of negative and positive freedom have argued that what I have here called positive or enabling conditions may be subsumed under the rubric of negative freedom. For, it may be argued, the absence of a necessary condition for the realization of one's choice or purpose may itself be understood as an impediment or a constraint on one's action. On one such view, that of MacCallum, all freedom is of one kind, not of two, and may be understood in terms of a triadic relation: "X is free from Y to do Z."[10] In this context, positive or enabling conditions would have to be characterized as what one is free from the absence or lack of. This seems, at best, an oblique and strained way of referring to the positive conditions. But more important, MacCallum's formulation fails to distinguish between the freedom from constraint, which requires the forbearance by others from interfering, and the freedom to realize one's purposes, which also requires the positive provision of necessary means of action by others. To ignore this distinction would be to conflate forbearance from action with action. It would be like saying that the action of others in providing the positive conditions for one's own actions is nothing else than a forbearance from inaction. While this might make sense in terms of the logical equivalence of the affirmation and double negation of a proposition, it certainly makes nonsense of the ordinary distinction between action and inaction which is essential in this context.

Other commentators, namely C.B. Macpherson and Lawrence Crocker, have proposed enlarging the concept of negative liberty to include freedom from economic exploitation and social domination as well as the narrower notions of external constraint characteristic of traditional democratic theory.[11] Both argue that since such exploitation or domination is the result of institutional arrangements that have been constituted by the actions of other people, these may also be seen as interference by others with the freedom of the individual. Thus Macpherson writes, "[W]e may conclude that the unequal access to the means of life and labour inherent in capitalism is, regardless of what particular social and economic theory is invoked, an impediment to the freedom of those with little or no access. It diminishes their negative liberty, since the dependence on others for a living, which deficiency of access creates, diminishes the area in which they cannot be pushed around."[12] Such an extension of the meaning of negative freedom to include freedom from economic exploitation or social domination seems to me warranted, for these would certainly seem to be impediments or external constraints imposed by others. However, freedom from domination or exploitation is not equivalent to the availability of the conditions of one's action, for it is conceivable that a person may be free from domination and exploitation and yet lack the means to realize his or her purposes. Thus, as in the case of MacCallum, Macpherson's characterization here fails to distinguish between the freedom from such impediments or restraints and the positive provision of those means – economic, social, personal – that would be needed for the full exercise of one's freedom. Thus these attempts to assimilate economic and social freedom to negative freedom do not sufficiently recognize the importance of the availability of such enabling conditions.

It should be noted that Berlin recognizes that liberty may in fact be ineffective without the presence of the conditions for its realization. Thus, for example, he notes that poverty or lack of education may render liberty useless. However, he makes a sharp and categorical distinction between liberty and the conditions of liberty. He writes, "The obligation to promote education, health, justice, to raise standards of living, . . . is not made less stringent because it is not necessarily directed to the promotion of liberty itself, but to conditions in which alone its possession is of value, or to values which may be independent of it. And still, liberty is one thing, and the conditions for it are another."[13]

Macpherson criticizes Berlin's distinction here on the grounds that it only holds when negative liberty is defined so narrowly as to exclude by definition any of the positive conditions necessary for its exercise. Moreover, he points out that Berlin is inconsistent in his admission that there are cases in which the absence of social and economic conditions of liberty has led to violations or diminutions of such liberty itself.[14]

I believe that Berlin is right to distinguish negative liberty from the conditions of its exercise and to insist that negative freedom is an important value in itself, as a protection against interference or coercion by others. Further, even if the positive or enabling conditions were available but if the freedom to make use of them were not protected, these conditions by themselves would be of no use in achieving one's purposes. However, with Macpherson, I think that Berlin is wrong to separate these conditions from the meaning of freedom, which, I would argue, in its full sense requires not only negative liberty as the absence of constraining conditions, but also positive liberty as the presence of or access to enabling conditions.

What sort of conception of freedom is it which has these multiple requirements that I have posed here: capacity for choice and its exercise, absence of constraining conditions, and the availability of means? I may begin by briefly characterizing it as self-development, that is, as the freedom to develop oneself through one's actions, or as a process of realizing one's projects through activity in the course of which one forms one's character and develops capacities. This conception may be related to what has been called positive freedom or "freedom to." Such concrete freedom goes beyond particular acts of choice or the fulfillment of short-term purposes and involves a process of the development of the person over time. Thus this notion of freedom, as we will see, has a biographical or historical dimension in that it concerns the individual's self-transformation through the course of his or her life, and also has a social dimension in that social relations and common purposes provide a fundamental context for such self-development. This conception, like that of negative freedom, also presupposes that people have the capacity for free choice and for acting to realize their purposes. However, the concept of positive freedom that I propose here emphasizes that in order to effect such choices concretely a wide range of actual options need to be available to people, for only through such activity is self-development possible. Thus this conception stresses the importance of the availability of the objective conditions – both material and social – without which the purposes could not be achieved. Among the material conditions are the means of subsistence as well as the means for labor and for leisure activity. The social conditions include cooperative forms of social interaction, reciprocal recognition of each one's free agency, and access to training, education, and various social institutions.

Yet the characterization of freedom in this sense as positive freedom does not mean that negative freedom is dispensable. Rather, as the absence of external constraint by other persons, negative freedom is also an essential presupposition for self-development. Thus the guarantee of civil liberties and political rights is central in the view I propose. I shall regard such negative liberty not only as compatible with positive freedom but as part of the meaning of self-development or of positive freedom in the full sense. This integral relationship of the meaning of negative freedom as "freedom from" with the meaning of positive freedom as "freedom to" is not a semantic shift that simply substitutes talk about the presence of a lack of constraint for talk about the absence of constraint. Rather, while retaining the distinction between constraining and enabling conditions, I want to suggest that it is the substantive interpretation of freedom as freedom to develop oneself that presupposes freedom from constraint as one of its necessary conditions. Thus I am using positive freedom in the full sense to refer to self-development and not only to positive or enabling conditions.

What justification is there for proposing this alternative view of freedom in place of such conceptions of it as the liberal individualist view of freedom of choice and the absence of external constraints, or the essentialist view of freedom as activity in accordance with one's nature? First of all, as I have already argued, those interpretations of freedom that see it simply as a capacity for willing or choosing or as the absence of external constraints are inadequate in that they are compatible with the person's being unfree to realize his or her purposes in practice. Further, these interpretations of freedom fail to take into account such plain cases of the violation of freedom as, for example, domination. Social and economic domination may not entail direct or forceful coercion of one person or group by another as an exercise of external constraint but rather control over the range or direction of one person's (or group's) actions by another, by means of control over the conditions that are necessary to carry out those actions. Thus domination is not a causal relation between agents in which one agent causally produces the actions of the other. (It is only in the extreme case of violent coercion where one may speak of a causal relation, in which one agent physically causes or constrains the other's bodily motions; but here, the person subject to such coercion is not engaging in any action.) Commonly, domination proceeds through control of conditions, either objective or subjective. Thus the means involved may be economic, political, social, or psychological. For example, it may take such forms as control over means of production or over the means of political expression (e.g., the press or political parties), or again it may operate through the power to impose punitive social or psychological consequences on others for their action.

An example of such domination is the case of racism, where there is control by a dominant group over access to the means of education or of earning a living, and where access to these means is denied or meted out in a discriminatory way to the members of the dominated racial group. In this case, social as well as political and economic domination does not proceed (for the most part) by direct personal coercion or control but rather indirectly through control over the means of action and self-development. Further, those who are victims of racial domination are not thereby stripped of their free will or capacity for choice, but rather are denied means of exercising it in ways that are necessary for their self-development. Thus the views of freedom as simply free choice or as the absence of external constraint, because of their abstractness, have no way of systematically accounting for or being critical of such lack of concrete freedom.

A second traditional view of freedom interprets it as activity in accordance with one's nature. That is, an action is said to be free if it follows from the innate character or the natural tendencies that mark an individual or a species. Such views, which one may characterize as essentialist, generally presuppose the existence of a fixed nature or essence that determines a priori the range and type of those actions that will be regarded as free or as rightly manifesting this nature. Although there are many different versions of this view, one may take issue with its general premise of a fixed human nature that defines freedom. It is not at all clear how one could establish whether there is such a fixed human nature, or what it is, simply on the basis of empirical knowledge of what human beings do and what the limits are of their actions. One cannot know this inductively, on the basis of how human beings have acted in the past, since under changed conditions or circumstances or with different conceptions of what choices are possible, it is entirely conceivable that human beings would act differently or in unanticipated ways. For just as history shows certain constancies in the forms of human action over time, it equally shows that human beings have radically changed their previous modes of action, developing new or transformed characteristics, or transcending the limits that were previously thought to be immutable. Thus it seems to me that the claim that there is a fixed nature and the claim as to what it is on the basis of history or past experience lack any persuasive grounds.

43

A further consideration that puts such essentialist theories in doubt is that the conceptions of human essence or nature that they have put forth have not only been historically variable but have tended in the main to be ideologically oriented to the interests of those in power. Such conceptions have tended to support notions of race, social class, or gender superiority of the dominant groups in society by proposing that historical relations of domination and subordination were grounded in essential human nature. Other arguments for a fixed human nature have been based on biological or genetic foundations, on rationalist or phenomenological intuition of what is essentially human, or on theological arguments concerning divine creation of human nature. The rejection of such arguments would require a full review and criticism, which I cannot give here. I can only note here that I find them equally unpersuasive on various grounds.[15]

There is a further argument against these essentialist views of freedom, which attempt to specify what capacities or traits are the essential ones, the realization of which alone would make someone free. For any such specification would seem to constitute a prescription for what allegedly free agents must necessarily do in order to qualify as free. But who, after all, is to make this decision about what is essential for free agents other than the free agents themselves? Who, other than the individual himself or herself, is to decide what capacities the individual is to develop freely? The requirement for a criterion for "action in accordance with one's nature" could easily serve to justify the imposition of some favored set of "essentials" by some people on others. This does not mean, however, that there are no determinate conditions that are universally required for freedom. But these are only of the most basic and general sort, e.g., means of subsistence, civil liberties, basic health care, and some education or training. Any determinate list beyond this of the sort that essentialist theories of freedom propose would constitute a prescription of approved purposes, capacities or forms of activity, and this would go counter to the very idea of freedom.

The inadequacy of these traditional views of freedom,

whether the liberal individualist conception of free choice and the absence of constraint or the essentialist conception of action in accordance with one's nature, suggest that an alternative conception is required. I would propose that the view of freedom as self-development is this required alternative. In order to see why this is so, it is necessary to give a fuller analysis of this view. In the course of this analysis, I will also consider problems that arise within this conception and objections or criticisms that have been raised against it. It will then be possible to show the ways in which this conception of freedom is more adequate than the traditional alternatives.

In the view that I am proposing here one may distinguish two aspects of freedom: first, what I would call freedom as capacity, and second, freedom as the exercise of this capacity in the form of self-development. Freedom as capacity refers to a fundamental characteristic of human action, namely, choosing among alternatives. Such choice is a constitutive feature of action which is manifest in the intentionality or purposiveness of such action. Thus, what marks off human actions from mere bodily motions or causally determined responses is that they are consciously oriented to some end or goal or express some intended meaning. Such actions are understood in terms of reasons that people have for acting as they do, rather than in terms of physical or physiological causes. Of course, such conscious purposiveness may be tacit much of the time and need not be explicitly reflected on or deliberated about in order for the action to qualify as intentional. Moreover, this intentionality or purposiveness is what individuates or identifies an action as being the action that it is. Thus, for example, though it may be the same bodily motion that is involved in waving one's hand in the air in order to ask a question or in order to greet someone, these are clearly different actions and are distinguishable as such on the basis of understanding the intentions of the agent and their social context. This characterization of human action has been the subject of a broad and intensive discussion in contemporary philosophy, which I will not pursue further here. One might only mention some of the phi-

45

losophers whose contribution to this understanding of action has in my view been most significant. In the Anglo-American tradition, one might mention Wittgenstein, Anscombe, Melden, Peters, Winch, Taylor, and Toulmin, among others. Among phenomenologists and existentialists, a related position has been developed by Husserl, Heidegger, Sartre, Merleau-Ponty, and Jaspers.

Self-development presupposes this characteristic of human action, namely, that it essentially involves choice and intentionality. That people do in fact develop cognitively, socially, and in other ways, that they transform themselves and realize some of their purposes, at least to various degrees, is an evident fact of our experience. But it may be seen that a precondition for the possibility of this activity of self-development is that individuals possess freedom as a capacity, which I am identifying with choice as a basic feature of action. It is though making such choices in their actions in particular situations over the course of time that people come to be who they are and develop their qualities and character. However, the capacity for freedom, as distinguished from self-development, may be described as abstract, in the sense that it does not yet specify concretely which choices contribute to one's self-development and which do not, but rather only that all actions involve choices. It is also clear that not all actions contribute to self-development, for some choices may in fact be pernicious for self-development or inhibit it, and a large majority of actions may neither help nor hinder it. Yet it is only through choices and actions of some sort that self-development can proceed and the capacity for freedom be realized in practice. It is in this sense that negative freedom, as the protection of the exercise of this capacity of free choice from external constraint, is a necessary condition for, and thus a presupposition of, positive freedom as I am defining it here.

Freedom as self-development, however, involves more than merely making choices or engaging in isolated actions. As suggested earlier, self-development connotes the process of concretely becoming the person one chooses to be through carrying out those actions that express one's own purposes and needs. This is not to say, however, that in such activity people realize some fixed, innate, or pre-given nature, or that their capacities or characters unfold from preformed potentialities, but rather that they create or develop their natures through their activity. Nor does self-development necessarily mean that there must be some single end-in-view or life-goal that a person pursues inexorably, for goals and life-plans may change. This process of self-development thus consists in the formation of new capacities and in the elaboration or enrichment of existing ones. In this process, individuals may be said to widen their range of actions and social interactions and intensify or improve the quality of particular modes of action or social relation. The development of intellectual, moral, or artistic capacities, or of practical and technical skills, as well as the cultivation of forms of social relations such as friendship and cooperation, would be examples of this process. In this development of capacities, individuals may be said to achieve a greater freedom of action, in the wider range of choices that are opened for their action and in the power to realize their purposes which their increased competence affords. Such a cultivation of capacities is, as suggested, a relatively long-term or continuous process and not merely the result of some set of disconnected actions.

In addition to this growth of capacities, self-development also connotes the achievement of a person's projects or long-term goals. This aspect of self-development is likewise an expression of freedom in one of the main ordinary senses of that term, namely, that one is free in doing what one chooses to do and being able to achieve what one sets out to achieve. This is the sense of freedom as the power to effect one's purposes. However, as in the case of the cultivation of capacities, the serious sense of freedom in this context involves a process of realizing relatively long-term projects or goals, and not simply realizing some ad hoc or disconnected desire. For it would be an inadequate sense of freedom if a person could only realize particular, disconnected intentions and desires and could not also attain such continuous and cumulative achievements.

It is not entailed here that such projects or goals are to be taken as narrowly individualistic or that the person's activity is to be understood as aiming at self-improvement. In fact, such projects may often be social or common ones. Further, projects, whether individual or social, normally involve not simply internal self-transformation in a subjective sense but also objective changes in the world in which the agents act to effect their purposes. Thus, for example, in the pursuit of a profession or trade, individuals may, over a period of many years, aim at a degree of excellence or success, which in turn requires not only their own self-improvement but also their practical activity or work. Moreover, in this case, their own self-development can only proceed in and through their participation in joint activities with others in common projects. Further, although processes of self-development cannot take place apart from particular projects and the cultivation of specific capacities, there may nevertheless be a supervening feature or coherence that marks such processes. That is the development of the person as a whole, which involves an integration of the variety of the person's intentions and actions and the formation of a character. Such an integration does not necessarily require some strong unilinear coherence or pattern of action. It may in fact exhibit itself in a manner or way of acting that characterizes a variety of different undertakings, or this coherence of the developing self may exhibit itself in a common conception that underlies diverse projects or activities.

It may be the case that many actions that people engage in are not undertaken for the sake of their own purposes or needs but are rather imposed upon them by others. Where a person is constrained, coerced, or manipulated to act on behalf of another's interests or aims, then it may be said that such actions do not contribute to the person's self-development. These are cases of domination by others, and the conception of freedom as self-development is incompatible with such domination. This is to be distinguished from those cases in which one person acts in another's interest without being coerced to do so.

What specifically counts as self-development obviously varies from one person to the next, since it is determined in large part by a person's choices. Thus it is always an individual who is self-developing or free in this sense rather than social groups or society as a whole. Yet such individuals are not isolated, but rather are social individuals. That is, they express who they are and become who they want to be in large part through their relations with others. Moreover, many of their actions are such that they are essentially social; that is, they are joint actions which could not be carried out by individuals alone. To this degree, their own self-development depends on these social relations and, as we shall see, on the extent to which these others are themselves self-developing. In the next chapter, I will consider in some detail the nature of such social individuality in terms of what I call social ontology. Here, however, I simply want to emphasize the role of social relations in individuals' self-development and therefore as a condition for their freedom, and later in this chapter, I will also consider the social categories of reciprocity and common activity as they bear on the argument for the extension of democracy.

Social relations enter into an individual's self-development in several ways. In the first place, it is clear that many of the intentions or purposes that individuals form are social in their origin. Clearly, a person's conception of what is valuable or important is affected by his or her process of socialization, and by the understandings and practices that constitute the social milieu. Thus, there is a fund of language, knowledge, skills, and techniques that is socially transmitted and which serves as the framework of individual activity. Second, relations with others in joint or cooperative activity as well as social institutions—e.g., economic, political, educational—provide objective conditions or means which are necessary for carrying out an individual's aims. Thus it is obvious that the contexts of work, politics, family life, and social interaction more

49

generally serve as means for self-development. Third, beyond the individual purposes or intentions that a person may have, there are social or common purposes that are shared in by many individuals and which a person may adopt as the aim of his or her actions. Here, the self-development of an individual takes the form of participation in such joint activity. Such collective activities as collaboration on common work projects or participation in political movements are examples of these contexts of self-development. Fourth, an individual's self-development depends to a large extent on the recognition by others of the individual as free. In social life, this recognition by each individual of the other's freedom is a relation of reciprocity, which stands in contrast to the nonreciprocal social relations of domination and exploitation. A fifth way in which social relations directly enter into an individual's self-development is through the mutual support that individuals may contribute to each other's self-development. Such mutuality may be defined as a social relation characterized not only by a reciprocal recognition by each person of the other as free and equal, but one in which each takes the enhancement of the other's self-development as a conscious aim. Sixth, there is another sort of mutuality, which, unlike the one just discussed, operates only indirectly. It consists in the contribution that is made to an individual's self-development by all those individuals who, in the development of their own capacities, have enriched the range of possible human actions, intentions, skills, and practices. This cultivation of human capacities provides an individual with options or models for his or her own development. Thus any high achievement, in the arts, in science, in sports, etc., sets new standards for what is humanly possible.

Several objections may be raised against the view of freedom as self-development that I have been presenting here. The first, and perhaps most obvious, criticism is that the concept of self-development is vacuous. That is, it seems to be applicable to every possible course of action which an individual may undertake. Thus for example, rote performances such as assembly-line work or household drudgery, or dead-end jobs such as much secretarial work, would appear to count as cases of self-developing activity. Since it would not be reasonable to regard such activities in this way and since the proposed concept of self-development does not appear to exclude them, the concept thus seems to be trivial or empty.

This objection would be correct and the concept would indeed be vacuous if it applied indiscriminately to any possible course of action or if it were to count the examples just given as instances of self-development. But in fact, as I have already suggested, the courses of action that would count as self-developmental are only those that express the agents' own purposes and are not imposed upon them by others; that involve the growth of capacities or the enrichment of the individual's range of activity; and that serve to realize long-range projects, consciously undertaken. Such courses of action may also contribute to the development of an integrated character over time. What I have just proposed are clearly normative requirements, which not every action or course of action meets. Thus the cited examples of rote performances or dead-end jobs fail to meet these requirements and do not qualify as self-developmental. Such activities normally do not involve any growth of capacities by virtue of their repetitious quality, and thus are taken to be stultifying. Similarly, they are most often under the control of others and thus are not expressions of the agents' own purposes or realizations of their own long-range projects. There may be aspects of such activities which in a larger context do contribute to an individual's self-development as, for example, one's relations with coworkers, or earning a living in order to be personally independent, but taken in themselves the cases cited would not generally be instances of self-development.

But, the objection may be raised, aren't the proposed normative requirements themselves so vague as to leave the concept almost as vacuous as it seemed to be before? Aren't such requirements as "the growth of capacities," "the agent's own purposes," and "long-term projects" too broad and general to articulate any useful conception of self-development?

My answer to this objection may seem somewhat strange in that it appears to grant the objection: On the view of freedom that is proposed here, the normative requirements for what counts as self-development must of necessity remain broad and general. For any further specification would preempt the very freedom to choose one's own path of self-development that is the value at stake here. Furthermore, on the grounds of my earlier criticisms of essentialism – the view that human beings have a fixed and specifiable nature – one may see that self-development cannot be properly interpreted as the realization of any particular set of capacities regarded as given or essential. Rather, what specifically counts as self-development has to remain open to the self-definition or self-determination of individuals if it is to embody the value of freedom. Yet, since not every course of action satisfies even the broad requirements for self-development, as I have argued, there are limits as to what remains open to the self-determination of individuals if such determination is to count as self-developing. Thus, although the criterion is broad, it is not vacuous.

Nevertheless, one may object, if what specifically counts as self-development has to remain open to the self-determination of individuals, as suggested here, doesn't this leave self-development completely relativized to whatever any individual might choose? Isn't this, then, an asocial or even antisocial conception of freedom and wouldn't it justify what are normally regarded as morally reprehensible courses of action, which are pernicious or destructive to others in the name of self-development? Against this objection, it may be recalled that human beings are here taken to be social individuals who realize their purposes through interaction with others and thus self-development has social interaction as one of its conditions. This requirement provides some constraint on those courses of action that would be destructive of the possibilities of social interaction. For if one pursued some course of action that harmed or alienated others, then one would be denied the support and cooperation that these others could otherwise provide for one's own self-development. This is a variation of the Socratic argument in the *Apology* that harming others harms oneself. Yet it may be objected that this support could be obtained by coercing others to do what one required of them as the means for one's self-development. Such coercion, however, would be so preoccupying in order to be effective that the coercer would be diverted from the pursuit of his or her ends by concern with the means. A stronger normative requirement, which would clearly exclude those actions that purport to be self-developing but that are destructive to others, is proposed later in this chapter as the central principle of this account of democratic theory, namely, the principle of equal rights to the conditions of self-development or equal positive freedom. In terms of this principle, it will become clear that the self-development of each individual ought to be compatible with the equal right to self-development on the part of the others. Anticipating that the argument for this principle has been made, it follows that pernicious, destructive, and antisocial modes of action are normatively excluded. For it is just such actions that, by harming others, undercut or deny their possibilities for self-development and thus violate their equal right to such development.

There is a further problem, however: Suppose that an individual, acting alone and without harm to others, were to choose, as a means of his or her self-development, some long-range project or course of action that was self-destructive. What would prevent us from accepting this as a bona fide instance of self-development, for it appears to meet the criterion that leaves the specific course of self-development open to the self-determination of individuals? The argument against this view is fairly straightforward. It is that any course of action that is self-destructive or harmful to the agent in effect undercuts or destroys the very possibility of further self-development, by endangering either the life or health of the individual or by inhibiting the cultivation of capacities. Such debilitation of an individual as a result of his or her chosen activity cannot in any reasonable sense be taken as self-developing. (This is not of course to say that there is any right to interfere with an individual's choice of such activity if it does not harm others, even if it is self-destructive and not self-developing.) However, suppose one were to count the cultivation of what one might call perverse capacities as instances of self-development, for example, the cultivation of such emotions or such capacities for feeling as hatred, self-revulsion, or cowardice. Could one then allege that an individual could become a virtuoso of hate or self-revulsion? Without going into any detailed moral or psychological analysis of these hard cases, I might suggest that such "cultivation" would tend to be all-consuming in such a way as to severely constrict the range of one's possible experience, and thereby deny the openness to alternatives and to self-change that is necessary for self-development. Further, it seems clear that in cases of this sort, such an individual could psychologically or morally harm others and thus inhibit or impede the exercise of their capacities, thereby violating their equal right to self-development, as noted earlier.

A further objection may be raised against the view of freedom as self-development. It may be argued that any requirement for the development of capacities as a condition for freedom imposes a constraint upon the free choice of individuals: In effect, it tells people what they have to do in order to be free. In contrast with the previous objection that the conception of freedom as self-development is too vacuous, this objection asserts that it is in fact too determinate. In effect, this conception of freedom seems to imply that unless people make the "right" choices, they are not free. In addition, it may be asked: Why suppose that people have an interest in developing their capacities or that they ought to? More generally, one might object: What evidence is there that people are interested in self-development at all, or what argument is there that they ought to take this as a goal of their activity?

If the first objection suggests that the requirement for self-development constrains free choice in the sense that only those actions that contribute to self-development are taken to be free, then this objection may be answered as follows: Concrete or positive freedom has as its presupposition the capacity for free choice, as noted earlier. The exercise of this capacity is neither qualified by nor constrained by the normative requirement for self-development. That is, it is not only the "right" choices, in terms of some notion of self-development, that are free in this basic sense. "Wrong" choices, choices that are indifferent to or even destructive of self-development, must also count as free if freedom in the first sense, that is, as capacity, is to have any serious meaning or value. Thus the first objection confuses the two senses of freedom that I have distinguished. One may by choosing freely, in the first sense, act in such a way as to constrain or inhibit one's freedom, in the second sense as self-development.

If, on the other hand, the first objection connotes that the requirement for the development of capacities (as a condition for the realization of freedom in the full sense) is imposed upon people as an external prescription for their activity, for example, as an exhortation to realize oneself, then the objection in this form may be answered as follows: This "requirement" is not an external imposition but rather arises out of the very nature of human activity itself, namely, out of the fact that people normally tend to act in the pursuit of their goals and to some degree toward the achievement of long-range plans. They also tend to one degree or another to develop the capacities that are instrumental to the pursuit of their goals, or indeed to develop capacities for their own sake, i.e., for the pleasure or satisfaction that skill or accomplishment affords. Thus, for example, individuals pursue their education, learn a profession, raise families, develop hobbies, and work at developing their skills in sports or other leisure activities. Such tendencies are the norm rather than the exception in ordinary life and it is precisely in such concrete and specific forms of activity that self-development as I described it earlier takes place and that capacities are cultivated. It is in the integrated sequence of such choices through time that the potentiality for self-development, which is ingredient in the capacity for choice, realizes itself. Thus, inasmuch as all human beings (with rare exceptions) develop such fundamental capacities as the acquisition of language, sociability, basic skills, and a measure of common sense, simply in order to get along in the world, and also pursue some long-range plans, they may be said to be self-developing to a degree. They have acquired the elements of freedom through their activity, though not necessarily the fuller realization of it.

This is not of course to say that there is any essential or universally fixed pattern of development inherent in human nature. Such development depends rather on individual choices under given circumstances. Nor is it to say that such self-development is inevitable. For the tendency toward self-development, which manifests itself in purposive activity, may be thwarted if agents lack control over the purposes or ends of their activities or have no share in determining these ends; or if they lack control over the activity itself; or if they are systematically discouraged from pursuing their ends, for example, through improper socialization; or, again, if the material means or social conditions for their activities or for the cultivation of their capacities are not available to them. Self-development, therefore, is not simply a matter of free choice, though it presupposes it. To say that self-development is a tendency in human activity, then, is not yet to say that any such activity, even if purposive, realizes this tendency fully. Yet, one may say, in a counterfactual mode, that if people were to have the opportunity to formulate and to pursue long-range ends and to develop their capacities, and if they had access to the requisite means, then for the most part they would in fact realize their freedom as self-development more fully.

It is nevertheless true that some people choose not to act on such relatively long-term goals even if the necessary conditions are available, or are simply driven by circumstance or by weakness of will to subject themselves to purposes other than their own; and it is certainly the case that some people for whatever reason fail to develop their capacities or simply choose to mark time. Thus not all human activity is inherently self-developing. However, what I am claiming here is that there is a tendency in ordinary human activity toward such self-development, and thus it is not an externally imposed norm. If this is true, then it also provides an answer to the second objection, as to whether people have an interest in self-development as a goal of their activity. For self-development is an inherent goal of that important segment of human activity that aims at the achievement of fully chosen purposes.

However, it may be questioned whether people are in fact explicitly interested in so lofty-sounding an aim as self-development as the central goal of their activity rather than in such more commonsensical and concrete ends as making a living, enjoying themselves, getting an education, and having friends, all of which are clearly purposeful activities. Such an objection misconstrues the conception of self-development that I have proposed by abstracting it from those modes of activity in which people pursue just such concrete ends. As I have suggested, freedom as self-development is precisely the process of realizing projects of one's own choosing and cultivating capacities in specific contexts, of which the particular ends cited above are examples. It is nothing over and above specific forms of activity, except in the special case where someone self-consciously takes self-development as an aim and sees these other activities as instrumental to it. But such a self-conscious articulation is not a requirement of the conception as I have presented it (no more than, say, a conscious awareness of Peano's axioms is necessary for doing arithmetic).

In response to the further query as to why people *ought* to take self-development as the goal or as the normative imperative of their activity: It depends upon how one interprets the "ought" here. If the question is why people ought to take freedom (interpreted as self-development) as the goal of their activity as against such traditional other ends as pleasure, virtue, power, duty, or happiness, then one might reply that the question is wrongly formulated to begin with. For self-development is not an alternative goal to these others. Rather, self-development is entailed by any goal-seeking activity if the goal is a long-term one which is chosen by the agent and if the activity to realize such a goal involves the growth of capacities or the enrichment of the individual's range of activity (provided the activity is not destructive to others, as discussed earlier). The pursuit of such other ends as those cited above would therefore be occasions for self-development or instances of it. Thus, for example, if pleasure were taken as the end of one's activity, then this would require the development of one's capacities for pleasure as well as of other capacities that would be needed to attain pleasure. Moreover, the pursuit of pleasure or happiness or any other such long-range goal is the mode of expression of one's self-development.

However, if the question is whether people ought to take self-development as the norm of freedom rather than interpreting freedom in some other way (e.g., as simply free choice) then I believe I have already answered this question in large part by pointing to the ways in which positive freedom as self-development is a more adequate conception than the other prevailing views. I would suggest that this conception of freedom – which involves not only choice but access to material and social conditions, freedom from domination, and a conception of the realization of projects, the cultivation of capacities, and the formation of character over time – represents a more serious and richer view of freedom than the others. In fact, one may characterize this as a conception of *complex* freedom, as against the notion of *simple* freedom which characterizes negative freedom inasmuch as it connotes unconnected episodes of individual free choice. If the question remains as to why people ought to value freedom at all as the norm of their activity, then the answer lies in an analysis of the normative status of the act of choice. The discussion of this question is given in Chapter 3. Here, however, I may suggest in short that the exercise of free choice is not simply a descriptive characteristic of human action, but is also what gives such action its normative value, and is itself the ground of other values. For, as I argue later, the act of choice posits its own value reflexively, that is, choosing is valuing or endowing with value. But, as we have seen, the full realization of this freedom of choice, or the fullest elaboration of its possibilities, is concrete freedom or self-development. For it is by means of the cultivation of capacities and through access to the means of activity, and in the achievement of one's purposes, that one widens the range of available choices and thus realizes more fully the value inherent in the act of choice itself. Thus one may say that the normative imperative that is ingredient in the act of choice is self-development.

It is appropriate at this point to return to Isaiah Berlin's objection that the concept of positive freedom provides a justification for a coercive imposition by the state or the "social whole" of what is best for the individual. His claim is that the concept of positive freedom entails the idea that what is rationally necessary is embodied in a higher consciousness or self, which then becomes identified with the state. It is clear that this view has nothing to do with the concept of positive freedom as I have presented it and in fact is antithetical to it. First of all, the conception I have proposed rules out any specification of what is "best" or "rationally necessary" for individuals and refuses to suggest what they ought to choose. It is left to individuals to determine what is best for them. This is evident from the earlier discussion in which I criticized the view of freedom as "action in accordance with one's nature," because of its essentialism, as well as from my argument that the requirements for self-development must remain broad and general so as to accommodate the various choices of individuals. Further, my view rules out any paternalism in the name of some "higher good" inasmuch as my conception of positive freedom presupposes negative freedom or freedom from external constraint on an individual's free choice as its necessary condition. Second, the view I propose rejects the holism that Berlin alleges to be characteristic of the concept of positive freedom. Thus I criticize the view that there is an overarching totality or organic whole, of which individuals are members or parts. Rather, as I shall argue in the following chapter, I regard both the state and society as constituted entities, which have no existence apart from the individuals who make them up. Beyond these differences between Berlin's view of positive freedom and my own, there is an additional criticism that may be made of his view. It is that the conception of the state as the legitimate interpreter of what is best or rationally necessary for individuals is not entailed by the original conception of positive freedom as being one's own master or being self-determining. It may rather be seen as an illegitimate transformation of the original idea (based on one historical interpretation of it), which Berlin picks on to make his point. This criticism has been developed by C.B. Macpherson.[16]

THE PRINCIPLE OF EQUALITY

The concept of positive freedom as self-development presented above entails that people must have access to the material and social conditions for their activity if they are to realize their freedom. They have to be able to appropriate these conditions or lay claim to them in order to use them for their purposes. But this gives rise to the problem of adjudicating among these claims in the contexts of social interaction in which the claims of one individual (or of a group of individuals) can be effective only if they are recognized by others. Such mutual recognition among individuals, each of whom must make such claims in order to carry out their activities, is required in two ways: one, with regard to the appropriation of material means, and the other, with regard to the acknowledgment of the individual's social status and roles. The question therefore arises of what principle or rule ought to govern such recognition. Such a principle or rule functions as a principle of distributive justice concerning the proper allocation of material and social resources. It thus addresses the validity of claims to these conditions or the rights that people have to them. I shall argue here that justice should be interpreted as a principle of equal rights to the conditions of self-development, or equal positive freedom. The principle of equal rights is familiar in traditional liberal democratic theory, but there it appears as a principle of political equality, that is, equality in voting and in civil liberties and rights. Here, however, the principle of equal rights applies not only to such political contexts but to social and economic ones as well.

What, then, is the basis for this principle of equal rights to the conditions of self-development? It may be seen to be derived from the conception of freedom as capacity (the first sense of freedom), which I discussed earlier. It will be remembered that this is a conception of free choice as a basic feature of action, manifested in the intentionality or purposiveness of such actions. As such, it is a constitutive feature of human actions. Such free choice may therefore be said to be a universal feature of human agency, which all human beings possess by virtue of being human. As I indicated earlier, this free choice is to be understood as the capacity for self-development, inasmuch as it is in the making of such choices that people realize their purposes and develop themselves. Although different individuals will of course exercise this capacity differently in their self-development, one may speak of it apart from such differences as an abstract capacity which all human beings have equally. That is, since it is defined as free choice, which is the bare capacity for self-development however differently anyone may exercise it, there can be no difference in degree or kind in this capacity among individuals.

Since human beings are all equally agents in this way, and further, since their full or concrete freedom as self-development (the second sense of freedom) requires conditions, it follows *prima facie* that no agent has more of a right to these conditions than does any other. Thus there may be said to be a *prima facie* equal right of access to the conditions of self-development. The basis, then, for arguing that no individual has more of a right to the conditions than any other is, in the first place, that no distinctions can be made among individuals with respect to their agency or their bare capacity for self-development. A possible counterargument to this view is that agents have differing capacities for freedom and that therefore their rights should be commensurate with their capacities. Against this I would argue that a distinction needs to be drawn between the general capacity for self-development and the particular talents and abilities in which indi-

61

viduals may clearly differ. Though it may make sense to claim that one individual has a greater capacity for musical or athletic development than another, this must be distinguished from the general capacity for self-development as such, which, I will argue, provides no basis for discrimination among individuals. The fuller discussion of this question of differential capacities in relation to equal rights to the conditions of self-development is the subject of a later chapter. (See Chapter 5.)

In the second place, the argument that every person, being equally an agent, has an equal claim to the conditions that are required for the exercise of this agency in self-development follows from the fact that the mere possession of the capacity for self-development is not sufficient for the realization of freedom. Rather, this capacity has to be exercised in concrete actions, which require material and social conditions. The normative imperative to realize one's freedom in this way is, as I argued earlier, posited in the very nature of human activity itself. But without the availability of the conditions for such self-development, the imperative remains empty. Thus the force of any individual's claim to the conditions derives in part from this imperative.[17] And because this imperative holds equally for each agent, their claims to the conditions are also *prima facie* equal.

However, it may be objected that such equal claims do not yet amount to equal *rights* to the conditions. Again, the mere fact that someone needs or desires a condition for his or her self-development, or that it is a value for him or her, does not imply that he or she has a right to it. To answer this objection, one would have to show how rights are integral to, or may be derived from, the conception of freedom as self-development. If the premises are true that the concrete freedom of human beings is an activity of self-development and further that free choice as a capacity for such self-development is what characterizes human beings as human, then it follows that the recognition of someone as a human being entails at the very least a recognition of that person as having this capacity (whether it is exercised or not). One may object that to recognize a capacity does not require that one recognize the validity of the claims to its exercise and thus that it is conceivable to recognize that individuals have the capacity for self-development and at the same time deny that they have a right to its exercise. But this objection is mistaken. For, as I argued earlier, the recognition of free choice is a normative recognition of its value and therefore of the imperative to realize it in the activity of self-development. To recognize someone as human in this sense, therefore, is to recognize the value of his or her humanity in his or her free activity. But, as I have argued, individuals cannot exercise this freedom of choice as a capacity for self-development without the requisite conditions. That is, this freedom remains abstract and unrealized unless the concrete means for the activity of self-development are available. Therefore, to recognize persons as free to develop themselves but not to recognize the validity of their (equal) claims to the conditions of this freedom would be empty. It would be a failure to recognize what is entailed by the concept of free choice as a capacity for self-development. To claim to understand A and also that A entails B and then to refuse to conclude therefore *that-B* would be to fail to be rationally consistent (where A is the [compound] proposition that free choice is a capacity for self-development and that there is a normative imperative for its exercise and that such exercise requires conditions, and where this entails B, that there is a normatively valid claim to these conditions). Therefore, we may conclude that since the availability of conditions is an essential part of what constitutes the meaning of the freedom of individuals to develop themselves, the recognition of this freedom entails a recognition of the validity of their claims to the conditions for self-development. But a valid claim is what we mean by a right. It follows that the recognition of human beings as human entails the recognition of their rights to the conditions of their freedom. But there is one more essential step to this argument. Freedom as free choice or the capacity for self-development is, as I argued earlier, equally possessed by all persons by virtue of their being human. Therefore, they may be said, *prima facie*, equally to have valid claims on the conditions. That is, all

63

individuals have *prima facie* equal rights to the conditions of self-development. This is the principle of equality that I would propose as commensurate with the conception of freedom presented earlier. It may be characterized as the principle of equal positive freedom.

In characterizing rights as valid claims, I am following a certain tradition in social and legal philosophy, which distinguishes between claims *simpliciter* and those that are justified or valid, where the justification is in terms of reasons, a system of rules, or general principles.[18] In particular, I would adduce Feinberg's notion of valid claims, as involving (in the case of moral rights) justification in terms of moral principles.[19] In the argument I have just made for equal positive freedom, the validity of the claims that an individual has to the necessary conditions of self-development derives from the requirement for the recognition of human beings as free agents and, as such, as having the capacity for self-development. This is the moral principle from which rights are derived and, as we have seen, is based on the argument that what characterizes human beings as human, that is, as being what they are, is freedom.

The claims which are validated by this moral principle are claims *to* conditions, as described. Yet, claim-rights have often been characterized as rights-against, that is, as involving correlative duties on the part of those against whom the claims are validly held, while rights-to have been characterized as entitlements. I do not see that these need be mutually exclusive and agree here again with Feinberg in his view that "All rights seem to merge *entitlements to* do, have, omit, or be something with *claims against* others to act or refrain from acting in certain ways."[20] While it is clear, with respect to equal rights to the conditions of self-development, what these are rights *to*, the question arises: *Against* whom are such rights held? If, as was argued, the recognition of human beings as human entails a recognition of their equal rights to the conditions of their freedom (and if we make explicit the obvious but unstated premises that human beings *ought* to be recognized as human and that they ought to be so recognized by each other reciprocally), then it follows that these rights are held by each human being against every other human being. However, since many of these rights cannot be satisfied distributively by each human being separately, and since the conditions for the self-development of any individual are often social conditions that can be met only by a community or society, then it may be said that in these cases the individual holds these rights as rights against society in general.

Returning to the notion of *rights-to* as entitlements, it has sometimes been argued that such entitlements are absolute, that is, that they are rights that cannot be overridden.[21] This is not how I conceive of such entitlements and, specifically, not how I conceive of the equal rights to the conditions of self-development. Instead, I have characterized these latter as *prima facie* rights, since, as I shall argue, this principle may be qualified under certain conditions by other principles, for example, distribution according to social need, talent, or desert, though the burden of proof for overriding the *prima facie* rights always remains on the claim being made against them. In certain cases, therefore, a differential distribution of specific conditions may be justified. But as will be seen, this does not undermine the general force of this principle of equality. It should perhaps be noted here (though it is discussed later) that I do not interpret the principle of equal rights itself as requiring across the board an equal distribution of goods or conditions in any simple quantitative or enumerative sense. Rather, in some of its applications, it will involve a notion of the distribution of equivalent conditions.

In speaking of these rights as *prima facie* equal rights, a difficulty is that they may be so qualified by other principles or rights that they retain no priority. If they are merely provisional or presumptive, then there is nothing that keeps them from being abrogated or subordinated as circumstances arise. Against this, it has been argued that the presumption in favor of a *prima facie* right over conflicting rights is to be regarded as so strong that it may be overridden only in the exceptional cases when moral reasons can be given for overriding it

65

(Brandt); or when considerations of justice demand it (Frankena); or, more stringently still, when the only acceptable moral reasons for just exceptions will be those that are the very same reasons that support the *prima facie* rights themselves (Vlastos).[22] My own view tends toward the stronger end of this spectrum, as will be seen in a later chapter.

· Another clarification of the sense in which I am using *"prima facie"* here concerns the distinction between the general principle of equal positive freedom and the interpretation of this principle in terms of particular rights (e.g., rights to life or subsistence rights, on the one hand, and rights to advanced professional training or to employment, on the other). I would suggest that in the case of those rights like the first two mentioned here, which I will characterize as basic rights, the rights to which each individual has an equal claim may not simply be *prima facie* but may be absolute, whereas in the second case of nonbasic rights, these rights may in some circumstances be overridden. Thus the general principle, which serves heuristically as a guideline for the determination of specific rights to conditions as equal rights, needs to be qualified as *prima facie*, even though some of the rights that it covers may not be.

The conditions to which these equal rights extend, under this general principle, include both negative and positive ones. Thus there are equal rights to the absence of constraint, as well as equal civil liberties and political rights. These traditional negative liberties and political rights are indispensable to my conception of freedom. There are also rights to be free from exploitation and domination. Beyond these negative conditions, there are equal rights to the positive or enabling conditions of activity, such as means of subsistence and labor, as well as access to education and training. A full discussion of all these rights is offered in Chapter 7.

In arguing for equal rights to the conditions of self-development, I have proposed that these rights are ultimately grounded in the equal freedom that all human beings have simply by virtue of being human. This is not to say that the argument for these rights consists in the mere assertion that

66

people have them by virtue of being human. Rather, the rights have to be derived from this ground. And the analysis I have offered of the nature of freedom, together with the argument concerning the validity of claims and the normative imperative for the recognition of these claims, is intended as such a derivation. Other philosophical views about rights have adduced different grounds and have offered different arguments, and it may be useful to situate my own view in this context.

Arguments on the ground or justification of rights typically divide into naturalistic or deontological sorts; that is, they assert either that these rights have some natural or empirical basis from which they can be derived, for example, interest or need, [23] or that they are a priori or are given as intuitively self-evident, or are derived from other more fundamental rights. [24] A number of major theories of rights, however, fall between these types. One alternative type derives rights from some normative rather than merely factual ground, but one which is not understood as a right. Thus, for example, a number of theorists have based their justification of rights on the value of human dignity or worth, [25] on the rational necessity of recognizing human beings as ends rather than means, [26] or on the normative presuppositions or requirements of human action or freedom. [27] Still another approach, which is methodologically rather than ontologically oriented, grounds rights in some sort of institutional or social decision procedure, whether this is taken as conventional or as based on some deep principles of rationality. [28]

Ronald Dworkin, in *Taking Rights Seriously*, proposes that rights are based on the equal concern and respect which are due to every citizen. He sees equality as the fundamental right and analyzes it as having two aspects: namely, a right to treatment as an equal and a right to equal treatment. Dworkin characterizes the right to equal treatment as "the right to . . . the same distribution of goods or opportunities as anyone else has or is given," whereas the right to treatment as an equal is "the right to equal concern and respect in the political decision about how these goods and opportunities are to be distributed."[29] Dworkin argues that the right to treatment as an equal is more fundamental, and that the right to equal treatment holds when it follows from this more fundamental right. Further, he argues that the right to equality is the ground for other rights and specifically of rights to distinct liberties, which follow only when the more basic right to treatment as an equal can be shown to require them. According to Dworkin, then, there is no general right to liberty, and he holds that the common conception of freedom as a fundamental right is confused and mistaken. Since liberty rights derive from equality, on his view, he maintains that there can be no conflict between liberty and equality understood correctly.

Dworkin frames his discussion of rights in the context of political morality rather than in some more general way and does not find any more ultimate grounds for the right of equality from which the others are derived. Rather, he presumes that we will all accept the postulate that the government must treat people with equal concern and respect, which he holds to be basic to the liberal conception of the state. Dworkin's argument proceeds to the view that rights thus based are rights of individuals against the state and that they cannot be overriden by any considerations of social utility or by majority rights.

I have offered this brief exposition of Dworkin's view on the origin and basis of rights for the purpose of situating my own view. It may be seen to contrast with Dworkin's in several main respects, two of which may be noted here. First, whereas I propose that equal rights have their origin in the equal agency of persons and offer an argument as to how they may be generated on this basis, Dworkin, by contrast, presupposes the right to equality as a postulate of political morality. He offers no argument for this postulate other than the presumption that we will all accept it as the belief in the equal human worth and dignity of people, which is shared by members of a political culture like ours. A second difference concerns Dworkin's derivation of rights to specific liberties from the right to equality, and his denial of a general right to liberty. I have argued that liberty or freedom is the fundamental ground of rights and that equal rights are themselves based on the equal freedom of agents. Therefore, there is a commensurability in principle between freedom and equality. Thus, like Dworkin, I also see no fundamental conflict between freedom and equality (such as that alleged by Nozick and Charvet, among others[30]). But I do not argue for this compatibility on the same basis that he proposes (namely, that liberty rights derive from equality). The relation between freedom and equality is discussed further in Chapter 7.

An elaborate argument on the grounds of rights is developed by Alan Gewirth in his *Reason and Morality*, and in some of the essays in his collection *Human Rights*.[31] I will not attempt to reconstruct or criticize that argument generally here, but will focus on some crucial points of difference between my own view and his. In briefest form, Gewirth proposes to derive human rights from an account of what an individual agent must claim as the necessary conditions for his or her action. From the agent's own "internal, conative perspective," in which he or she must claim the rights to freedom and well-being as a matter of prudential necessity, Gewirth proposes to move to the moral domain, in which each individual must, on pain of self-contradiction, recognize these rights as rights that every other human being has, by virtue of being a prospective agent.[32] Gewirth thus characterizes these rights to freedom and well-being as generic rights and argues that the logical principle of universalizability entails that in acknowledging his or her own rights as generic, this same recognition must be accorded to all other prospective agents.

As several critics have pointed out, however, there is at least a difficulty if not a failure of the argument in the move from individual prudential considerations to moral ones, in which there is a recognition of the rights of others, a move which Gewirth characterizes as "a subsequent step in the argument."[33] The transition from the merely prudential to the moral status of the individual's rights-claim comes, according to Gewirth, from the fact that the agent claims the rights to freedom and well-being as generic rights, as rights which hold for all prospective agents as necessary conditions for their action. But this is already to include in the notion of agency something more than Gewirth himself allows in his account of the individual agent acting prudentially in pursuit of his or her own purposes. For if the right claimed by the agent is a generic right, then it is already surreptitiously moral at the outset, and its universalizability is assured even as the agent acts presumably only prudentially. In this way, Gewirth's argument seems to be question-begging, since he builds in the moral status of these rights at the outset. That they can then be derived by a logical argument is not surprising.

My own approach to the ground of rights differs significantly from that of Gewirth, though it may superficially appear to be similar. I believe that two of the main ways in which it differs show how my view can avoid the criticism just made concerning the question-begging character of Gewirth's argument. First, I take the freedom of agents not to be a necessary condition of their agency, but rather its constitutive feature. Therefore, the recognition of their rights to the exercise of this agency is not based on the recognition from an individual's "internal, conative view" of what is required for his or her successful action, but rather upon the ontological features of agency or what makes agents what they are. In starting from the first-person perspective, as he does, I do not think that Gewirth can get to the generic features of agency, which, according to him, are the basis for the moral status of the rights. Thus I propose that the ground of rights or their justification, instead of emerging as a dialectical consequence of an individual's recognition of what is rationally entailed by the pursuit of his or her own interests, is inherent in the identifying feature of this individuality itself, that is, freedom.

Related to this is the second difference that I want to note. It is that Gewirth's account begins, almost as Hobbes's does, with isolated individuals prudentially pursuing their own interests. Its starting point appears to be egoistic, both in the

characterization of individuals and in Gewirth's methodological construction. Sociality emerges there as the logical consequence of a rational reflection on what is required if individuals are to avoid self-contradiction in the assertion of their
rights to freedom and well-being. But these rights, though
generic on Gewirth's account, are claimed fundamentally as
the rights of agents in pursuing only individual ends. Thus,
sociality is a consequence rather than an ingredient of an
agent's actions, and it is this sociality that is the basis for the
transition from merely prudential to moral rights. My account, by contrast, proposes that individuals are social from
the start, both in the fact that social relations are an essential
mode of their individual self-development and that they char-
acteristically engage in common activities, oriented to common and not merely individual ends. It seems to me that one
aspect of Gewirth's difficulty in moving from the prudential
nonmoral to the moral character of rights is coordinate with
this lack of a social characterization of individual agency.
Because it is missing in the original account of individual
action, he has to introduce it in a rather ad hoc way, by
means of the concept of generic rights. Since my account sees
this sociality as an ingredient of the character of agency, the
ground for what Gewirth calls moral rights is already built in.
Likewise, in the view I present, reciprocal recognition by
agents of their equal agency, which arises as a logical consequence of rational reflection on Gewirth's view, is already
part of the practical contexts of social interaction which are
the framework for individual self-development. Thus the recognition of the rights of others has its basis in the relation of
reciprocity as a characteristic feature of the structure of action
in everyday life.

SOCIAL RELATIONS OF RECIPROCITY AND COMMON ACTIVITY

Equal rights to the conditions of self-development require a
certain form of social relations if they are to be realized, for as

I argued above, it would require the recognition by each individual of the equal freedom of the others. Such a relation is therefore one of reciprocal recognition of their equal agency. This relation of reciprocity, which may be seen as one of the social conditions for self-development, needs further analysis here. As will be seen, such a reciprocal relation among agents is an important characteristic of democratic decision-making, as I will discuss it in the final section of this chapter. Another form of social relations that has import for the conception of freedom as self-development and also for the form and scope of democratic decision-making is what we may call common or joint activity, namely, activity in which a group of individuals act to realize a common or shared aim. A brief analysis of these two forms of social relations – reciprocity and common activity – will serve to make clear the crucially social dimension of the concept of freedom that I am proposing and will also provide some of the grounds for the argument for democracy, which concludes this chapter.

The relation of reciprocity is grounded in the need that individuals have for the cooperation and support of others in the activities in which they realize their individual or common purposes. This sociality is thus one of the conditions of freedom as self-development. The question is what exactly constitutes a relation of reciprocity and what normative claim can one make for the requirement of reciprocity in a theory of freedom and of justice? For indeed, it could be argued commonsensically, against the view that reciprocity is a requirement, that the self-development of an individual may be achieved not only without reciprocal relations with others, but indeed by means of the nonreciprocal relation of the domination and exploitation of others in the service of that individual's own needs and purposes. This would mean subordinating the development of the others and limiting their freedom to whatever degree necessary so as to satisfy the requirements for the self-development of the privileged individual. This is in fact not merely a hypothetical case but historically a common one. Obviously, however, it violates the principle of equal positive freedom or of equal rights to the conditions of self-development, which I argued for earlier. This principle requires the recognition by each individual of the equal freedom of all the others and such recognition constitutes the relation of reciprocity. It is through such reciprocal recognition that individuals can meet each other's needs in a noncoercive way by voluntary cooperation. But beyond the normative imperative of equal positive freedom, it could be argued – in a way related to the earlier discussion of sociality and self-development – that without reciprocal recognition, individuals would deprive each other of the resources and support that each would afford the other in the achievement of their purposes; or else, they would have to divert much of their energy and attention to coercing the others to provide the needed cooperation. In this way, reciprocity may be said to serve as a social condition for self-development. Further, even in the case of a coercive relation between individuals, and despite its predominantly nonreciprocal character, there remains an element of bare reciprocity, in that each must recognize the other as an agent, if only in the relation of enforcing one's will upon another or of acceding to the will of the other. Therefore, even where self-development is based on coercion, reciprocity in this minimal sense remains a condition.

In one mode of such reciprocity, one individual may meet another's needs simply for the sake of getting the other to meet the needs of the first. The motive for the reciprocal actions of each may therefore be limited to what each sees as his or her own interest or benefit and the form of such exchange may be characterized as "tit for tat." In this mode, although there is a tacit recognition of the other as an agent insofar as the other is free to respond in kind or not, one agent does not yet recognize the other's interests except as it serves his or her own. The other is therefore viewed only as an instrument or means to realize one's own purposes or ends, and indeed the entire relation may be characterized as instrumental reciprocity.

This form of reciprocity may be seen to be compatible with,

and indeed to characterize, the nature of the relations between individuals as it is conceived in liberal democratic
theory. This theory has most often been understood as entailing a model of rational egoism or of enlightened self-interest,
in which each individual is free to pursue his or her own
interest up to the limit of impinging on the like freedom of
others. This model implies an interpretation of reciprocity as
instrumental, in that agents are seen to relate to each other
only insofar as they are useful to each other in some way.
Such an interpretation of reciprocity does not, however, exhaust the forms that this relation may take. It is inadequate to
account for the noninstrumental forms of reciprocity that
may characterize the social relations of agents engaged in
geniunely common activity or those relations in which a-
gents regard each other's interests as having value and demanding respect in themselves.

Such a noninstrumental form of reciprocity may be called
social reciprocity. It may be described as a social relation in
which the recognition by one agent of the other (or of others)
involves an explicit acknowledgment of the other's agency
and of their interests and judgments as demanding respect
and thus readiness to take the other's purposes and views into
consideration in one's own judgments and actions. This may
also be characterized therefore as a reciprocity of respect.

Such social reciprocity is also involved in relations among
people engaged in common or joint activity, where this activity is undertaken for shared purposes that they have voluntarily agreed upon. In associating themselves in this way,
every member of a group is minimally bound to recognize
the equality of the others as agents freely choosing to join in
the activity and to contribute to the realization of a common
aim. What is reciprocal in this form of cooperation is first of
all just this recognition of and respect for the other's status as
a voluntary participant in the process. Beyond this, each
member of the group contributes reciprocally to the others
insofar as they each contribute to an end that they all share in
common. Such a genuinely common aim, however, is one
whose achievement realizes a common good or satisfies a

common interest, which is not merely an aggregation of particular goods or individual interests.

It is clear that not all activities by a group are reciprocal in this way. Those acting together to achieve a purpose not chosen by themselves but imposed on them by others, and those who are joined in a group by force or coercion (e.g., slaves) may indeed be cooperating toward some end but cannot be said to be in a social relation of reciprocity. (They may, of course, enter into relations of reciprocity and mutual respect among themselves even in such circumstances, but this would go beyond their original constitution as a group.)

In both of these forms of social reciprocity – as involving relations of respect and common activity – this mode of social interaction is to be distinguished from instrumental reciprocity or "tit for tat" relations. First, as I have noted, where instrumental reciprocity is a relation in which agents are related to each other only insofar as they are useful to each other's individual ends or interests, in social reciprocity agents take each other's aims as worthy of respect in their own right. Second, the conception of individuals here, as distinguished from that of instrumental reciprocity, is that they are genuinely social beings with common interests, rather than only individual interests. As will be seen, these features of social reciprocity provide one of the bases for the account of the form and procedures of decision-making in the new democratic theory that I am proposing, and which contrasts with liberal democratic theory.

The forms of the relation of reciprocity are not exhausted by the instrumental or social types which I have discussed. Because of its centrality to the understanding of social relations, it would be useful to give a more formal analysis of the concept of reciprocity here and to distinguish more systematically among its various modes.

A reciprocal social relation may most generally be defined as one in which each agent acts with respect to the other on the basis of a shared understanding, and a free agreement, to the effect that the actions of one with respect to the other are equivalent to the actions of the other with respect to the first.

A necessary condition for reciprocity, therefore, is that it can be a relation only between agents, that is, between individuals who have the capacity for free choice. It also entails that these agents freely agree (whether tacitly or explicitly) to regard each other's actions as equivalent in some relevant dimension (of quality, quantity, benefit, etc.). A further necessary condition of reciprocity is that each agent share with the other an understanding of the actions of each of them. For without such a shared understanding, one action cannot be said to be in reciprocation for the other. That is, the relation of reciprocity is essentially an intentional one: The actions are equivalent in being understood to be equivalent and are reciprocal in being understood to be reciprocal by the agents themselves.

Reciprocity, generally defined here, may be seen to be differentiated in social practice into several specific forms. These may be summarized briefly here as follows: (1) *Customary reciprocity* is the relation in which the equivalence of the actions among agents has been established by traditional or ritual social practices. Examples of this would be the customary reciprocation of gifts, of the handshake and other forms of greeting or politesse such as, "Hello. How are you?" / "Fine thanks. How are you?" or "Thank you" / "You're welcome". (2) *Formal reciprocity* is the relation in which there is an exchange of equivalents, in which the equal value or assessment of the things exchanged or of the actions of each of the agents is not established by custom but by the explicit agreement of the individual agents themselves. An example of such an exchange of equivalents in formal reciprocity is the exchange of goods or services or the purchase of things in the marketplace. Other examples would be any mutual agreements to abide by rules or procedures, or to observe certain boundaries, or again, contracts of any sort. (3) *Instrumental reciprocity* is a mode of formal reciprocity in which the exchange of equivalents is undertaken by each agent solely for the sake of each one's own gratification or for the satisfaction of his or her own needs. Each takes the other into account, but only as a means to his or her own ends. (4) *Social reciproc-*

ity, as discussed above, goes beyond formal and instrumental reciprocity in that it requires, in addition to a recognition of the agents as free and equal, a respect and concern by each agent for the aims and interests of the other as having independent value. Where social reciprocity is manifest in common activity, this respect and concern is shown for the aims that the agents share in common and is reciprocated in that each one's aim is the same as that of each of the others. (5) Finally, *mutuality*, or full reciprocity, is a relation in which (a) each agent recognizes the other as free and as capable of self-development, (b) each acts with regard to the other in ways that enhance the other's self-development on the basis of a consideration of the other's needs, and (c) both agents take such mutual enhancement of each other's agency as a conscious aim.

It may be seen that these types of reciprocity arrange themselves in an ordered way in what may be called stages of the development of this relation. Though I am not ready to propose an argument that these are stages of historical development, there is a sense in which these types can be understood as stages of a normative development, that is, from customary to formal to social reciprocity and, finally, to mutuality. I would qualify this normative progression in one way, however: Recalling that relations of reciprocity are among the social conditions for freedom as self-development, I would not go so far as to propose that mutuality in social and political life is a condition for such freedom. As we shall see, social reciprocity suffices as the social and political condition for freedom and for the extension of democracy that I propose in this book. Mutuality goes beyond what is required for democracy but remains as a norm for personal relations among individuals and for some forms of voluntary association (such as groups set up for purposes of cultural, intellectual, or athletic improvement and advancement).

By contrast with all of these forms of reciprocity there are forms of nonreciprocal social relations that inhibit freedom or impede self-development. These may be analyzed as relations of domination. Domination may be defined as a relation in which one agent or group of agents controls the direction or range of the actions of another agent or group of agents by means of control over the conditions that the others require for their activity and in such a way as to deny or inhibit the equal freedom of these others. Depending on the conditions that are thus controlled, domination may take psychological or cultural, as well as economic, social, or political forms. On this definition of domination, it should be clear that it is distinguished from those nonreciprocal relations in which there may be said to be a legitimate exercise of authority.

Before turning to the argument for the extension of democracy in the last section of this chapter, I want to consider briefly the second form of social relations which serves as a condition for self-development, namely, common or joint activity. As in the case of reciprocity, the analysis of the nature and structure of common activity will have important bearing on the account of democratic decision-making and the argument for its extension.

Common activity may be defined as activity in which a number of individuals join together to effect a given end. This end or aim may be a shared end in the sense that they have all freely chosen it together, or it may be shared only in the weaker sense that they all cooperate to effect an end set for them by someone else or even imposed on them from without and which they have not chosen. Further, such common activity may either be aimed at the common good of all those who participate in it, or it may be aimed at some private or external good. Insofar as it is aimed at the common good, this end may be chosen by the members of the group themselves who jointly determine it, or it may be chosen for them or on their behalf by someone else (on the presumption that they are not competent to choose it for themselves or on the paternalistic premise that someone else knows better what is best for them). However, it is only where they choose for themselves what the end of the activity shall be and what the good is which it is intended to serve that we shall speak of genuinely common activity in the strong sense, as distinguished from common activity in general.

Common activity obviously contrasts with individual activity undertaken for individual ends and also from any mere aggregation of individual activities in pursuit of such ends. Such common activity essentially involves the cooperation and coordination of many individuals in the realization of their joint projects or purposes. Though there may be ends that could be achieved either by individual or by common activity, there nevertheless is a large class of projects that can only be realized through such cooperation. Moreover, such socially achievable projects constitute an essential part of what human beings require for meeting their life needs and for their self-development. Thus, for example, any branch of economic production requires such socially organized forms of activity, and so too does any political system. Further, as suggested earlier, the experience of participating in, and cooperating with others in common tasks serves as one of the conditions of individual self-development. In such contexts, individuals have the opportunity to exercise and develop their social, moral, and intellectual capacities.

The question might be raised concerning whether such common activity subordinates the individual to the group as a whole and delimits his or her freedom and initiative. Both the historical and the recent experience of the supervenience of the authority and power of totalities over individuals make this a sharp issue for any theory of democracy in which common activity or sociality plays an important role. The relation of the group to the individual in common activity would appear to be holistic in nature if the choice of the ends of the group's activity were imposed upon its members by some external power or authority over which they had no control; or if the members themselves, having originally determined their common purpose and their rules of operation, so fetishize or reify the group as to relinquish all future power of decision. Totalitarian states or religious cults easily come to mind as egregious examples of such supervening authority and power of the group over its members, and many lesser examples may be cited as well.

However, even in such cases, the individuals retain the

79

capacity to choose to reject the external authority or to dissolve the group. As I will discuss it later, such a choice may not be a rationally feasible one under all conditions and may require the creation of the conditions for realizing such changes. Thus it will be seen in the following chapter that the account I give of the relation of individuals to the groups, or to the social wholes or institutions of which they are members rules out any holistic interpretation of this relation.

Of course, the possibility of such a holistic interpretation of common activity or of groups does not arise in the case of what I have characterized as genuinely common activity. For here the choice of a shared or a common good is always determined by the individuals who constitute the group and who recognize each other reciprocally as free and equal members of it. There is thus no possibility of a supervenient or external authority, which can impose its will upon the group. However, there remains the danger that the members of such a freely constituted group may reify the group's own authority and relinquish all participation in decisions about its aims and activities. The holistic interpretation of such a reified authority would simply reflect this same misconception, mistaking the apparent reified authority for the real authority of the individuals who constitute the group.

AN ARGUMENT FOR EXTENDING DEMOCRACY

At the outset of this chapter, I indicated that I would argue for four theses: first, that freedom should be understood as an activity of self-development, requiring the availability of conditions; second, that the principle of equality should be understood as one of *prima facie* equal rights to the conditions of self-development; third, that reciprocity and common activity serve as social conditions for freedom, and also have implications for the form and scope of democratic decision-making; and fourth, that democracy should apply not only to the political domain, but to the economic and social domains as well.

Having argued for the first three theses in this chapter, it remains to show how the fourth thesis concerning the extension of democracy and of participatory forms of decision-making may be derived from the principles established thus far.

It may be useful to begin here by characterizing the conception of democracy in traditional liberal political philosophy in order to clarify the sense in which I am proposing an extension of democracy and to illuminate the differences between this conception and the one I will develop. Traditional political theory has taken democracy to be a form of government in which people govern themselves either by direct participation in decisions affecting all of them or by the election of representatives. On this theory, all those individuals who are taken as constituting the political community, i.e., as citizens, have equal political rights and liberties. This entails that, regardless of any differences in social or economic status, all citizens (with a few specified exceptions, e.g., minors or prisoners) have an equal right to participate or be represented in the making of governmental decisions. Political authority thus ultimately reposes in the citizens, either directly in their power to make decisions or indirectly in their consent to be governed. Further, on this theory, each individual is regarded as free to do what he or she chooses without being constrained by others to the extent that such actions do not interfere with the same freedom to act that the others have. This is the conception of negative freedom discussed earlier. One of the main purposes of government on this view is to protect this negative freedom through institutions that prevent one individual from harming another or that punish those who have harmed others. As this traditional theory develops, democracy is further seen as a means for protecting the negative freedom of individuals by preventing the government itself from becoming a constraint on the freedom of individuals. Control over the power of government to make arbitrary decisions or to impose constraints on the citizens is provided by periodic elections through which the people have control over their representatives. Further, the equal representation of all the citizens is meant to ensure that no one group or faction can control the government for its own interests at the expense of the others.

On this traditional view, democracy has in principle been conceived as limited to the political sphere, that is, to the form and processes of government. It is seen as not pertaining to the contexts of social and economic life, which are taken to be spheres of private, rather than public, activity. This restriction of democracy to the political sphere is based on the conception of negative freedom and specifically on the idea that the only legitimate constraint that can be imposed on the freedom of individuals is to prevent their actions from interfering with the like freedom of others. This gives rise to the conception that government is principally for the purposes of protecting the civil liberties and rights of individuals and the protection of individuals against criminal harm by others. Therefore, government is not to interfere in any way in those functions that are taken to be the proper domain of private activity or judgment (including the personal, the religious, the social, and the economic). Thus, as a form of government, democracy is taken to be restricted to the political sphere taken in this narrow sense. This view is perhaps best expressed in the aphorism, "That government is best that governs least."

It is quite clear that this theoretical form of democracy is not the one which exists in practice. Thus, as we know, government often acts in the interests of the economically powerful; all are not equally represented in the political process; government interferes in the lives of its citizens beyond the limits described above; and the government plays an active role in economic, cultural, and social life. But I am not primarily interested here in an empirical critique of current political practices. Rather, I am principally interested in a reconstruction of the theoretical foundations of democracy and therefore in a critique of the traditional theory. Nevertheless, a reflection on the prevailing practices of democracy not only reveals a discrepancy between democratic theory and political practice but also points to some of the shortcomings of the traditional theory. Thus, while it is a central tenet of the theory that all citizens have equal political rights, in practice this equality has often remained merely abstract or formal, because many people lack the political or institutional means through which they could exercise these rights effectively. In contemporary practice, effective participation in political decision-making is often dependent upon access to economic means and organizational structures, e.g., lobbying, advertising, and the media. This lack of effectiveness is expressed in voter apathy and in feelings of political powerlessness by ordinary citizens in the face of organized and well-financed political bureaucracies. One might also suggest that such political inequality in practice results from inequalities outside of the political sphere, namely, economic and social inequalities. Thus, for example, poverty, discrimination in educational or job opportunities, or unemployment make it difficult for people to exercise their political rights effectively. The traditional theory, in limiting itself to the purely political sphere of voting and representation, must necessarily fail to take into account the effect that such inequalities, existing outside the political sphere, have upon the political process. It thus fails to protect the very political equality that it enunciates in its principles. This consequence also follows from the traditional theory's underlying presupposition of negative freedom, which disregards the social and economic conditions for freedom as well as for the exercise of equal rights.

The critique of the traditional liberal theory of democracy suggests that an alternative theory is required, namely, one that answers to the criticisms that I have made of the foundations of the traditional theory. The new theory of democracy, as I have suggested, takes as its foundation the alternative conception of freedom which includes negative freedom as a necessary condition but goes beyond it to include positive freedom or self-development as well, where this requires access to material and social conditions of one's activity. The principle of equality is likewise conceived as extending beyond the conception of political equality of the traditional theory to include also *prima facie* equal rights to the social and economic conditions of self-development. It will be seen that the theory I propose does not reject the traditional forms of political democracy but rather develops the conception of democracy and extends it to new contexts.

The principle of democracy to be established here is the following: every person who engages in a common activity with others has an equal right to participate in making decisions concerning such activity. This right to participate applies not only to the domain of politics but to social and economic activities as well. The scope of such decision-making includes both the determination of the ends of the common activity and the ways in which it is to be carried out.

The argument for this principle of democracy begins from the proposition argued for earlier, that freedom as self-development is grounded in agency, or the capacity for choice, and that it can be attained only through activities that individuals freely determine. Human beings are therefore fundamentally characterized as agents who choose or make decisions concerning their actions. Further, I argued earlier that all human beings are equally agents in this sense and that they have an equal right to the exercise of this agency and a *prima facie* equal right to the conditions necessary for its exercise as a process of self-development. Further, I have previously distinguished between the context of individual activity, where individuals act with respect to their own personal ends, and common activity, where individuals jointly engage in action toward a common purpose. I have also argued that such common activity is one of the conditions for self-development – in providing a social context for reciprocity and in making possible the achievement of ends that could not be achieved by an individual alone.

These serve, then, as the premises of the argument. But if individuals have an equal right to determine their own actions, and further, if engaging in common activity is one of the necessary conditions for an individual's self-development (where self-development, and not agency alone, is the meaning of concrete freedom), then it follows that there is an equal right to participate in determining the course of such

84

common activity. For if an individual were to take part in common activity without having any role in making decisions about it and under the direction of another, then this would not be an activity of self-development, since such self-development requires determining the course of one's activity. It is only in this sense that common activity can be a condition for self-development. And since there is an equal right to the conditions of self-development, it follows that there is an equal right to make decisions about such common activity.

Clearly, since the form of such common activity differs from individual activity, in which one makes decisions about one's own actions independently of others, the nature of decision-making in common activity must also differ. It cannot simply be the aggregate of individuals' decisions about their own separate actions. Rather, as joint activity defined by common purposes, it requires a form of participation in the common decisions which bind all the members of the group. Thus, its appropriate form is codetermination or shared decision-making among equals. The general conclusion of this argument, as stated above, is therefore that all individuals who are engaged in a common activity have an equal right to participate in the decisions concerning it. But this is to say that, in principle, there is a normative requirement for the right to democratic participation in decision-making in all the contexts of common activity. Therefore, this argues for the extension of democracy beyond the context of political life alone to decision-making in economic and social contexts as well, for so much of common activity takes place in these contexts.

An objection may be raised against the argument for the extension of democracy as it has been presented here. It is that while it may be granted that engaging in common activity is a condition for self-development, it doesn't follow from this that every common activity in which an individual takes part is a necessary condition for that individual's self-development. Therefore, lacking this premise, there is no basis for concluding that every individual has an equal right to participate in decision-making concerning all the common activities in which they are engaged. Indeed, some of these activities may be indifferent with respect to an individual's self-development and others may even be pernicious.

This objection is correct in holding that not all common activities in which an individual takes part necessarily contribute to his or her self-development. However, what may or may not contribute to the self-development of the individual often cannot be known in advance; nor can one know what any given individual will choose as a path of self-development. Therefore, there would be no basis for one person or group of persons to decide for another what the "proper" common activities are that would be required for that other's self-development. Moreover, any such attempt to decide for another in this way would undermine the very condition of free choice or agency that, as I argued earlier, is necessary for self-development. In order to guarantee this condition of agency, the options for participation in decision-making have to remain open, and the only way to secure this in practice that is compatible with equal agency is through equal rights to participate in decision-making in all those forms of common activity in which an individual takes part. In later discussion, it will be seen that there are qualifications on this equal right to participate in social decision-making, but they do not derive from considerations concerning the relation between a common activity and an individual's self-development on which this objection is based.

The proposed extension of democracy beyond the political sphere to the arenas of economic and social life has some important implications for changes in the organizations and institutional structures in these domains. These will be discussed in subsequent chapters and especially in Chapters 4 and 9. As will be seen, perhaps the most important implication is the requirement for workers' self-management, as the institutional form of the extension of democracy to the workplace or the firm. I will also argue that democracy should apply as well to decision-making concerning the broader contexts of economic policy. Further, it will be seen to extend to forms of common activity in social life such as educational and cultural institutions and local community organizations.

The equal right to participate in social decisions also has implications for the form and nature of the democratic process. Specifically, it implies that where feasible, the form of democratic decision-making should be participatory rather than representative. That is, it should directly involve the members of a group in deliberating upon and making decisions, rather than having them elect representatives to make these decisions on their behalf. The reasons for this are first of all that direct involvement of the individuals provides the opportunity for the exercise of their agency in determining the nature and course of their common activity and this, as we have seen, is a condition for their self-development. In addition, participation would serve to develop the range of choices that an individual has, as well as the individual's capacities to deal with diverse situations, and in this sense could serve as a means for fuller self-development. Moreover, a participatory form is the surest and most accurate way of taking into account each individual's judgments and concerns about the common activity and thus would most genuinely realize his or her equal rights to participate. For even the fairest form of representation can only approximate to the direct expression of the will or judgment of the members of the group, since the representative must construe what the common judgment would be if it were directly expressed, and this is plainly open to error.

The realization of equal rights in social decision-making thus requires the extension and development of participatory processes. However, such processes of direct participation clearly cannot be instituted in all contexts, as for example in large-scale and centralized policy-making in government, industry, and cultural affairs. Here, what is required is a system of representation based on participation at the lower levels. In such contexts, the equal right to participate in decision-making is satisfied insofar as every member of the group or institution has an equal right to participate in the election of representatives. Furthermore, the representatives or delegates would be held accountable to those whom they represent by periodic elections and regular consultations with those whom they represent, as well as being subject to recall. Such forms of representation, as well as of direct participation, have been discussed primarily in the context of political processes. However, in the account given here, they would apply not only to this context but also to decision-making in economic, social, and cultural life.

It will be remembered that I introduced reciprocity as one of the social conditions necessary for self-development and that I suggested that it has important implications for the form and practice of democracy. The democratic process in decision-making, as it is usually understood, already may be seen to embody this relation of reciprocity. Thus where people democratically participate in a joint decision, this presupposes that each one in principle must take the others as having equal rights to voice their views and an equal vote in effecting the outcome. In this sense, the individuals take their relations to each other to be equivalent, that is, each one reciprocally recognizes the others as agents and as having equal rights in the process. But beyond this, it follows from my account that the deliberative process of democratic decision-making requires that each participant not only permit the others to express their views and offer their judgments but take the others' views seriously into account in arriving at his or her own judgment. Clearly, this does not require agreement with the views of others, but rather serious attention to, and respect for, their views. Such reciprocal respect also presupposes that disagreements be tolerated and not suppressed. In effect, this exhibits the relation of social reciprocity that I discussed earlier. Thus the form of democratic decision-making is not simply an instance of formal reciprocity nor is it an instance of instrumental reciprocity or "tit for tat." It is not instrumental in two senses: first, that the participants are not simply pursuing their own interests but are taking the interests and views of others seriously into account; and second, that they share a common end or interest as the object of their decisions. The result of such reciprocal recognition is that individuals taking part in democratic interaction may learn to take each others' needs and purposes into account and to respect differences among themselves and this may contribute to the self-development of each of them. More generally, in realizing the various dimensions of social reciprocity noted above, the practice of democratic decision-making itself serves as a condition of self-development.

These considerations of the role of reciprocity in democratic processes suggest a further point. The reciprocal recognition and respect for the other which defines social reciprocity is most fully realized in the direct or face-to-face interactions which characterize participatory forms of decision-making. This provides further support for the view that wherever feasible such participatory forms rather than representative ones should be implemented. However, this does not mean that the procedures of representative democracy fail to provide any opportunities for reciprocity. Even in the ordinary practice of political elections, there is the tacit and formal recognition of the equal rights and agency of the citizens. And if representative democracy were more fully developed and extended, the deliberation and discourse among citizens or among the participants in any other common activity, or again, between representatives and those who choose them, would provide opportunities for the growth of social reciprocity and for the respect among persons which it connotes.

It may be useful to stress one further implication of the general analysis given here. The scope of democratic decision-making is social, that is, it pertains to those decisions that have to do with the common ends or purposes of a group or with determining the course of its activity. The private lives of individuals are not the province of such social decisions nor may such decisions intrude on the privacy or the self-development of individuals, except insofar as such private actions impinge on the equal right to self-development of others. Except in such a case, any intrusion upon the privacy of individuals would contradict the very purposes of democracy as a social condition for the realization of the freedom of all individuals.

Rethinking democracy

Democracy has been redefined in this chapter as deriving its normative justification from the principle of equal positive freedom or equal rights to the conditions of self-development, and as providing the institutional form of decision-making that most fully serves as a condition for freedom. The extended account of the concept of freedom as self-development offered here, which takes freedom as a preeminent value, is intended to provide the ethical foundations for a theory of democracy which argues for its extension beyond the political realm to all forms of common activity.

Chapter 2

Ontological foundations of democracy

Every social and political theory presupposes, whether explicitly or tacitly, an ontology, that is, a conception of the nature of the entities and relations that constitute social life. Thus every theory works with some conception of the nature of individuals or persons, of the social relations among them, and of the sort of reality that is constituted by such complex entities as social institutions and their processes. The analysis and criticism of the ontological commitments of such theories therefore ought to be part of the philosophical examination of them. Furthermore, I would hold that the development of an adequate political or social theory requires a coherent ontology at its philosophical foundations, which may thus be characterized as a *social ontology*. By this I mean the construction of a systematic theory of the nature of social reality in terms of its basic entities, relations, and processes, and correlatively, the examination and critique of the ontologies implied by alternative social and political theories.

In this chapter, I will consider what the ontological foundations of an adequate theory of democracy would be. In order to do this, I will begin with a criticism of the ontological presuppositions of three prevailing theories of democracy and show how these three criticisms also bear on their shortcomings as political theories. Then I will propose an alternative ontology which underlies the conception of democracy that I presented in the previous chapter. This ontology, I would claim, avoids the shortcomings of the ontologies that underlie the alternative theories that I discuss. In the next chapter, I will consider some of the philosophical problems raised by such an approach, which I have earlier called quasi-foundationalist, in the context of a general consideration of foundationalism in ethics.

In the first part of the chapter, I examine the following three theoretical models of democracy: (1) liberal individualism, with its conception of political democracy as a representative form of government with universal suffrage and equal rights; (2) pluralism as a theory of political democracy in which the conflicting interests of diverse groups are mediated through the mechanism of political parties and periodic elections; and (3) holistic socialist theory, with its conception of democracy as a centralized political and economic system through which society as a whole is said to exercise popular control not only over the political sphere but also over the production and distribution of goods.

CRITICISM OF THREE PREVAILING
THEORETICAL MODELS OF DEMOCRACY
AND OF THEIR ONTOLOGICAL
FOUNDATIONS

LIBERAL INDIVIDUALISM

This view is represented in such traditional formulations as those of Locke, Jefferson, Bentham, James Mill, and J.S. Mill, and is analyzed in such recent discussions as those of Benn and Peters, J.R. Pennock, and C. Cohen.[1] As we have discussed it earlier, on this view, democracy is a form of government in which the ruled rule themselves through their freely elected representatives. Laws are made by these representatives and thus derive their authority from the consent of the governed. This conception sees democracy as a protection of the individual against the arbitrary powers of government and takes the function of government as protecting the freedom of each of its citizens from harm or constraints imposed on them by any of the others. In its fully developed form, this model of democracy proposes the universal equality of all the citizens and the equal rights of all citizens to take part in the political process. Thus this view may be characterized as that of "one-person, one-vote."

The ontology that is presupposed by this theory of political democracy is what we may call abstract individualism. It takes individuals or persons as the basic entities that constitute the social world. However, this view abstracts from the particular qualities that make each individual concretely different from each of the others, and instead characterizes all of them in terms of their universal human properties alone, that is, those properties that they all share in common and that make them the kind of individuals they are. On these grounds, liberal individualism takes all individuals as equal in their basic liberties and rights. Further, these individuals are taken to exist independently of each other and to be related to each other only in external ways. That is, each individual is understood as an independent ego, seeking to satisfy its own interests or to pursue its happiness. The relations among these individuals are external relations in that they do not affect the basic nature of these individuals and leave them essentially unchanged. Thus this nature is regarded as fixed and at the same time as a universal nature, common to all individuals. Among the basic features of this essential human nature are freedom, rationality, and self-interest. Thus these individuals are understood as free agents in the sense of possessing free choice. The motives of each individual's actions are taken to be each one's self-interest, which is pursued by rational choice among alternatives. This is understood to require negative freedom, or the absence of external constraint, as its appropriate condition.

The first criticism I would make of this model as an ontology of social reality concerns the abstractness of these individuals. While on the one hand it is true that human beings have certain features in common, insofar as they are human, and that these are the ground for their equal rights, on the other hand abstract individualism does not account for the differences among individuals that constitute them as the distinctive beings that they are. The uniqueness of individuals, which consists in their differentiated qualities and capacities, is not accidental to their individuality, and it is just this particularity of real individuals that abstract individualism fails to capture. In fact, I have proposed in the previous chapter that it is the development of each individual's distinctive qualities that is the full meaning of freedom and for which democracy serves as a condition. This does not mean, however, that such differences among individuals are to be taken as innate characteristics of their individual natures or as fixed essences. Rather, individuality is understood here as the product of a person's choices and actions in his or her circumstances.

Further, in conceiving of individuals only in terms of their common or universal properties, an abstract individualist ontology disregards the concrete social differences among individuals, without reference to which their actions cannot be adequately explained or their social institutions understood. Thus the fact that some have greater social or economic power than others or are able to dominate the political process cannot be explained without reference to the concrete differences in wealth or social status that characterize their situations.

A second criticism of this abstract individualist ontology concerns its conception of individuals as isolated egos and as related to each other only externally. This fails to take into account the fact that in social life, the purposes and actions of individuals develop and change in their relations with others and are affected by these interactions. Thus these individuals are not isolated, but rather become the individuals that they are through their social relations. These relations therefore are not external but ought to be characterized properly as internal relations. That is, individuals who stand to each other in these relations are essentially changed in and through them. This is not to say that there are no external relations that such individuals may enter into, but rather that social relations are

94

fundamentally internal. (This conception of internal relations obviously requires fuller analysis and I will discuss it further below.) Furthermore, the conception of these individuals as isolated and self-seeking does not account for the fact that they often have common purposes which are not reducible to aggregations of their separate self-interests.

The view that individuals are isolated and self-seeking and that their relations are external gives rise to the idea that society is no more than an aggregate of such externally re-lated individuals. But this conception fails to recognize that the association of individuals in social institutions or projects is often interactive and not summative. For one thing, these institutions are constituted by the shared understandings of these individuals and not by the accidental correlation of private views. Thus, for example, when I write a check at the bank and give it to the teller and the teller in return gives me dollars and not my hat or a quart of milk, it is because both of us share a common understanding of the social institution of banking and of the rules by which it operates. The actions of individuals within such institutions are social rather than private in that the individuals have to take each other's un-derstandings and actions into account in their own activity. In this way, the social relations among them are internal relations, and society as the totality of such social relations cannot be understood as an aggregate of external relations among private individuals.

A third criticism of this model concerns its assumption that individuals have a given or fixed nature. It may be argued that what human beings are has itself changed historically, that is, that there has been development and change in their characteristics and capacities which has made an essential difference in who they are. It may also be suggested that part of what constitutes human beings as what they are is their own self-conception, and that this plays a role in changing their nature. Thus, for example, at one time, people tended to believe that their social roles or their station and its duties were determined by God or constituted their natural and necessary place within the community. This was not merely a matter of belief but was embodied in social structure and informed their actions. In important respects, then, people were what they were in virtue of these social definitions and roles, for example, slaves, serfs, lords, kings. But clearly, these changing definitions and roles are historical and people no longer act in accordance with them. For these reasons, the presupposition of a fixed human nature is, at the very least, problematic.

This first model of political democracy is problematic not only for its abstract individualist ontology but also for its practical consequences. As we noted earlier, in failing to recognize in theory the relevance of economic and social inequities and constraints to the political sphere, this model tends in practice to permit them to intrude into the very political process that was intended to exclude them. Thus, contrary to its intention of political equality, this representative form of democracy has often led in practice to rule by powerful minorities.

It may be seen that these practical shortcomings are in part attributable to the ontological view which takes individuals as only abstractly the same and as related to each other only in external ways. Since this view abstracts from the concrete differences and internal relations that mark social interaction in personal, cultural, and economic life, it cannot account for the role these differences play in the political process itself. The restriction of democracy to the political sphere can also be related to the understanding, in this ontology, of freedom as merely freedom of choice, rather than also as freedom of development. This freedom of choice is seen to be protected by government, the function of which is taken to be the prevention of interference by others in the exercise of this freedom through the protection of civil and property rights and the prevention of criminal harm. Government therefore has the negative function of preventing such interference and is not regarded as legitimately concerned with the social and economic conditions which lie outside the political sphere.

Despite these criticisms, this first conception of democracy has several positive features which I preserve in my redefinition of democracy. One crucial feature that is central to my view as well is the emphasis on the universality and equality of rights and on their corollary, equal representation in the political process. Here, the ground for this equality is seen to be the equal agency of all individuals. This has much in common with the abstract individualist characterization of all humans as equally free; but my view differs in rejecting egoistic self-interest as the fundamental and universal features of individuals. Another feature of liberal individualism that I retain in my account is the centrality of free choice and negative freedom. Finally, I share with the liberal individualist ontology its emphasis on the ontological primacy of the individual, but as will be seen, I characterize the individuals differently.

PLURALIST POLITICAL DEMOCRACY

The second theoretical model, that of pluralist political democracy, is presented in various forms by such theorists as Madison, Dewey, Schumpeter, Dahl, and Berelson.[2] In contrast with abstract individualism's emphasis on the self-interest of isolated individuals, pluralism focuses upon the aggregation of individual interests as group interests and the representation of these often conflicting group interests in the political process. Political democracy is therefore interpreted as a system of governance that mediates these competing interests for the sake of maintaining social equilibrium. These group interests are represented in the political process either in the form of political parties or voting blocs, or by permitting extrapolitical groups (e.g., those based on particular economic, social, regional, or ethnic interest) to influence political decisions. In this way, according to pluralist theory, political democracy maximizes the representation of those individuals whose interests would otherwise not be adequately represented through the power of the groups in which they are united. Thus pluralism acknowledges differences of interest principally in terms of their political manifestations as interest groups or political blocs and therefore

97

tends to treat such groups as internally undifferentiated entities or as wholes, for example, "the Labor vote," "the Southern vote," "the Black vote," "the Eastern establishment," or "the military." Like the first theory, pluralism also sees democracy as a protection of the freedom of the individual against the unchecked power of a centralized state and thus as a condition for negative freedom from constraint. In this case, however, the protection is by means of the checks and balances provided by the representation of different interests through regular elections. Further, the theory claims that pluralism protects the free choice of individuals by preserving the political alternatives that the plurality of interest groups or parties represents. It attempts to do this by a political structure which militates against the hegemony of any single group or party. In many versions of this theory, political leadership is understood as a professionalized activity in which political elites compete for the support of different interest groups in periodic elections.

The social ontology that the pluralist theory presupposes may be characterized as a mixed ontology, by contrast with that of liberal individualism. On the one hand, the entities of social life are individuals who pursue their self-interest as rational choosers. On the other hand, the effective entities that constitute social life are groups rather than these individuals themselves. Thus, while pluralism recognizes differences among groups in society, it leaves out of account the differences among individuals within a group and characterizes these individuals abstractly only in terms of their group membership. In this way, this second view may be seen to substitute an ontology of groups for the ontology of abstract individuals that characterizes the first view. The social relations that are of consequence for this model are relations among groups rather than among individuals. These relations are external relations in the sense that each group is taken to be defined as what it is with reference to an abiding or fixed interest that remains essentially unchanged in its relations with other groups, where these relations are fundamentally those of conflict, coalition, or compromise. Furthermore, society as a whole is seen not as an aggregate of individuals, but as an aggregate of groups. The ontology that underlies this view is thus a mixed one, for while it retains an element of individualism at its base, it combines this with an emphasis on holism at the level of groups.

The first criticism that I would make of the ontology that underlies this pluralist model is that in defining individuals fundamentally in terms of their group membership, it does not recognize the importance of the concrete differences among individuals within a group. These differences make the individuals what they are as unique individuals. Second, in failing to see the internal relations among individuals within a group, this view cannot see the respect in which these relations are essential both to who the individuals are as well as to what the group is. For in order to understand what a group is, it is necessary to understand the constitution of the group in terms of the shared understanding of the interests that the members of the group have in common and some form of agreement among them as to the actions which the group undertakes on their behalf. Without this, the group would be no more than an extensionally defined aggregate of individuals. However, a political or social group is intensionally constituted in virtue of the consciousness that each member of the group has of himself or herself as a member of the group in relation to others who have a similar consciousness. Further, in taking themselves as members of a group, individuals also define themselves to some extent in terms of the relation to other individuals whom they take to be like themselves. Analogously, in seeing groups as related to each other only externally, the pluralist model does not grasp the internal relations that characterize the dynamics of interaction among groups. For example, in the case of conflict between two groups, each one is in part constituted and changed by this relation of conflict with the other. Thus a group representing the interest of tenants is in large part defined by its relation to another group representing the interest of landlords in the sense that there cannot be tenants without landlords nor can there be landlords without tenants. Thus the interest of each group is in part constituted by its relation to other groups with whom it vies for power or a measure of control over limited resources. In this sense, the relations among groups are internal. In addition, insofar as the pluralist view sees democracy as a condition only for negative freedom and insofar as it sees the individuals as externally related and as acting from self-interest alone, this view is also subject to the same criticism that I make of these features in the first view.

Here too, as in the first case, features of the ontology are related to practical problems associated with this pluralist view of democracy. Thus, because of the failure to recognize the concrete social relations among groups and among individuals within groups, this theoretical model does not provide a ground for criticizing the inequitable relations of power and domination that may exist among individuals within a group, among groups, and among individuals outside of their group membership. Thus, within the political sphere, pluralism may tacitly condone in practice the reproduction of the power relations that obtain in the social and economic realm.

HOLISTIC SOCIALISM

The third view, that of holistic socialism, is one of a set of approaches that emphasize economic democracy and that arise in response to the neglect of concrete social and economic relations in liberal individualism. This set of approaches generally addresses those needs for economic opportunity and for the equitable distribution of goods that fall outside the political process. Thus economic welfare is seen as a condition for political democracy itself and there is an emphasis on the importance of some form of democratic participation in decisions about the distribution of economic goods. The principle of equitable economic relations outside the political process is sometimes extended also to include democratic control over the processes of production and not merely distribution.

This general view is represented by two main types of

theories. The first tends to see economic democracy primarily as a mode for the more equitable distribution of goods and opportunities in the context of one or another of the forms of political democracy discussed above. This is generally a liberal rather than a socialist view. Recent formulations of this view include those of Galbraith and Rawls. The second sort of theory emphasizes democracy in control over production as well as distribution. This view has traditionally been associated with socialist theories. Here too, we may discern two different types of theories. The first emphasizes participation by individuals in the decision-making processes of economic as well as political life. The second, by contrast, regards the community or the social whole as primary and sees the political forms of governance as subordinate to economic life. For the purpose of this analysis, I will consider only this second version of the socialist view. It may be characterized as a holistic conception of economic democracy.

On this view, society is essentially organized for the purpose of the production and distribution of goods to satisfy socially determined needs. Although it is the concrete needs of the individuals that have to be satisfied by this activity of production and distribution, this activity is seen as social in the sense that it is the project of the society as a whole. Thus the ends of production and the forms of distribution are to be decided upon by the community as a whole. In the predominant versions of this view, the state becomes the instrumentality that acts on behalf of the community in directing and controlling social production. This centralized authority is thus understood as expressing the general will or the best interests of the individuals. This view is developed as a theory of democracy inasmuch as it holds that decision-making is based on popular control of the economic system either directly or through the state apparatus.

The ontological presuppositions of such a view are that the basic entity of social life is the whole or the social totality. Individuals therefore have their existence as parts of the whole and in terms of the roles and functions that they play within it. The whole is identical with the set of relations within it. These are all internal relations in the sense that each entails all of the others and is entailed by all of the others. These relations are therefore wholly interconstituting. Individuals, then, are nothing but what they are constituted as by their relations and in this sense are parts or functions of the totality. On this view, freedom is seen as the freedom of the whole to actualize its potentialities through the activities of individuals. The freedom of individuals, therefore, is realized to the extent that their activities contribute to the actualization of these potentialities of the whole.

In its emphasis on the primacy of production and distribution in social life, this theory tends to be ontologically reductive in that it interprets all forms of social activity as ultimately based on the economic needs of society.

My criticism of the ontology implied by this third view is that in its holism, it disregards the ontological status of individuality. In attributing the fundamental agency and freedom to the community as such or to the whole, this view reduces the agency or freedom of individuals to a derived or merely reflected status. But it is patently implausible to say that "the whole" is an agent or that it acts; and it is not even clear what this would mean. For agency requires intentionality and the capacity for choice, and thus could only be the property of a conscious entity. To ascribe such consciousness and intentionality to "the social whole" is ontologically extravagant if not completely obscure. What is clearest to say and what is evident from everyday experience is that it is individuals who act and have purposes. Against the view that the state as such or society as such has agency, or that the institutions of a society have agency or purposes, I would argue that these are shorthand expressions for the joint or combined actions of individuals within these institutional frameworks. Thus, for example, to say that "The Supreme Court reversed itself" or that "The United States sent an envoy" is not to be taken as meaning that "reversing" or "sending" are actions of abstract entities but rather that the nine individuals who constitute the Supreme Court voted in a certain way in accordance with those rules that make it an action of the court, or that the appropriate authorities in the Department of State, or the President, took the action of sending the envoy. To speak otherwise is to reify or to hypostatize the abstract entities in the sense of regarding them as having the properties of concretely existing individuals. The agency, purposiveness, or freedom of a whole should thus be understood in terms of the actions of the individuals who make up this social totality. To attribute this agency to the whole is to commit the logical fallacy of attributing to a class the properties of its members.

A related criticism concerns the conception of the whole as a totality of internal relations, in which the individuals or parts are totally interconstituted by their relations. Such an ontology of pure relations is implausible concerning social reality since the relations in the social world are among concretely existing individuals, and these relations cannot exist apart from the individuals who stand to each other in such relations. Furthermore, these individuals as agents can choose many of these relations and can also change them, as I will argue shortly. In these respects of concrete existence and agency, individuals are more than what is constituted by their social relations.

A third criticism of this view is that it takes individuals and society in general in a one-sided and reductionist way, namely, as fundamentally economic. Thus it fails to do justice to the many-sidedness of social life, in subordinating the social, the political, and the cultural to the economic.

The practical criticisms of socialist holism are related to the ontological criticisms sketched above. Despite its emphasis on community and on popular control, this third model of democracy tends to give rise to authoritarian and nondemocratic forms of social decision-making. Decisions for the totality come to be made not by participatory or genuinely representative means but rather by an elite which presumably speaks for the whole or knows what the good of the whole is. Furthermore, such decisions then come to be imposed upon individuals who are required to function for the good of the whole as it is thus defined and whose individual liberties and rights are subordinated to this end. The ontological holism of this view thus supports a tendency to authoritarianism in practice, in the name of the popular or general will.

The strength of this view lies in its emphasis on economic sufficiency as a condition for freedom. Moreover, some conception of economic democracy is an essential aspect of a full conception of democracy and is a necessary supplement to the one-sided emphasis on political democracy that characterizes liberal individualism and pluralism. However, economic democracy should not be interpreted in the holistic way just described, which gives rise to highly centralized and authoritarian practices, but rather should be interpreted in a truly representative and participatory way, which I will discuss later.

Just as the mere combination of a theory of political democracy with a theory of economic democracy does not yet constitute a coherent alternative theory, so too the combination of elements of the ontologies implied by the views thus far considered does not constitute a coherent ontology. What is needed in support of the redefinition of democracy offered in the previous chapter is a new ontological foundation which coherently accounts for both individuality and sociality.

PROPOSAL FOR AN ALTERNATIVE
ONTOLOGICAL FOUNDATION FOR
DEMOCRATIC THEORY

The views thus far examined represent two basic ontologies, namely, individualism and holism (since the pluralist view as I have indicated has a mixed ontology borrowing from both of these approaches). These two alternative ontologies focus respectively on the primacy of individuals who stand to each other in external relations, or on the primacy of the whole within which there are internal relations that constitute the individuals. This makes it appear as though one has to choose between individuality and external relations, on the one hand, and holism and internal relations, on the other, as basic principles for understanding social life. However, I believe that there is a third way, namely, a coherent ontology in which individuality is given its full due but not at the cost of regarding individuals as isolated and abstract egos, standing in only external relations to each other; at the same time, in this ontology, internal relations are seen to obtain in a way that preserves the importance of sociality, but not at the cost of an overarching totality or whole of which individuals are mere parts or functions. It will be suggested that such an ontology is necessary in order to account for the fundamental features of social reality. Moreover, I would argue that the normative implications of this ontology for a theory of society help to constitute an adequate conception of the good in social life. That is, in its account of free individuality, on the one hand, and of the importance of sociality for self-development, on the other, this ontology avoids the defects of the alternative one-sided views and provides for the integration of these two principles in social life.

The fundamental entities of this proposed ontology are individuals-in-relations, where these individuals are human beings and their relations are social relations. Thus these fundamental entities may also be called social individuals. The other entities that make up social reality, such as groups, social institutions, social structures, processes, and practices, as well as society as a totality, are derived entities that are constituted by the activities of, and relations among, such individuals. To say that individuals-in-relations are the fundamental entities is not to say that there are two sorts of fundamental entities: individuals, on the one hand, and relations, on the other. Rather, these individuals are such that their characteristic mode of being, that is, their activity, is relational or essentially involves their relations with others. Thus these individuals act fundamentally in and through social relations. The individuals are therefore ontologically primary, but the relations among them are also essential aspects of their being. However, these relations do not exist independently or apart from the individuals who are related. Rather, they are relational properties of these individuals.

Thus, for example, being a teacher is such a relational property, in that it is a property of an individual that is defined in relation to another individual, namely, one who has the property of being a student. However, this teacher–student relation cannot exist independently or apart from the individuals who are either teachers or students. It has no abstract existence, except perhaps conceptually, as an object of thought, or as it may be institutionally defined in terms of social roles. Thus one may think about the relation of teacher to student abstractly, apart from any given individuals, and even if no existing individuals were to stand in this relation. But the relation would not exist or have any reality except in and through the individuals who are related in this way.

There is an alternative interpretation that takes both individuals and relations to be real but, instead of seeing relations as relational properties of individuals, regards them instead as basic or independent ontological entities, on a par with individuals. Such an interpretation raises a traditional problem of an infinite regress (as discussed, for example, by F. H. Bradley[3]): If individuals are to stand in relations to each other or to other entities, and if the relations themselves are to be taken to be independently real entities, then there must be relations between the individuals and their relations, in order to coordinate them. Further, there must then also be relations relating the relations, since each relation would itself stand in a relation to the things that it relates; and between each of *these* relations there would in turn be some relation, and so on ad infinitum. In the ontology I present, this problem does not arise, since relations cannot be said to exist independently but only as relational properties of individuals.

These individuals are who they are (or become who they are) fundamentally through their social relations. In this sense, these relations may be said to constitute them as being who they are. However, this does not mean that individuals are wholly constituted by their relations, for individuals are agents who themselves choose or create many of the relations into which they enter. That is, they have an original capacity for choice and purposeful activity, which is not itself a function of these relations. In this respect, these individuals may be said to be self-constituting. Furthermore, these individuals are concretely existing beings who are the bearers of, as well as the creators of, their relational properties. As bearers of these properties they cannot be reduced to the sum of these relational properties or to the relations into which they enter, nor can these relational properties exist independently or apart from the individuals who have them.

The basic mode of being or the life activity of these individuals is purposive or intentional activity. Thus, these individuals are agents who have the capacity for conscious choice. However, to say that individuals have such a capacity is not to say that they always exercise it, that is, that they always do in fact choose their relations. Nor is it to say that individuals can choose all of the relations into which they enter, for some of these relations are given and not open to choice. For example, one does not choose one's parents or one's native language. Yet even in these cases, these relations are at least in part the historical result of the choices that other individuals have made. Further, individuals may choose to change many of the relations in which they find themselves, and there is also a wide range of relations that agents can create or choose for themselves.

An important consideration regarding the agency of individuals is that their activity is often joint or common, that is, involves many individuals acting together with a shared or common purpose. Such common activity may be seen to be ontologically distinct from the individual activity of agents acting to realize their separate purpose. Further, as I suggested in the previous chapter, common activity is not to be understood as simply an aggregation of individual activities, which may be accidentally coordinated. Rather, it is defined by a shared aim and joint activity to realize that aim. Thus, what marks such common activity as ontologically distinctive is that no adequate or coherent account of such activity can be given in terms of the actions or intentions of individual agents alone, but only by reference to the shared aim. This would be true of both of the cases of common activity that I distinguished earlier, namely, that which I characterized as genuinely common activity, in which members of the group freely choose their own shared purpose, and the case in which the common purpose may have been chosen for the group or imposed upon it by some external authority or agency.

In the latter case, it may appear that what is called common activity is not really common at all but is simply the subordination of the individuals to a group conceived of holistically as a supervenient entity. This would be contrary to the conception I have proposed that groups are entities essentially constituted by their members; and it would undermine the proposed ontology of individuals-in-relations. Yet even in the case where the common purpose of a group's activity is imposed by an external agency, the group remains a constituted entity inasmuch as its members retain the capacity to change it or dissolve it through their joint action. For even in this case, the individuals retain their freedom as capacity in the sense discussed in the previous chapter. Of course, such a choice to reject the aims imposed upon the group or to dissolve it may entail such great risk that it may not be rational to choose such a course of action. Without the enabling conditions to realize such a choice, this freedom remains abstract. For such a choice to be rational, it may require the creation of conditions that would enable such a radical change to take place. Yet in principle such an option remains open. For example, under conditions of slavery, the group of slaves is under coercion to act in common to realize the purpose of the slavemaster as an external authority. Nonetheless, on risk of life or punishment, slaves in such coercive circumstances have chosen to revolt or to escape the group and, under certain conditions, have succeeded in dissolving the group and indeed the very institution of slavery itself. Or again, members of a group who have acted under ideological pressure or fear and have participated in the group's immoral aims and actions, nevertheless, could have chosen to refuse to act in this way or could have attempted to change the aims of the group. That is, they retain the capacity to choose to act otherwise than as they did. Thus even in such extreme cases of external coercion or authority, a holistic ontology, which concedes primacy to the group over and against the individuals, would not give an adequate account of the social reality. At a deep level, the agency of the individuals remains primary, even under duress, and the group remains a derived entity ontologically.

The choices that agents make – both individually and in common – are with respect to purposes or ends that the agents posit. In their activity, agents seek to realize these purposes through social interaction and through the transformation of the natural world. In the course of this activity, agents transform the objects of their activity or bring new objects into being. Also in the course of this activity, the agents enter into or change their social relations with other agents. Moreover, in this process, individuals also may transform themselves by changing or developing their capacities and qualities or creating new ones.

The free choice of agents is in itself not sufficient for the realization of the purposes that the agents have. In addition, as I argued in the first chapter, there are conditions that are necessary, if the purposes are to be concretely realized and not merely entertained. What is required is both the absence of constraining conditions and the presence of enabling conditions. I have characterized the former as negative conditions and the latter as positive conditions. Among the negative or constraining conditions are harm, physical coercion, or domination. Enabling or positive conditions include the means required for the agent's actions such as raw materials and tools, as well as the forms of social relations through which or upon which agents act, such as institutions, social practices, and forms of social cooperation, as well as such more immediate forms of social interaction as friendship and other informal relations.

I have argued elsewhere that agents are causal in their action upon natural objects, but that agency itself is not caused and is free.[4] If this is the case, then it also follows that agents cannot cause the actions of other agents. What they

109

can do, however, is to control the conditions (both natural and social) that others need for the realization of their own purposes. This gives rise to the possibility of constraint and domination in social life. The freedom of agents to realize their purposes thus requires social relations that are free of such domination and that provide access to the positive conditions of agency. I have argued in the previous chapter that the form of social relations that permits agents to realize their purposes most fully is democracy, understood in a broader way than on the earlier views.

It should also be clear that the account of freedom as self-development given in the previous chapter is relevant to the ontology proposed here. In this account, self-development is taken to be the ultimate end of the activity of individuals. Thus, individuals-in-relations as the fundamental entities of the ontology are understood as free in the sense of having the capacity to create or change their own natures through their activity.

A further set of questions concerning the ontology that I am proposing arises with respect to the nature of relations. I claimed earlier that individuals become what they are largely through their social relations. That is, their mode of being is an activity that essentially involves their interaction with others. I have also claimed that these relations among individuals are internal relations and that in these relations the individuals are fundamentally changed. But I have also suggested that the individuals are not wholly constituted by their relations. I would like to develop this view of internal social relations somewhat further here.

On one traditional view of internal relations (associated with F.H. Bradley, among others) all relations are internal relations and individuals are essentially constituted and changed by their relations.[5] This view goes too far, as G.E. Moore[6] and C. Baylis[7] among others have argued. Thus Moore argues that some relations are external and that changes in these relations do not essentially change the entities in the relation. And Baylis argues for a principle of partial interdependence of the characters or properties of an entity such that a change in one character or relation of a thing does not totally change the thing. Further, I have argued earlier in this chapter that the strong interpretation of internal relations fails to preserve the ontological independence of individuals and cannot do justice to the fact of their agency.

I take social relations to be internal in the sense that individuals entering into these relations become who they are in and through their relations with each other. As Aristotle already pointed out in the *Categories*, "Those things are called relative, which, being either said to be *of* something else or *related to* something else, are explained by reference to that other thing. . . . All relatives have correlatives: by the term 'slave' we mean the slave of a master; by the term 'master,' the master of a slave."[8] Aristotle presumably means here that the entity in the relation is the kind of entity it is only with respect to its correlative, and that apart from this relation it would not be what it is but something else. Thus the master would still be a man outside the relation but would not be a master except in relation to a slave. I believe that social relations may be analyzed in a similar way in terms of what Aristotle in the *Categories* calls "the reciprocity of correlation."[9] In such social relations, the characters or natures of the entities in the relation are interdependent.

Social relations are internal in another sense as well. The relation of conscious agents to each other in their activity presupposes that each one understands the actions of the other with respect to some shared understanding of the situation. Minimally, each understands the other to be an agent like him- or herself and to be acting intentionally. Such a relation is therefore internal in that each one, in his or her actions, takes into account the understanding which the other has. To this degree, the actions of each are affected by how these actions are understood by the other.

However, although agents may be fundamentally changed by changes in their relations with other agents, what remains unchanged by the relation is the agency or the capacity for choice which the individuals have, as well as the existence of the individuals who enter into these relations. Because of this, individuals are not totally constituted by their relations. Indeed, social relations presuppose this agency on the part of individuals. That is, the agency of individuals does not arise out of their relations but rather is a precondition for their entering into the relations. Yet such social relations are fundamental to the concrete expression of this agency. In general, then, the concrete realization of purposes as the mode of activity of agents requires social relations as its condition.

Thus it may be concluded that what remains essentially unchanged through any changes in the relations that individuals have is the fact that they are agents and that they are individuals. Because the existence of such individual agents is a precondition for the existence of the relations into which they enter or choose to enter, these individuals may be taken to be ontologically prior to the relations. Yet their individuation or the realization of their distinctive character depends on how they exercise this agency in and through concrete social relations.

Such social relations take not only the form of immediate and direct relations among persons, but also what we may call objectified forms, namely, those that are embodied or structured in institutions. Examples of such objectified forms of social relations are rules, customs or practices, social roles and functions, social classes, forms of governance, laws, and forms of property ownership, as well as the whole range of particular institutions such as schools, hospitals, and courts. Such social relations are objectified in the sense that they exist as institutional facts or as abstract social conceptions and not only implicitly in actual relations among persons. Thus, for example, the institution of property has its objectified form in property laws, social practices, and in those things to which property right is taken to apply, and at the same time is manifest in the social relations among persons who stand to each other with respect to property in such relations as owner, user, renter, and lessor, and who have rights and duties to each other in these contexts. Though it sometimes appears that such institutions have an independent existence apart from social relations among persons, it should be evident that such institutions or objectified forms are socially constituted, i.e., they have been brought into being by the decisions and actions of agents and can also be changed by them.

Further, if one takes that set of social relations that makes up the state or the political and legal system, such an "objective" entity is nevertheless also constituted by individuals in relations. The state would be nothing but an empty abstraction if in fact people did not stand to each other in such concrete relations as citizens, representative, judge, and legislator. Moreover, the state is also instituted by a process of social decisions (though, historically, not with the participation of all those who are subjects of it), and is also subject to change by such a social process. Finally, without going into it further here, one may speak of the totality of social relations or of the society as a whole. On the view proposed here, this is an entity constituted by the manifold social relations entered into by the individuals within it.

Chapter 3

Social ontology and the question of foundationalism in ethics

Foundationalism in philosophy has come under severe attack in recent years. The idea that philosophy can either discover or construct the ultimate foundations of knowledge or science or morality has been criticized from a variety of perspectives. This criticism has been articulated most fully in the philosophy of science and in epistemology, where it has been directed against essentialist approaches in these fields, that is, against the view that philosophy can determine the necessary and sufficient conditions for any knowledge whatever or can discover the universal and unchanging structures of knowledge, belief, or action. A similar trend is increasingly manifest in ethics as well (though, of course, the foundations appealed to in this domain most often differ from those appealed to in the case of knowledge of the natural world). In ethics, the traditional appeal to universal foundations and standards of morality has been countered by relativisms of a cultural, historical, or individualistic sort;[1] moral pluralism held to be implied in practical reasoning; or theories of consensus as the normative basis for moral judgments. Although this antifoundationalist critique seems well taken with respect to such essentialist or realist approaches to morality as natural law and natural rights theories and intuitionist theories, it seems to me that the antifoundationalist and relativist alternatives are themselves inadequate. What I would propose in their stead is an approach in terms of what I have called social ontology, which I would suggest can provide a grounding for moral values that avoids the antifoundationalist criticisms. The argument here is based on the view that ethical norms are grounded in the activity of individuals who constitute the social world through their interactions. The "real world" to which ethical principles apply, and from which they derive, is therefore taken as a socially and historically constituted reality and as one that changes by means of the human activity that constitutes it. Thus the ontology proposed here is not an essentialist one.

TRADITIONAL FOUNDATIONALIST VIEWS
AND SOME RECENT ALTERNATIVES

Before considering the implications of the social ontology that I presented for a foundation for ethics, I would like to briefly review some traditional foundationalist views and the criticisms that may be made of them, for the purpose of articulating my own view more clearly. I will then look at two contemporary alternatives concerning the grounding of moral judgments which may be thought to avoid the problems of foundationalism, namely, the approaches of Rawls and Habermas. I consider these two because my own project is in some respects similar to theirs inasmuch as they seek to determine the norms or values of a good or just society and yet seek to avoid traditional foundationalism.

The traditional foundationalist views include natural law and natural rights theories as well as intuitionist theories in ethics. Natural law theories seek to ground moral values on objective and universal standards that are taken to be given in the natural order of things (or in the divine order, on theological versions). On such views, what is right or good is so because it is in accordance with nature or with God's will. Thus classical Platonism, with its conception of an objective form of the good, which good things or just actions exemplify, and traditional Stoicism, with its idea of natural necessity as the norm of right action, as an injunction to "follow nature," both represent this approach. Further, on two of the major Christian theological views – Augustinian and Thomistic – something is good because God wills it, or alternatively, God wills it because it is good. In both approaches, the essential objectivity of value is asserted. A related view is the Aristotelian one which sees the good for each sort of being as determined by its specific nature or kind. Thus with respect to human beings there is a fixed nature or essence that defines them as human and determines what will be morally appropriate to the realization of their essence. Both of these versions of natural law ground natural rights as moral requirements derived from the nature of things itself rather than from conventions or from cultural constructions. Modern natural rights theory from the 17th century on sees such rights as life, liberty, and property as essential and inalienable and as inhering in each individual by virtue of his or her human nature. The recognition of these rights is thus taken to be required for the constitution of just states.

Epistemologically, "natural rights" approaches such as those of John Locke or Thomas Jefferson take these rights to be "self-evident," that is, either such that reason alone dictates what they must be or that they follow from the philosophical understanding of the essence of human nature, as what it requires or enjoins as its "natural" due; or in other intuitionist versions, such that our "moral intuitions" or our "moral sense" know these to be rights immediately, that is, by a direct and veridical apprehension of these values. In Kantian ethical theory, both these elements of rational necessity and intuitive immediacy play a role in the apprehension and justification of rights and goods, as well as in the moral feelings that ground our obligations or duties to respect them and act in accordance with them. But as we shall note shortly, Kant is a foundationalist with a difference.

Such a very brief sketch of traditional essentialist or foundationalist theories cannot claim to represent them adequately. I offer it here only to suggest the object of the antifoundationalist critique and also its relation to my own view.

Some of the criticisms that have been made of these foundationalist views, and which I think are well taken, concern the question of the order of nature as a moral ground and the question of a fixed human nature. Thus it may be argued that the religious or cosmological notions of an order of nature which were proposed in support of natural law theories are merely speculative and unfounded. Further, it is not clear how one could derive moral imperatives from an account of the natural order, nor is it clear that one can simply impute moral values to this order itself. One may also argue that there is no fixed or essential human nature on which one may base a categorical doctrine of human rights.[2] Rather, what constitutes human nature may itself be seen as changing as a result of the self-transforming and self-developing activity of diverse individuals in a variety of social and historical contexts. Indeed, it has been argued that the 17th-century conception of human nature, with its characteristics of possessive individualism, is an expression of a particular social and historical form of human existence.[3]

An alternative foundationalist approach in ethics is that of intuitionism. This view, developed in its modern forms by G. E. Moore, W.D. Ross, and A.C. Ewing, among others, holds that morality can ultimately be grounded only on simple and immediate intuition of moral properties like goodness and rightness. However, as has been pointed out, it is far from clear that all moral agents will share the same intuitions, and if, as is likely, there are differences, there is no way to adjudicate among them.

The critique of foundationalism in ethics has led to several non- or antifoundationalist positions, the most radical of which is moral relativism. This theory holds that there are no universal grounds or norms for moral judgments but that instead moral values differ from one culture to the next or even from one individual to the next and that each culture or individual is equally justified in holding to its own norms. Moral relativism can take the form of an anarchist or indeed a nihilist approach to ethical values: that they are radically ungrounded, except in the will or choice of individuals (or groups) and that therefore there can be no justification for one position against another, other than that it is willed or chosen or represents an existential act of commitment or faith. Thus Max Stirner, Nietzsche, and even Kierkegaard are 19th-century representations of such a "relativist" view, though each had a strong sense of what the moral content of such creative acts ought to be. However, moral relativism also may take the form of a relativization of ethical norms to context: What's good or right is what is good or right for X in circumstances C with the (cultural, historical, social) framework or convention F, and there is no appeal beyond such frameworks and circumstances. In either approach – whether ethical norms are grounded in acts of choice or of faith, or are relative to context and convention – relativism holds that there are no universal grounds or norms for moral judgments and no fixed or essential list of goods or rights.

Two standard arguments have been advanced against moral relativism: First, it permits the justification of any action as moral and thus allows for no moral discrimination or criticism whatever; for discussion across or between alternative (relativistic) moral frameworks has no rational basis for criticism or persuasion, since these frameworks are taken to be conceptually and practically incommensurable by the relativist. Thus for example, such relativism would seem to condone slavery, massacres, murder, or rape if it happened that these are defined as morally permissible within the value system of a culture or individual. Second, it may be argued that moral relativism is self-refuting since it itself makes a universal and nonrelative value claim about the relativity of values.[4]

The two major frameworks of modern ethical theory, namely, utilitarianism and Kantian deontology, do not fall entirely neatly within a foundationalist perspective and certainly cannot be classified as relativist either. Without going into an analysis of these views here, one may note with respect to Kantian ethics that although it does make a claim for universality and necessity in ethics, this claim is grounded on what would follow from the requirements of rationality itself and the correlative presupposition of the freedom of the will. Thus there is no external or underlying foundation for morality other than the capacities that define the moral subject. With respect to utilitarianism, one may observe that insofar as it is a naturalistic or psychologistic theory of the origin or ground of values it might be regarded as foundationalist. Nevertheless, by leaving open to choice what it is that people will determine as good, the principle of utility does not specify an external or objective basis for determining the good. Rather, on J.S. Mill's view, it is what people who have experience of the alternatives would choose. In *Utilitarianism*, he writes:

> Of two pleasures, if there be one to which all or almost all who have experience of both give a decided preference, irrespective of any feeling of moral obligation to prefer it, that is the more desirable pleasure. If one of the two is, by those who are competently acquainted with both, placed so far above the other that they prefer it, even though knowing it to be attended with a greater amount of discontent, and would not resign it for any quantity of the other pleasure which their nature is capable of, we are justified in ascribing to the preferred enjoyment a superiority in quality so far outweighing quantity as to render it, in comparison, of small account."[5]

Beyond this rapid overview, it would be useful to examine somewhat more carefully two major contemporary theories of social ethics with respect to this question of foundations. These are the theories of John Rawls as set forth in *A Theory of Justice* and his Dewey Lectures, and that of Jürgen Habermas as he develops it in his theory of communicative action. We may begin by noting that both Rawls and Habermas develop their views largely within the framework of a Kantian ethics, a point that both of them acknowledge in various ways. In Rawls's case, this is evident in the grounding of his construction of the principles of justice in the freedom and rationality of individuals and in the priority that he gives to the right over the good. In the case of Habermas, a strong Kantian element may be seen in the transcendental grounding of the ideal speech community in universal and necessary conditions of speech or communication. Both of them, however, want to go beyond Kant in various ways and to meet some of the objections and criticisms that have been raised about Kantian ethics. Specifically, one may note three respects in which both Rawls and Habermas differ from Kant. First, both claim to be giving a social, rather than an individualistic account of moral principles. Thus Rawls's theory concerns the principles that would apply to a social structure; that is, it is a theory of justice as applied to social institutions. Likewise, Habermas gives what he calls a dialogical rather than a monological theory of ethics, and one that has its foundation in social interaction rather than in individual action. In the case of Rawls, one may question the degree to which his is truly a social account. For although his theory applies to social structures, the principles of justice have their origin in the deliberations of mutually disinterested individuals in the original position. A second difference from Kant which both Rawls and Habermas share is that they both claim to base their theories on actual or empirical persons rather than on the transcendental subject. However, while it is true that both take the subjects of morality to be concrete empirical persons with interests and life plans, yet one may argue that both retain a transcendental emphasis: on the universal conditions of communication in the case of Habermas and on the abstraction from all particular interests in the original position in the case of Rawls. The third difference from Kant which both manifest is the proceduralist emphasis in their grounding of moral norms. Thus Rawls regards his view as a kind of constructivism in which the principles of justice emerge from a decision procedure carried out by individuals presupposed as free and equal. Similarly, Habermas sees the emergence and validation of moral norms, particularly that of justice, as deriving from a procedural ideal of undistorted communication leading to consensus in an ideal speech situation. Having noted these agreements and differences with Kantian ethics, it remains to consider the question of the extent to which either Rawls or Habermas is providing a foundationalist approach to ethics despite their rejection of traditional foundationalism, and further, if they are, whether such neofoundationalist approaches are adequate.

Given the highly systematic nature of Rawls's theory of justice and the wide and elaborated discussion of it in the literature, it should be understood that my consideration of Rawls's view here and elsewhere in this book is intended neither as a general analysis of his theory nor even as a detailed critique of one of his arguments. Rather, I propose to elicit those features of his view that bear specifically on the issue under discussion (in this place, foundationalism in ethics, and in later chapters where I deal with Rawls, on aspects of economic justice and on the relation of reciprocity), and which show its relation to my own view. In Rawls's original formulation in *A Theory of Justice*, he explicitly seeks to provide what he calls "an Archimedean point for assessing the social system without invoking a priori considerations."[6] The original position is intended to provide such a standpoint from which principles of justice would be reasonably arrived at and to which everyone would agree. The presupposition here, however, is that the persons in the original position who would reason to the principles of justice are free and equal and mutually disinterested individuals. Another presupposition in the construction is that there would be agreement on the list of primary goods as goods that everyone would rationally want regardless of whatever differences there might be in his or her particular interests or life plans. Although Rawls introduces these presuppositions as reasonable and in accordance with our commonsense intuitions, nonetheless, they do serve as foundations in his construction. Rawls's argument for their not being a priori foundations is that the test of their validity or force is the plausibility or reasonableness of the theory as a whole.[7] Thus in *A Theory of Justice*, Rawls provides what might be called a qualified foundationalism. It is qualified because the justification for its fundamental presuppositions is neither a priori nor naturalistic but derives from the coherence of the whole construction and the degree to which it serves to represent our "considered moral judgments in reflective equilibrium."[8] It has been argued that in such a "wide reflective equilibrium," the elements to be brought into equilibrium–our moral judgments, our moral principles, and the relevant background theories–are brought to bear on each other critically and reflectively so that there is no single and privileged unrevisable foundation upon which the theory rests.[9] Nevertheless, it seems to me that this coherentism as an alternative to foundationalism willy nilly preserves a foundational appeal to validate its procedure. It remains foundational with respect to Rawls's appeal to some set of moral judgments or intuitions as the test of our moral principles[10] and in the presupposition of the rationality of the disinterested individuals who would reason to the principles of justice.

In his Dewey Lectures, Rawls seems to depart from this qualified foundationalism in suggesting that the theory may only apply to "a democratic society under modern conditions." Thus, he says, ". . .we are not trying to find a conception of justice suitable for all societies regardless of their particular social or historical circumstances."[11] In those lectures, Rawls characterizes his project as a concrete and situated task of formulating principles that we could all agree to abide by in our present circumstances. He writes:

> The search for reasonable grounds for reaching agreement rooted in our conception of ourselves and in our relation to society replaces the search for moral truth interpreted as fixed by an a priori and independent order of objects and relations, whether natural or divine, an order apart and distinct from how we conceive of ourselves. The task is to articulate a public conception of justice that all can live with who regard their person and their relation to society in a certain way. . . . Apart from the procedure of constructing the principles of justice, there are no moral facts.[12]

What seems to me to be problematic in Rawls's original qualifiedly foundationalist account is that he introduces what are in effect a priori presuppositions or postulates under the guise of commonly accepted and reasonable conceptions. As I have noted, this applies to his conception of the persons in the original position as free, equal, and mutually disinterested and his list of primary goods (i.e., rights and liberties, opportunities and powers, income and wealth, and self-respect). Rawls claims that these are weak assumptions and grounds them in the wide acceptance they are presumed to command. But in fact these are rather strong premises and not all that widely shared, especially if they are to be taken as more than merely slogans or common platitudes. Moreover, they presuppose a certain conception of moral personality. I would argue that Rawls is surreptitiously appealing to an ontology of persons and society, namely, a particular view of what is true about the nature of individuals and social reality, and that this ontology ought to be articulated explicitly.

Rawls's later position, in the Dewey Lectures, makes more explicit his appeal to consensus as the justification for his moral theory. Thus the normative force of both his starting points and his conclusions rests on the condition that they would be widely accepted. However, it is not clear why consensus should serve to validate a norm or an ideal conception of a person. If a consensus is taken simply as a matter of fact or descriptively, then of course it would have no normative force, on the grounds of the argument against naturalism in ethics which Rawls himself accepts. And if the consensus is taken to have normative weight then it would have to be on the basis of some argument or ground that would have to lie outside the consensus, or else it would be self-certifying. But Rawls does not give such an argument. Moreover, the emphasis on consensus and on what is widely accepted in our social and cultural circle limits the theory to a representation of prevailing views and does not permit it to be critical in a radical way. But the possibility of such radical revision in light of alternative conceptions is what Rawls himself sees as requisite for the "kind of reflective equilibrium that one is concerned with in moral philosophy."[13] And to be fair to Rawls's intention, one must add that his view has an incipiently critical dimension insasmuch as it requires that those who come to agreement on principles in the original position are bound to the specific consequences of these principles. Therefore, if they fail to act on such consequences of autonomously arrived at principles, they may be criticized for moral inconsistency or self-contradiction. Yet Rawls's view does not provide for the possibility of a fundamental criticism of either the premises or the principles derived from them.

Parenthetically, I should note that I take exception substantively to Rawls's account of the person. First, I think that his conception is not social enough in its initial formulation, that is, with respect to the original position, where individuals are understood as mutually disinterested, that is, as each pursuing his or her own particular interests without regard for the others. Although he later recognizes the importance of shared aims and of mutuality, these features do not enter into the original conception sufficiently and thus do not play a role in the development or formulation of the principles of justice. Second, although Rawls characterizes persons as free in the sense of possessing free choice or the ability to choose and to change their life plans, he does not yet see that freedom is also a matter of the self-development and self-transformation of the person through these concrete choices.

Habermas also eschews traditional foundationalism in his rejection of any pre-Kantian metaphysical foundations for norms. His approach is rather to give an account of how moral norms are grounded in certain modes of human activity itself, in particular, in what he calls communicative action. He holds that there are universal and necessary – indeed, transcendental – conditions which underlie the very possibility of language itself. The very use of language on this view presupposes a relation among speakers such that, in making utterances, they are implicitly making validity claims of four sorts: namely, that what they say is comprehensible, that it is true, that their intention in uttering it is truthful or veracious, and that their utterance is appropriate or in accordance with prevailing norms.[14] On Habermas's view, communicative action aims at a shared understanding (by contrast to strategic action, which aims at success). Where there is disagreement about truth or rightness, the presupposition of communicative action is that such disagreement can be resolved by rational discourse in an "ideal speech situation." Such an ideal speech situation thus represents the counterfactual norm according to which consensus or agreement can be reached by everyone's having a chance to take part in the dialogue. Habermas sees the ground of the ethical and particularly of justice in this communicative action. The limitations on the realization of this norm are the "distortions" of the ideal speech situation that are imposed either by social or political constraints, for example, domination or institutionalized inequality, or by ideological or psychological constraints. The validation of moral norms is grounded in the formal preconditions of the ideal speech situation and depends on the achievement of consensus based on rational discourse concerning such norms. Thus the validation of such norms arises from the determination of which interests and needs are generalizable and would therefore provide the grounds for general agreement. Anything that remains recalcitrantly particular is excluded from the ideal speech situation as inappropriate.

Habermas's approach to the genesis of ethical norms may be characterized as a qualified foundationalism (despite his rejection of traditional foundationalism) and one that is strikingly similar to that of Rawls in many ways. Here, as with Rawls, the claim is made that moral norms concerning what is right or just do not themselves have any specific foundations in a priori or naturalistic sources but rather are grounded in a procedure that validates them. Nevertheless, in Habermas's construction, there is a transcendental normative ground of this procedure itself in the ideal speech situation and in the validity claims implied in the use of language. This ideal situation entails that speakers are rational and that they are capable of exchanging dialogue roles, sharing perspectives, and equally entering into the discourse. Thus the speakers are presupposed to be rational, free from coercion, and equal with respect to speaking. Again, this is strikingly similar to the presuppositions that Rawls introduces concerning the original position, which is the ground for the formulation of principles of justice. However, Habermas's view remains more universalistic and thus perhaps more foundationalist than Rawls's later view inasmuch as he sees the grounds of a universal ethics in the universal pragmatics of language.[15] Yet both of them are only foundationalist in a limited way because they construe the grounds of moral values as lying in the characteristics of persons or their activity, rather than in any extrapersonal or extrasocial "reality."

Whereas Habermas, like Rawls, appeals to consensus for the validation of values, he does not seem to be open to the same criticism that I made of Rawls. For Habermas offers an argument as to why the norm of consensus has validating force. This argument depends upon his view of the transcendental conditions present in any act of speech, namely, that there is the normative presupposition or expectation of understanding and of the possibility of agreement. Thus consensus is seen as the ideal end toward which rational discourse would tend and which would ultimately serve to validate moral norms.

Although I agree with Habermas's general strategy of grounding moral values or norms in features of human activity and sociality itself, I would take exception first of all to the restricted mode of this activity to which Habermas appeals, namely, speech or what he calls communicative action. This seems to me too narrow a conception of the forms of activity that ground morality. Because of Habermas's excessively rigid distinctions between labor or production on the one hand and social interaction on the other, and between what he calls strategic action and communicative action, he is unable to take into account the role of creative, productive, and purposive activity and the role of self-development and self-transformation as grounds for morality. That is, the forms of practice that he does admit as relevant to the grounding of moral norms are too exclusively linguistic. Furthermore, in his account of the ideal speech situation, he stresses exclusively only those interests of individuals that are generalizable or common to all the others, and he fails to see that the recognition of particular interests and differences also falls within the domain of morality. Thus I would argue that his view does not take sufficiently seriously the moral value of individuality.

Yet another criticism is that Habermas's appeal to consensus as the validation of moral norms is not compelling even as a counterfactual norm. The moral validation of the consensual judgment arrived at cannot simply rest on the fact that the consensual procedure has been duly observed, for even if this procedure presupposes undistorted communication, moral claims cannot be grounded on such a consensus without circularity. For if the moral claim derives its validity from the consensual procedure, then one cannot argue that the consensual procedure is validating because it embodies moral grounds within it that serve to make it a validating procedure. Therefore, I would argue that the normative ground that validates any consensual judgment must lie outside the consensual procedure itself in some wider context of human activity. Moreoever, though this procedural criterion may well be acceptable as a way of arriving at rules to govern collective action – inasmuch as it is a kind of democratic decision procedure – it remains unclear why the judgments arrived at in this way should be regarded as morally right rather than as merely accepted. This suggests a possible relativist reading, despite the fact that Habermas's view has a strong universalistic emphasis.

SOCIAL ONTOLOGY AND ETHICAL NORMS

The approach to ethics in terms of a social ontology that I propose differs both from traditional foundationalism and from the recent alternatives of Rawls and Habermas. It may be distinguished from traditional foundationalist views in several respects. First of all, it differs from traditional natural law or natural rights views in that it does not appeal to any transcendent or external ground beyond the human, that is, to neither a divine nor a natural moral order. It also does not appeal to any intrinsic ground of values in biological nature as such. Moreover, it is not an essentialist theory that derives its normative force from a conception of action in accordance with a fixed human nature or natural kind. For the view proposed here is rather that human beings create and transform their own natures in the course of their activity. Their nature is therefore not fixed but self-transforming. This very capacity for self-transformation in activity will be seen to be the ground of value. The view I am proposing is therefore not to be taken as a traditional metaphysical one in which the moral reality exists or subsists *in se* and is then read off by reason or intuited in moral feelings. Rather, the reality which our moral beliefs and judgments are concerned with is here taken to be a social reality constituted by intentional and interacting human beings.

Second, the approach here differs from the foundationalism of moral intuitionism. That is, a social ontological approach to ethics does not base the conception of value or of right on any immediate, apodictic, and incorrigible moral intuition on the foundations of which one then constructs a moral theory. Rather, my approach here is to reconstruct the genesis of value and the ground of rights from an analysis of the nature of human activity as free. Such an approach involves a rational reflection on the experiential or empirical knowledge of human action and interaction.

Third, this approach to the grounding of a social ethics is not naturalistic in the sense of deriving "oughts" from "is's" or values and rights from nonmoral facts. The empirical facts to which it appeals are what I would characterize as normative facts, that is, facts the description of which entails a valuative component.

Fourth, the approach here is not a purely Kantian one in that it does not appeal to transcendental or a priori arguments concerning what is rationally necessary to presuppose as conditions for there being rights or values. Further, I do not follow Kant in sharply distinguishing between a sensible and a supersensible realm. On the other hand, there is a

Kantian element in the argument here in the appeal to the freedom of the agent as the necessary and universal condition for values.

A final difference I would like to point to is that between the construction I am proposing and that of both Rawls and Habermas. It seems that in the final analysis both Rawls and Habermas propose that the ultimate ground for the validation of norms is consensus or agreement. The approach I present argues instead that there are fundamental values that have an objective basis. As Kant says in the Preface to the *Critique of Practical Reason*, ". . .universality of assent does not prove the objective validity of a judgment, i.e., its validity as knowledge, . . . even if sometimes that which is universally assented to is also correct, this is no proof of its agreement with the object; it is rather the case that only objective validity affords the ground of a necessary universal agreement."[16] However, the objectivity I am adducing does not lie outside the activity of human individuals but rather derives from the very nature of this activity itself as free. This claim must now be made clear.

The question that presents itself, therefore, for such an ontological approach to the construction of a social ethics is how values are generated by human activity. The premise that I begin from is the fact of human freedom. As I discussed this earlier, this freedom is in the first place the activity of choosing or purposive activity. This premise is not merely an assumption nor is it a transcendental postulate necessary for the argument. Rather, I would argue that the fact of choice is empirically shown and is experienced phenomenologically. Such choice is not mere randomness or spontaneity but is rather an intentional endowment of one alternative among others with value, or with greater value than the others. That is to say, the act of choice itself necessarily entails a valuation. But such valuation is typically relative to the purposes, needs, or wants of agents, and as such, cannot lay claim to objective validity. Even if such valuations are socially constituted by a group or a community of agents by some consensual procedure, this would not give them any greater objective validity than if they were the choices of individuals (though I would hold that if such choices were democratically arrived at, they would have a claim to be binding on those who participated in making them).

Acts of choice are, however, not merely the ground or source of those values with which the things chosen are endowed. In addition, they are reflexive affirmations of the agent's capacity of choice as characteristic of his or her mode of activity or mode of being. The act of choice thus necessarily affirms its own value in the act of choosing. The objective ground of freedom is thus the exercise of this freedom itself. And since the exercise of choice is, as I argued earlier, the characteristic mode of being human, this freedom has its objective ground in the nature of human activity as such. One may say further that this freedom as the characteristic mode of life activity of human beings is of primary value in the sense that it is a necessary condition for the possibility of any other value and is moreover valued in itself. Freedom is thus necessarily affirmed in the mode of being of human beings. As I argued earlier, the exercise of this freedom, however, is not merely a repetition of this bare capacity of choice in one instance after another but rather involves the development of the individual through the activities that such choices engender. It also involves the development of a world created by the activities of these individuals, a world which embodies the values that they have given it. Thus the capacity for choice becomes concretely realized in the self-development of individuals which thus constitutes the meaning and the value of freedom in the full sense. Self-development may therefore be seen as the highest value to which a process of individual acts of choice tends.

If freedom is the characteristic mode of the life activity of human beings and if it is a primary value, the question may then arise as to the value of life itself and its relation to the value of freedom in this scheme. This is a large and complex question and can be treated only briefly here. One may begin by saying that in a certain sense human life and freedom are generically identical, if one takes life not simply as a state of being, but as an activity characterized by choice. Clearly, however, one may distinguish life in the sense of biological existence from freedom and see it as a necessary condition for the free activity of human beings, since one has to be alive in order to act. Yet, to understand this biological existence as *simply* a matter of organic life would be to lose its distinctive character as *human* biological existence, or its value as human life, that is, as the existence of that kind of living being whose nature it is to exercise free choice. Thus life may be understood not as a separate precondition of agency but rather as ingredient in it and as expressed or realized in human activity. The value of life, like that of freedom, is thus affirmed in the very activity of human beings. Since life too is a necessary condition for the possibility of any other value – for without it there would be no agency – it also is a primary value.[17]

In addition to the fundamental value of freedom, the other principal values of the social ethics presented here, namely, equality, reciprocity, and democracy, may be seen to have an ontological basis in the nature of human activity itself. It remains to indicate briefly how the account of these values given in Chapter 1 is explicitly related to the social ontology that I proposed. It will be remembered that I interpreted equality in terms of the principle of equal rights to the conditions of self-development. Such equal rights are based on the agency or capacity of choice that every individual has by virtue of being human and which thus makes them equally agents. Since the exercise of this agency is realized in the form of self-development and since this requires material and social conditions, both the equality of individuals and their equal rights to the conditions may thus be seen to be based on the ontological nature of individuals and of their activity.

Similarly, the value of reciprocity has its ontological ground in the relational character of individuals, specifically, their interdependence in realizing their projects and satisfying their needs. I analyzed such reciprocity as one of the principal social conditions for self-development. As such, its normative force derives in part from the value of freedom. Beyond this,

Chapter 4

Economic justice, self-management, and the principle of reciprocity

Recent theories of economic justice have generally focused on the question of just distribution of goods or wealth.[1] Where they have focused on production and not only on distribution, such theories have generally operated with conceptions of property and specifically of private property, and of entitlement to the products of one's labor.[2] Very few, if any, of these theories have given significant attention to the question of justice in the organization of the production process, or to the distribution of powers and rights in this domain. In this chapter, I propose a conception of economic justice in which the right to participate in economic decision-making in the production process, that is, workers' self-management, is understood as a requirement of justice. Although other theorists have argued for such workers' self-management, they have not seen it as required by justice, but rather by such other values as meaningful work, property rights, or productive efficiency, or most generally, by the value of democracy itself.[3]

This requirement for worker participation emerges, on my view, from a more general framework of a theory of justice, in which justice is understood as fundamentally involving equal positive freedom, that is, the equal right to the conditions of self-development, including enabling material and social conditions in addition to civil liberties and political rights. Here I will develop this framework as it relates to questions of the production and distribution of goods and the allocation of economic rights. In this connection, I will also consider when inequalities may be justified.

In my discussion of the principle of equality, I will introduce the principle of reciprocity and argue that justice requires not only equality as an extensional principle of allocation or distribution, but also reciprocal relations among persons. This discussion of reciprocity will cast light on the earlier thesis that I proposed, namely that workers' self-management is a requirement for economic justice.

I begin with a consideration of some themes in two major recent theories of economic justice, namely those of Rawls and Nozick. I will focus on only a few leading points from a critical perspective in order to articulate the specific position that I am proposing in this chapter and which contrasts with both of theirs in important respects.

BEYOND RAWLS AND NOZICK

There are four relevant features of Rawls's conception in *A Theory of Justice* that I would like to discuss here. First, it seems to me that Rawls's "difference principle" – that justice requires that social and economic inequalities should be to the greatest benefit of the least advantaged – permits relations of economic exploitation and possibly of social domination, particularly as Rawls represents this principle in various examples. Because the principle focuses only on the relative standing of representative individuals in terms of their advantages and disadvantages, it does not take into account the nonreciprocal social and economic relations that hold between them. This results at least in part from Rawls's interpretation of relative advantage and disadvantage only in terms of how much or what quantity of the primary goods, for example, wealth and income, each possesses. This leaves out of account the ways in which these primary goods are acquired or used and also leaves out of account the internal social relations among the individuals. Thus the principle does not exclude a relation in which some individuals would benefit from the exploitation of the labor of others, so long as their enrichment by this exploitation increases the income or wealth of those exploited. In economic exploitation, the value produced by wage labor exceeds the rate at which it is compensated, where this difference in value is appropriated by those who own and control the means or conditions of productive activity.[4] This is therefore a nonreciprocal relation, in which one may be said to benefit at the expense of the other, inasmuch as one controls the conditions of labor and therefore the productive activity of the other and, further, that one appropriates without equivalent return a part of the other's product or contribution. Such exploitation thus violates the norm of reciprocity which, I would hold, is an aspect of justice. It is also not clear that the difference principle would exclude nonreciprocal relations of social or personal domination in which some are able to subordinate the actions or decisions of others to their own, whether through coercion or undue influence over them. Although Rawls does recognize the norm of reciprocity as involved in justice, he defines it simply as a requirement for mutual benefit without regard for the sorts of relations among persons in terms of which these benefits are acquired. But I will argue later that the quality of these relations is crucial to reciprocity.

One qualification to this discussion needs to be made, however: Rawls does include self-respect among the primary goods, and it would seem that this requirement for self-respect might prohibit domination or exploitation in social and economic life. But this is unclear, because Rawls suggests that self-respect would be effected primarily by the requirement of equal liberty in civil and political life. Furthermore, the examples that Rawls offers suggest that the difference principle is not meant to exclude economic exploitation, and he regards the principle as compatible with both systems of capitalism or of socialism.[5]

The second point in Rawls's analysis to be considered concerns the separation that he makes between the two principles of justice,[6] and specifically his restriction of equal liberty to the domain of civil and political affairs. Thus Rawls suggests that there would be rational agreement that justice requires equal basic liberties of citizenship, including the political liberties of the right to vote and to be eligible to hold office, as well as the liberties of freedom of speech, thought, and the right to hold property. However, he does not see a comparable principle of equal liberty as applying to the social and economic domain, where instead justice concerns the distribution of social and economic advantages. But one might argue that there are important respects in which the principle of equal liberty pertains to this domain as well, and that the restriction of this principle to the political and civil domain alone is arbitrary. Thus I would propose that equal liberty also requires an equal right to participate in decisions concerning the social and economic activities in which one engages, as much as it requires the equal right to participate in political matters. For such participation is just as important a requirement for the expression of one's free agency and for one's self-respect as is participation in political decisions. Thus I argue that workers' self-management and rights to participate in decisions concerning social institutions are required by equal liberty, just as is the equal right of political participation.

A third, and related, point is that Rawls fails to take clearly into account that equality with respect to certain social and economic conditions is necessary for freedom or liberty. This is partly because of the separation, noted earlier, that Rawls makes between the first and second principles, assigning equal liberty only to the first, and from the priority that he gives to the first principle, interpreted in this way. This account fails to recognize the way in which certain social and economic inequalities can undermine the equal liberty which Rawls regards as preeminent. This point has been made by Norman Daniels as a criticism of Rawls's distinction between equal liberty and the unequal worth of liberty,[7] where this unequal worth of liberty may arise from "[t]he inability to take advantage of one's rights and opportunities as a result of poverty and ignorance, and a lack of means generally. . . . "[8] Thus for example, as Daniels notes, the wealthy are more capable of influencing the political process or exercising their freedom of speech through the media than are the poor, and this discrepancy undercuts the supposedly equal liberties.

This criticism may be extended further by noting that certain social and economic equalities are necessary conditions not only for liberty, as Rawls treats it, but for freedom in the broader sense of self-development, which bears some relation to what Rawls calls the pursuit of one's plan of life. Such a conception of self-development is what I have called positive freedom, which goes beyond the abstract capacity for choice provided for in the requirement for equal liberty. Without at least minimal social and economic conditions and, most notably, minimal means of subsistence, such freedom remains empty. Thus although I believe it is correct to give importance to equal liberty, as Rawls does, I think one should also regard the equal right to minimal means of subsistence as of the same importance.[9] A similar point has been made by Shue, who argues that rational agreement on principles of justice would require a guarantee of some floor or minimal threshold of the provision of means of subsistence.[10] Beyond this, there may be other social and economic goods and resources that should be distributed equally as conditions for the full development of freedom. I shall consider these later, along with the question of the demarcation between those conditions for self-development that are required to be equal and those where inequalities may be justified.

A final criticism of Rawls's position that may be made here is that he limits the application of the principle of justice in the economic domain only to distribution and not to production. Thus, in the first place, he does not explicitly consider the organization and control of the production process nor its relation to economic rights with respect to the requirements of justice. Rawls does include rights, powers, opportunities, and self-respect as among the primary goods to be distributed, and these might seem to bear on these questions concerning production. However, he does not develop this relation explicitly.

Rethinking democracy

A second aspect of this criticism is that Rawls fails to take into account the relation between the economic products or goods which are to be distributed and those who have produced them. Thus one may argue that the producers of the goods have a claim to some return on the value of what they have produced, or that there is some form of entitlement. Thus it is not the case that economic goods are simply available for some distribution out of a common pool. Rather, those who have produced them have some prior right to control over the product or to recompense for their work in producing it. A similar point is made by Nozick who argues that "The situation is *not* one of something's getting made, and there being an open question of who is to get it. Things come into the world already attached to people having entitlements over them."[11]

Nozick is right in pointing out that the production of goods implies some form of entitlement on the part of the producers of these goods. However, he is wrong about the nature of this entitlement. Nozick's presupposition is that entitlement is originally based on an act of appropriation by an individual. What this account fails to consider is the fact of joint or social labor or acts of appropriation. That is, it is plausible to suppose that some of the earliest forms of appropriation took a tribal or communal form or were regarded as property of some subgroup who originally worked together.[12] Thus Nozick's appeal to an original act of just acquisition in terms of individual appropriation is at the very least one-sided. Moreover, contemporary forms of economic production are most often social or cooperative and thus would seem to give rise to some form of joint or social entitlement to the product.

Nozick does in fact deal with social cooperation in the economy in terms of the question of whether "individual entitlements apply to parts of the cooperatively produced product."[13] Here he translates the question of social entitlement to the social product into a question of individual acquisitions and transfers through market exchange. He does this either through a model of sequential exchanges among individuals each of whom participates in parts of a sequential production process (with each individual as a "miniature firm") or, more realistically, through a model of joint working together in which each is entitled to his or her marginal product. But according to Nozick, in this latter case, a free market approximates to such a distribution of marginal products through voluntary transfers. Thus according to him, the individual entitlements based on socially cooperative production are justly apportioned through voluntary exchanges in a free market.

However, contrary to Nozick's view, it can be argued that the exchange between the owners of capital and laborers is not in fact a fully voluntary one, but is rather constrained or coerced in fundamental respects. Although the laborer sometimes has a choice among alternative jobs, he or she does not in general have the reasonable option of refusing to work in some job under the conditions set by the owners and managers of capital, since this is the only means available to the wage worker for earning a livelihood. Therefore, Nozick's reliance on the notion of voluntary transfer in a free market situation as the ground for just distribution of the marginal product is not warranted. Nozick offers a counterargument here to the effect that whatever options or restrictions on one's choices result from a sequence of legitimate exchanges cannot be regarded as forced or coerced, even if they are unpalatable. But against this one may argue, as G.A. Cohen has done, that regardless of how a situation has been arrived at, if one has no real choice but to engage in a certain action that is necessary for one's existence or well-being, then one can speak of being forced to act in this way.[14] I would not use the term "forced" in this context, reserving it rather for contexts of direct physical control, but would speak of constraint, coercion, or domination instead. Nonetheless it seems to be a piece of semantic sleight of hand on Nozick's part to define away the notion of coercion by appeal to the legitimacy of previous acquisitions or exchanges. Furthermore, in the case at issue, namely that of the voluntariness of the exchange between wage labor and capital, one may put in question whether the original acquisition of capital and the ensuing exchanges are in fact legitimate.

One may argue that in the market exchange between capital and labor, the laborer does not receive recompense for the full value of what he or she has produced, but rather that the capitalist market form of exchange recompenses only a portion of this. To develop this argument, however, would require a fuller discussion of the economic relation between labor and capital than I can give here. Furthermore, with respect to the original acquisition, one may note that the historical cases of original acquisition of capital, that is, of so-called primitive accumulation of capital, include so many instances of appropriation by force or stealth, that one cannot base a legitimation of subsequent exchanges on such illegitimate original acquisition. Yet in Nozick's argument against the notion that labor is coerced to exchange in the market, there is a tacit appeal to just such legitimacy in the initial appropriation and the subsequent exchanges.

Thus far I have argued that Nozick fails to take into account adequately the notions of social production or social entitlement. While he is correct in recognizing that there should be some relation between the activity of producers and their entitlement to the products of their labor, he fails to recognize how much of productive activity is in fact social, and where he does recognize it, he misinterprets the entitlement that derives from it. I would argue that where labor is social, there is a right to joint control over the process and the product by all those who participate in the production. This amounts to a requirement of workers' self-management or worker control in the economy.

Before proceeding to a consideration of Nozick's objections to worker control, there is a point concerning Nozick's criticism of redistribution through taxation, which I would offer on the basis of the previous argument. Just as I have argued that someone may be constrained or coerced in a certain situation apart from the question of the legitimacy of how the situation arose, so too I would argue that one may speak of the injustice of a situation in which some are able to exert undue power over others or to dominate them, even if there were some sense in which one could speak of the sequence

Economic justice and self-management

of steps by which they attain to such power as legitimate or just. Thus in my view, as I shall sketch it later, one of the requirements of justice is freedom from such domination. This therefore becomes a ground for an argument for the legitimacy of the redistribution of resources through taxation, when the distribution of resources is such that relatively few have control over the livelihood and working activity of others through their ownership and control of the conditions for this activity. This requirement of justice also serves as a ground for an argument for the redistribution of economic power in the form of workers' self-management so as to exclude domination or exploitation. Against Nozick's further objection that such a redistribution would require continual interference with individuals' liberties and violations of their entitlements, one may note first of all that his view disregards the liberty of those who are dominated. Second of all, some justifiable redistribution would be in recognition of social entitlements not recompensed in market exchanges and thus would not be a violation of individual entitlements. Third, it is possible to be sensitive to the requirement for not interfering with individuals' liberties by devising social policies or institutions that require minimal intervention. That is to say, the distribution of rights and powers needs to be structured in such a way as to preserve equal freedom through the working of these institutions. The form that such institutions would take would be that of democracy not only in politics but in economic life, where it would more specifically take the form of workers' self-management.

Nozick briefly considers the question of worker-controlled firms, which would involve democratic decision-making in the firms and would extend to powers of ownership. Nozick suggests that workers' control is less efficient than capitalist forms of enterprise on the grounds that, if it were in fact more efficient economically, means would have been found to introduce it on a broad scale, for example, by the use of union funds or by attracting private investment. Nozick's argument here is flawed on several grounds. First, there is striking and rapidly growing evidence that worker participation in de-

141

of economic justice that avoids the problems that I have noted in their views. A theory of economic justice concerns the principles that ought to govern the distribution of rights, powers, and goods within the economic domain. The main principle of justice that I proposed earlier is that of equal positive freedom, defined as *prima facie* equal rights to the (social and material) conditions of self-development. Interpreted as a principle of economic justice, it would require equal rights of access to the economic conditions of one's self-development. It will be seen, however, that this *prima facie* equality is qualified by some permissible inequalities. Furthermore, I will propose that economic justice also entails a principle of reciprocity, in addition to the fundamental principle of equal rights. If economic justice is understood in terms of this principle of equal rights to the conditions of self-development, then it is clear that it pertains not only to the distribution of material goods but also to the distribution of rights and powers that are involved in economic production, since these rights and powers are among the social conditions necessary for agency. Central among such rights is the right to participate in decisions or choices concerning the productive activities in which one engages jointly with others. The argument for such a right of participation derives from the characterization of agency as the freedom to choose the purpose or direction of one's actions, a freedom that all agents equally share, as I have proposed earlier. Where activity is joint or social, as it is in the economic activity of social production, this equal right of agency implies a right by all who participate in an activity to jointly determine it, that is, to participate equally in decisions concerning it. This right to participate in decisions concerning joint activities of production is, in effect, the right to workers' self-management or to the democratic sharing of authority in economic production.

Such workers' self-management is therefore analogous to democracy in political life in which the equal right to participate in decisions concerning common actions is recognized. The argument is similar in both cases, namely, that free agents have a right of self-determination or self-rule, which therefore implies an equal right of codetermination concerning all common activities in which they engage, whether political or economic. In the case of economic democracy, I would define the locus of participation in decision-making more narrowly as in the first instance the basic unit of production. In most cases this would be the firm. The argument for this restriction is that the right of codetermination belongs to those who are themselves agents in this activity, that is, who are engaged in a common project. Thus I am not proposing that all those who are affected by an economic activity have a right to participate in decisions about production, but rather that it is the producers themselves that principally have this right. This formulation avoids the objection that has been raised against proposals for economic democracy to the effect that there is no way of demarcating who is or who is not affected by economic decisions. Thus it is argued that ultimately everyone is affected and therefore such participation in economic decision-making is unworkable and meaningless. On my proposal, the locus of decision-making in matters of production is principally defined as the firm, and participation is in the first instance delimited to those who are actively engaged in the firm. Therefore, the firm retains relative autonomy as the principal locus of participation in economic decision-making.[16]

Workers' self-management in this model would mean that the workers in a firm would have the right to decide jointly on questions of the planning and organization of production or the provision of services, including what to produce or what services to provide, as well as rates of production, allocation of work, working hours, work discipline, etc. They would also have the right to determine jointly how the firm's income is to be distributed, for example, how much of it is to be plowed back into the firm itself, how much distributed in wages, and how these wages are to be divided among themselves, that is, more properly speaking, how they are to share the net revenue. They would also control the decisions concerning sales and marketing of the product or service. However, this workers' self-management surely does not require that all the workers participate in every decision concerning all aspects of production and sale of their products. In any large firm, one would expect that they would delegate various functions to directors and managers whom they appoint. However, in this model, ultimate authority and decision-making power remains with all those who work in the firm.

It is clear, then, that workers' self-management as it is described here involves more than worker participation in the management decisions of privately owned corporations. Rather, it is understood as worker control, that is, as involving property rights of ownership, as well as management rights. In this way, this view entails a conception of social or cooperative ownership of the means of production by the participating workers in a firm.[17] I give the argument for this conception of property in a later chapter.

However, economic production involves more than the single firm as its unit. It typically involves complex interactions among many firms through a market or other means of exchange (e.g., in the acquisition or sale of raw or processed materials for production, of tools, of transportation, of warehousing, and again, of credit facilities). In such complex economic interactions, decisions are made through the medium of the market itself, where the joint decisions of the members of each firm come into play with respect to each other. Insofar as the market permits a free agreement based on the decisions of worker-controlled firms, it is compatible with such economic democracy. In the model proposed here, then, firms are free to buy and sell to other firms, institutions, or to individual consumers. The market is the locus for such exchanges and therefore adjusts supply and demand and influences the setting of prices. However, this model would generally exclude the market between capital and labor, since the wages would be determined in the process of self-management, by the workers' own allocation among themselves of the net revenue of the firm.

Yet, there is a domain of economic decision-making that involves questions of social policy, regional or national economic planning, and investment, taxation, and welfare. Since such questions involve the most general conditions for the economic activity of all those who are participants in the common economic life , for example, of a nation, the right to participate in decision-making concerning such matters properly extends to all those who are involved. Such participation should be direct, where possible, but may of course proceed through representation where necessary. Furthermore, it may be part of the political processes of decision-making in a democratic government. In the context of such regional or national economic policy, one may propose that there should be market-regulatory, and planning or investment, commissions, which are democratically representative. These would aim at serving general social interests, for example, by regulating abuses of the market system, by some long-range planning to meet expected social needs, and by fostering innovation. Such a model is discussed in further detail in Chapter 9.

Whereas my argument for workers' self-management has been grounded on a principle of equal rights to the conditions of self-development, as a principle of justice, other proponents of self-management have adduced different grounds. Among these are meaningful work, property right, productive efficiency, and democracy. Each of these is inadequate in one way or another in my view, though each expresses a value that workers' self-management serves to realize.

The argument for workers' self-management on the grounds of meaningful work asserts that work should be "challenging," "interesting," "skilled," "self-directing," and "varied," and in general "satisfying." As commonly understood in these ways, however, meaningful work could be achieved without requiring workers' self-management, by modifications or reforms within the framework of existing work relations. Such modifications have indeed already been introduced to overcome feelings of alienation, by such methods as participation in decision-making and quality-of-life improvements in the workplace. The common understanding of meaningful work described above leaves the concept sufficiently ambiguous so that it can hardly serve as an argument for workers' self-management. If, however, meaningful work is defined more narrowly as being autonomous or self-governing, or as "self-directing" in the stronger sense of having control over one's work activity,[18] then of course either workers' self-management is entailed by definition (since it is built into the concept of meaningful work) or there is a tacit appeal to values other than meaningful work, for example, to autonomy or even self-development as the ground for self-management.

Workers' rights to the product of their labor, as property rights, have also been proposed as the moral ground for self-management.[19] The argument runs that private ownership of the means of production by capitalists leads to expropriation of the value of the product of labor, which rightfully belongs to the producers. Workers' self-management, on this view, would return control over the product or result to the producers. One problem with this argument is that it is not made clear why participation in the activity of production should give one a right to appropriate the product. This is merely asserted or tacitly understood. Moreover, it is not made clear what the connection is between control over the product or result of one's labor and control over the activity or process of production. It is not self-evident that there is any connection between these two, and this would have to be established by further argument or analysis. Finally, it is likewise left unclear as to how such a labor theory of property right would support workers' self-management as a form of democracy involving equal rights to control the activity and products of labor. For if there are differences in the amount or quality of labor among workers, it might seem that they should have differential and thus unequal rights in controlling the process, stemming from their unequal right to the product. It is usually assumed that there are such equal rights of participation in self-management, but the ground for this is not given. However, it seems to me that property right can provide a ground for workers' self-management but only if the concept of property is itself derived from or grounded in some more basic rights or values. Further, I would hold that there is indeed an important connection between the concepts of property and democracy, but this needs to be explicitly shown. (I consider these questions in Chapter 6.)

A common and current argument for workers' self-management is that such an organization of work leads to greater productive efficiency than present forms of organization and may in fact be the cure for the ills of postindustrial society. The argument here is that traditional top-down hierarchical forms of work relations, with their features of domination and alienation, lead to such phenomena as high rates of absenteeism, worker resistance to increases in efficiency, and poor quality control. Workers' self-management, by contrast, would lead to greater job commitment and readiness to adopt more efficient methods of work, since the workers would have a say about the conditions of work, and the benefits of increases in productivity would redound to them.[20] Although it is not a model of workers' self-management, the Japanese model of participative decision-making in industry has been presented as a paradigm of how worker participation in decision-making leads to great increases in productive efficiency. I believe that workers' self-management would in fact lead to great increases in productive efficiency, as suggested in this view. However, even if it were not maximally efficient, self-management would still be normatively required on the grounds of the equal rights of participation, which I discussed earlier (as long as it were efficient enough to provide the material conditions of self-development to a reasonable degree). Further, increased productive efficiency by itself cannot serve as a normative argument simply on the grounds that more is better, unless it is made clear in normative terms *why* more is better and better for what. Without this specification, such an argument for workers' self-management is at best incomplete.

Perhaps the most general ground that has been advanced in support of workers' self-management is that of the value of democracy itself. If one is committed to the value of democracy, then it can be argued that one ought to recognize the importance of it not only in political life but in the economic domain as well, since the situation is analogous in both cases. Thus it is argued that just as the freedom and equality of individuals require political democracy, so too do they require an equal right to participate in economic decision-making. But the analogy between political democracy and workers' self-management as economic democracy does not go through simply on this basis. For the freedom and equality that are adduced here generally remain interpreted as negative freedom and abstract equality. As such, their extension to the economic realm becomes inadequate as a ground for workers' self-management, since these very conceptions can be interpreted – and indeed have been – as the basis for individualist free enterprise and capitalist forms of economic decision-making. If the extension of democracy to the economic domain is to be adequately argued, then the freedom and equality upon which democracy itself is grounded would have to be understood as positive freedom and as equal rights to the conditions of self-development.

There is, however, a form of the argument from the analogy between political democracy and democracy in the economic realm which explicitly rejects liberal conceptions of private property that underlie capitalist free enterprise and which have been used to argue against the extension of democracy to the economic realm. This is the view that has recently been proposed by Robert A. Dahl in *A Preface to Economic Democracy*. He argues that a country committed to the goals of a democratic society would choose to extend democracy to the economy. He writes,

If democracy is justified in governing the state, then it is also justified in governing economic enterprises. What is more, if it cannot be justified in governing economic enterprises, we do not quite see how it can be justified in governing the state. Members of any association for whom the assumptions of the democratic process are valid have a *right* to govern themselves by means of the democratic process. If, as we believe, these assumptions hold among us, not only for the government of

149

the state but also for the internal government of economic enterprises, then we have a *right* to govern ourselves democratically within our economic enterprises."[21]

Dahl's argument for this conclusion is, in outline, that if certain assumptions hold – for example, a principle of liberty, namely, that "each adult person in the association is entitled to be the final judge of his or her own interests"; and weak and strong principles of equality: "the good of each person is entitled to equal consideration," and "all the adult members of the association . . . are roughly equally qualified to decide which matters do or do not require binding collective decisions" – then it follows that people involved in such an association possess an "inalienable right to democratic self-government." He then argues that these assumptions do hold for economic enterprises and that therefore the right to self-government applies to this context as well. Against the view that such self-government in economic enterprises would violate a right to private property, and in particular, a right to private ownership of corporations, Dahl holds that "none of the well-known reasoned arguments for private property as a fundamental right, comparable to the fundamental right of self-government, is satisfactory. . . ."[22] Further, he maintains, following Becker,[23] that none of the arguments for private property justifies a right to the unlimited acquisition of such property nor do they successfully justify private ownership of corporate enterprises.[24] Beyond this, Dahl argues that the objections to the viability of workers' self-management (or what he calls self-governing enterprises) either do not hold up or leave the point moot.

Dahl's view that the rights of democratic self-governance apply not only to political life but to the workplace or to economic enterprises as well is one which I clearly share. However, I would suggest that without a fundamental reformulation of the basic concepts of freedom and equality – a reformulation that Dahl does not offer – and lacking an explicit conception of common or joint activity, Dahl's argument for workers' self-management remains somewhat tenuous and open to the sorts of objections he tries to avoid. Dahl offers a series of negative arguments in the form of answers to objections against workers' self-management, the upshot of which is to show that self-governing enterprises do not violate the rights of private property of corporate owners, or that workers' self-management is not less efficient than privately owned corporations, or that self-governing enterprises are not less competent in management functions than are traditional hierarchically run corporations. At most, however, such arguments have only the negative import of showing that workers' self-management is permissible or feasible, but do not yet constitute a positive or normative argument for the introduction of such self-management. For example, in arguing that rights to private property have not been successfully demonstrated, Dahl does not yet offer any positive normative ground for a conception of common property that would underlie a system of self-managing enterprises. I will argue in the next chapter that such a conception can be derived from the principle of equal positive freedom and from the idea of common or joint activity. It is true that Dahl proposes what he calls cooperative ownership of the self-governing firm by its members, but the considerations he offers for this are of a strictly empirical and instrumental nature. Moreover, aside from his refutation of the liberal arguments that have been given for a right to private property in the means of production, Dahl offers no principled argument against such a right, an argument that could follow from a conception of equal positive freedom. Further, although he suggests that a system of privately owned enterprises historically has led to (and would continue to lead to) discrepancies of wealth that tend to undermine political liberty, this objection to such private property remains a contingently empirical one and it might be argued that such discrepancies are remediable by some redistribution short of any fundamental changes in forms of ownership.

In addition to his negative arguments, Dahl does offer positive arguments for workers' self-management, but here too some questions arise. First, in his account of the assumptions about the nature of a democratic association and the people in it, which underlie the validity of a claim to self-government, Dahl implicitly appeals to conceptions of negative liberty and abstract equality without any fundamental reformulation of these concepts. Thus, the only principle of liberty that he enunciates here is that "Each adult person is entitled to be the final judge of his or her own interests."[25] But if this is the case, then the applicability of democratic self-government to the economic domain remains open to question. For, on the basis of these very conceptions, one can just as well argue, as traditional liberal theory has, that workers freely contract to accept hierarchical and nondemocratic forms of decision-making in firms, and that respect for their freedom of choice requires respect for the free labor contract in the economic domain, as it does for political liberty, as the expression of this freedom of choice in the political domain.[26] To be sure, at a few points Dahl does appeal to another conception of freedom, somewhat closer to the notion of positive freedom (e.g., in talking about economic freedom as involving "a right to gain access to adequate personal economic resources"[27]), but he does not develop these alternative ideas of freedom in any sustained or systematic way.

Second, one of the necessary conditions (or, as Dahl puts it, "assumptions"), which Dahl proposes as defining an association as a democratic one and therefore as entailing an inalienable right to democratic self-governance, is that "The collection of people in the association has a need to reach at least some collective decisions that will be binding on all the members of the collectivity."[28] Dahl goes on to argue that decisions taken in an economic enterprise are in fact binding upon its members,[29] which would presumably make such an enterprise eligible in this respect for designation as a democratic association by his criterion; but nowhere does he argue for the equally essential condition that he sets, namely, that there is a need that these decisions be collective. Indeed, this is precisely what is at issue in a valid claim to democratic self-governance in the economic domain, and this cannot be simply assumed without begging the question. Therefore, the positive argument justifying democracy in self-governing enterprises remains incomplete on Dahl's own grounds.

ECONOMIC JUSTICE AND THE
DISTRIBUTION OF GOODS

I have thus far argued that economic justice requires equal rights to participate in decision-making by those who are jointly engaged in economic activity. I would now like to consider what the implications of the principle of equal positive freedom are for the question of the distribution of economic goods. It is clear in the first instance that this principle requires equal rights to those goods and services that are minimal conditions for any human action whatever. Without such minimal conditions, the very possibility of exercising human agency or of self-development would not exist. Such minimal economic conditions would include means of subsistence, health care, and basic education. Because these are universally necessary conditions for any agent, each human being has an equal right to these minimal conditions by virtue of their equal agency. Since the allocation of goods in this case would be designed to meet basic needs, the criterion here would be one of distribution according to need.

Beyond these minimal conditions, however, it may be seen to follow from the principle of equal positive freedom that individuals have a right to conditions for their specific and differentiated forms of self-development. Because such self-development is what characterizes human activity, and because different human beings pursue individually differentiated purposes or ends in their self-development, the equal rights to conditions here are not rights to the same conditions in each case but rather rights to equivalent though different conditions. This right has to be qualified, however, as a right to only some of these differentiated conditions for self-development, rather than to all the conditions that would be necessary for full self-development. This qualification is necessary because it is a practical impossibility to achieve the level of abundance that would be required to meet everyone's needs for the conditions of full self-development without any limits. In this situation of relative scarcity, equal rights to individually differentiated conditions for self-development can realistically extend only to initial requirements for training in a particular vocation and initial opportunities to exercise it, as well as to minimal conditions for the development of some avocational interests. As to the distribution of resources for self-development beyond these – that is, the resources for full self-development – I would argue that the principle of equal positive freedom should not be interpreted to require an equal distribution of inadequate means, but rather that some other principle of differential distribution is required. The introduction of such a principle for differential distribution may be justified not only on the basis of practical considerations of relative scarcity, but also from considerations of desert or of social value, deriving from one's effort or contribution. Needless to say, where such differential principles of allocation of goods or resources are applied, there needs to be equality of opportunity with respect to the possibility of gaining them.

Such a principle for differential distribution of economic goods is based on the right of agents to control the products of their activity.[30] Therefore, it may be characterized as a principle of entitlement to the fruits of one's labor. However, since this labor is most often social, the entitlement in such cases is a social entitlement and is vested in the associated producers in a given firm. They therefore have the right to dispose of the product and to benefit from whatever they receive in exchange for it. The presupposition here is that the products will be sold in a market and that the net income from the sale will be allocated democratically by the workers as reinvestment in the firm or as shared profits. The criterion here is to some degree one of distribution according to work, where the value of the work is measured in economic terms by the social value of its products as it is determined in the market. It is a principle of distribution according to work to

154

the degree that it is by participation in the work process that the individual is entitled to the control over the product of that labor and to a share in the income deriving from its sale. However, since the workers in the firm would determine how to distribute the income among themselves, they need not choose to allocate it according to the amount of work each one has individually contributed, but may decide to share it equally or according to some other criterion. Thus the criterion of distribution according to work here refers to the allocation of income to the firm as a whole from the sale of its social product, rather than to the internal distribution of the revenue among the workers.

It is likely that the operation of such a market will lead to inequalities in income among different firms and even to the elimination or bankruptcy of some of them, leading to the displacement and unemployment of the workers in these firms. To counteract the effects of such inequalities without at the same time subsidizing inefficiency, I would propose that there be some means of opening up new opportunities for profitable production. One such means would be by public investment commissions, democratically elected, which would choose to disburse tax monies so as to fund new and promising industries.

Beyond the principle of differential economic distribution according to work, there should be a place for reward for those forms of achievement that are not adequately reflected in market response, and also for the promotion of activities that are socially needed but that may not be adequately supported by the operations of the market. An example of the first case, of achievement, would be that of the arts, in which excellence might be appropriately determined by expert or peer judgments rather than simply by mass popularity as determined by market response. An example of the latter case of social need might be theoretical research in the sciences or in medicine, where the market cannot be counted on to support such long-range and high-risk prospects for technological payoffs, or research carried on for its own sake, the social value of which consists precisely in this characteristic.

Thus I have proposed a conception of economic justice based on the principle of equal positive freedom which requires equal rights of participation in economic decision-making, that is, workers' self-management or worker control. As it applies to the distribution of economic goods, this principle of equal positive freedom requires equality in the minimal conditions necessary for any human action and equal rights to a basic level of equivalent conditions for individuals' self-development.[31] Beyond this, the differential distribution of goods and resources appropriately operates in accordance with a principle of entitlement to the fruits of one's labor, where this entitlement is understood as social. This was analyzed in terms of a principle of distribution according to work.

The conception of economic justice that I have advanced here thus differs in crucial ways from those of Rawls and Nozick. It seems to me also to avoid the difficulties in their views that I noted earlier. Thus where Rawls's difference principle does not exclude relations of exploitation or domination, the right to participate in economic decision-making which I have proposed precludes such relations of exploitation. It rules out the control by others over decisions concerning the economic activity of individuals or over the products of their labor. Further, whereas Rawls defines equal liberty as pertaining only to the sphere of political and civil rights, I propose that equal liberty extend as well to the domain of economic activity, where it requires equal rights to the basic conditions of human activity as well as equal rights of participation in economic decision-making. In this extension, freedom is defined more inclusively as self-development and not only as political liberty. Democracy is seen to be required in the economic as in the political domain. Further, it may be suggested that if the equal rights in the economic sphere that I proposed were in fact established, then political liberty and political democracy would be more fully realized. Finally, as I have already noted, Rawls's emphasis on distribution neglects the question of rights, powers, and entitlements in the domain of economic production. By contrast, on my view, economic justice is seen to apply to both domains.

With respect to Nozick's conception of economic justice, my view stresses the importance of social entitlement in addition to the individual entitlement which is his sole model. Beyond this, I propose an ongoing requirement for equal rights to basic economic conditions and to participate in economic decision-making, whereas he denies rights such as these in favor of what he calls a historical account of justice in terms of acquisitions and transfers. Further, I have maintained that, Nozick's claim to the contrary notwithstanding, it is possible to arrange economic institutions in such a way that they maintain equal rights and yet do not require constant interferences with individuals' liberties.

EQUALITY AND RECIPROCITY

In the final section of this chapter, I want to turn briefly to a consideration of the principle of reciprocity as an aspect of a theory of economic justice. Traditional theories have very often defined justice as a matter of treating equals equally and unequals unequally. In my discussion, justice is likewise seen as a question of treating equals equally, and in particular, with respect to their equal rights to the conditions of self-development, on the grounds of their equal agency. The requirements of justice would not be met, however, if the equal rights were thought to be satisfied by a merely extensional equality in the apportionment of goods and powers among individuals. For although such an apportionment might be objectively in accordance with the principle of equality, justice requires in addition a social relation among individuals in which each recognizes the equal rights of the others. For this mutual recognition itself constitutes one of the social conditions for self-development to which individuals have equal rights, since it entails the acknowledgment of their status as agents by their peers. Lacking such recognition, the demands of justice would not be met. Thus the requirements of justice include not only extensional equality, in terms of an external standard of distribution, but also an intentional social relation among agents, which entails a shared understanding and a mutual consciousness of each other's equal rights. For suppose, by contrast, that an apportionment of goods and powers were made which was merely extensionally in accordance with the principle of equal rights, either by a forcible imposition by an external authority or by the "invisible hand" of some perfect market distribution. In this case, though equal rights to some of the conditions could be satisfied, crucial social conditions which require intentional social relations among agents would remain unsatisfied, namely, the mutual recognition by agents of their equal freedom and, consequently, the recognition of their equal right to participate in decisions concerning the distribution of economic goods and powers.

Such mutual recognition constitutes the relation of reciprocity, which is thus required by justice. It will be recalled that I defined reciprocity as a social relation among agents in which each recognizes the other as an agent, that is, as equally free, and each acts with respect to the other on the basis of a shared understanding and a free agreement to the effect that the actions of each with respect to the other are equivalent. Insofar as each recognizes the other equally as an agent, each takes the other's rights as equal to his or her own. Beyond this, such a reciprocal relation involves the recognition by each of the other's differences. Where such reciprocal relations characterize a group of individuals engaged in a common project, this reciprocity involves a free and joint agreement among all the members on the common purposes and procedures.

This view of reciprocity differs from that of Rawls. For Rawls, the principle of reciprocity is also closely related to the principles of justice. He discusses reciprocity mainly in connection with moral development, but he also considers it in his discussion of the difference principle.[32] He interprets it as a principle of return for benefit done or as rooted in "a tendency to answer in kind."[33] Alternatively, he characterizes it as a principle of mutual benefit. But in both cases, reciprocity remains a response to a perceived benefit and thus is to some extent a principle of tit for tat, though the motives here may not be instrumental. His conception does not yet involve what I have characterized as social reciprocity, in which there is a recognition of another's distinctiveness as a value and a relation to others in terms of a common aim. Rawls may well be able to give an account of these features of social reciprocity in terms of his other conceptions, for example, the social conditions of self-respect, and social union, but he does not include them in his conception of reciprocity as I do.

The principle of reciprocity may be interpreted with respect to economic justice as requiring mutual recognition by individuals of each other's equal right to the basic economic goods that are necessary conditions for self-development. Further, it requires that each member of a group engaging in joint economic activity, for example, the members of a firm, recognize the equal rights of all the others to participate in joint decisions of the group. And since such equal rights to participate in common decisions is what I defined as democracy, reciprocity in this context would be realized in the extension of democratic decision procedures to economic life. Such democracy would in practice amount to what I have described as workers' self-management in the sense that all those engaging in a common economic enterprise would have the right to control the aim and course of such activity, either directly through their participation in decisions or through their appointment of managers.

Chapter 5

Equal rights, individual differences, and the ideal of self-development: paradoxes in the theory of democracy

The principle of *prima facie* equal rights to the conditions of self-development, I argued earlier, should serve as the guide for just distribution and for social and political organization. In this chapter, I want to examine some problems that arise from what seem to be contrary and mutually exclusive demands deriving from this principle. On the one hand, the full self-development of some individuals would seem to require an inequality of conditions, on the supposition that different individuals have greater capacities or different capacities for self-development than others and therefore have a right to more of the conditions than do others. Thus for example, it might be claimed that someone with a great talent for high-energy physics would require more conditions for his or her self-development than someone with a moderate talent in painting or even with a great capacity for this art, because in the former case the conditions, for example, of experimental apparatus and training, require much greater outlay of resources than do those in the latter case. Thus the equalization of conditions for self-development would seem to constrain the free self-development of such individuals. On the other hand, the principle appears to require full equality of rights to the conditions of self-development since, as I have argued, the agency or the capacity to choose, which is the basis for self-development, is found equally or in undifferentiated degree in every human being and thus requires equal recognition and equal rights. The principle, therefore, takes on a paradoxical dimension: Its two constituent aspects, namely, equality and the freedom of self-development, which are intended to be coherent, seem instead to be in conflict.

This conflict may be articulated more specifically in terms of two paradoxes, one that concerns the theoretical formulation of the principle, which I will call *the paradox of self-development*, and the other that concerns its practical implementation in social and economic life, which I will call *the paradox of distribution*.

The theoretical paradox is already suggested by what I have said. It is founded on the conflict between the concept of equal agency, which is the basis for the equal rights to the conditions for self-development, on the one hand, and, on the other hand, the concept that different individuals have different capacities for self-development and different modes for realizing themselves. Such special capacities would seem to demand unequal conditions for their full development. Such a claim to the conditions, however, would violate the principle of equal rights and with it the recognition of equal agency, which is at its foundation. Alternatively, if the principle of equal rights means that individuals have a right to an equal share in the conditions, then this would be in conflict with the differential claims based on the different capacities for self-development. Thus it would appear that the proposed principle entails self-contradictory claims to the conditions – that is, both equal and unequal claims – and therefore that it is paradoxical. This paradox bears some relation to the often formulated problem of how it is possible to preserve and encourage talents and individual excellences while at the same time maintaining or extending an egalitarian framework.

The practical paradox, which I have called the paradox of distribution, is related to the theoretical one. It concerns the problem of implementing the principle of equal rights to the conditions for self-development under the practical circumstances of scarcity of the means. Whereas the theoretical paradox is generated on conceptual grounds and would obtain even if there were unlimited resources or means, the practical paradox derives from the realistic supposition that such means will always be limited. In such a condition of scarcity, it would appear that the only solution to the problem of distribution that is compatible with equality would be a shared poverty of means and a limitation of the conditions of self-development to the lowest common denominator. Therefore, some individuals, requiring greater means than others, would be constrained in their development or would even be unable to realize their talents or capacities at all. Yet, if the requirement for self-development that the principle proposes is to be met, and if individuals are different in the means they require, then equality of conditions would have to be violated. Indeed, it would seem that the good of society as a whole would require the fuller development of certain talents or abilities and, under conditions of scarcity, this would necessarily require an unequal distribution of means.

In what follows, I want to show that the principle of equal rights to the conditions of self-development, or what I have called equal positive freedom, is not incoherent and does not necessarily lead to paradoxes. In order to do so, I will show that on a certain interpretation of the principle, and specifically of the concepts of self-development and of equal rights to the conditions, the problems and paradoxes posed earlier may be resolved.

While it is clear that individuals differ in the degrees of their self-development, such differences in degree do not provide a basis for differences in the allocation of social resources, though, as will be seen, different ways of self-development may justify differences in allocation. Beyond this, differential allocation may sometimes be justified on still other grounds. In order to see how this could be so, we need to introduce a distinction between self-development as such and particular achievements or excellences, which may, for certain purposes, be considered apart from their role in the self-development of the individual. By self-development as such, I mean first of all the realization, over time, of purposes of one's own choosing. Beyond this, I have characterized self-development as involving the cultivation of excellences, talents, or competences of one's own choosing, in a way, moreover, that contributes to the enlargement of the person's capacities. In either of these senses, the *particular* achievements of individuals (i.e., the particular actions, performances, excellences, or products of their activity that contribute to the process of their self-development) may for certain purposes be considered apart from, or abstracted from, this self-development. From the standpoint of an individual's self-development, particular actions and achievements are defined only with respect to the agent or self, regarded as continuing and developing through these actions. By contrast, these particular achievements or competences may also be considered separately from the life history of the agent and judged with respect to other values or standards than their contribution to the self-development of the agent.

Given such a distinction, I would argue that it is legitimate in some cases to provide individuals with differential means or conditions of activity on the basis of particular achievements or performances, whereas it is not legitimate to do so on the basis of differences in their self-development. In this way, merit or desert may sometimes enter as criteria for an unequal allocation of social resources, but one that is aimed at rewarding and encouraging activities that are socially, culturally, or aesthetically valuable and not on the grounds of their contribution to the individual's own self-development. The differential allocation according to achievement introduces a framework in which comparison must be made among different people's specific accomplishments, skills, or competences. By contrast, differences in the degrees of self-development among individuals cannot be used in a similar way to support differential allocation of resources. The reason for this is that self-development as the essential exercise of human freedom characterizes a relation between the agent's own choices and his or her activity to realize them and thus is fundamentally relative to such choices or pur-

poses. As such, one person's self-development is not comparable to that of another with respect to merit or desert. Thus
although there may be grounds for differential allocation of
resources on the basis of differences in individual achievement, there is no such ground in differences in degrees of
self-development. It will be seen that while this differential
allocation leads to a qualification of the principle of equal
rights to the conditions of self-development, it does not have
priority over it.

Further, it may also be seen that there is no basis for differential claims to resources on the grounds of differences in
capacities in self-development. The argument may be made
that people have different capacities for self-development as
shown by differences in the degrees and kinds of their self-
development, and that these differences provide a basis for
unequal distribution. It could then be argued that the principle of equal rights to the conditions, which is based on the
premise of equal capacities for self-development, is simply
wrong. This argument, it seems to me, has two major flaws:
First, it mistakenly reads back from differences in achievements or performances to differences in original capacities.
Thus, while it is certainly plausible to assert that if someone
accomplishes or achieves something he or she must in fact
have the capacity to do so, it cannot similarly be asserted on
the evidence of his or her failure to achieve or accomplish
something that he or she does *not* have the capacity to do so.
For in this latter case it may be that the capacity is present but
has remained unrealized or has been blocked in its exercise.
Thus, one cannot conclude from differences in achievement
that there are differences in capacities. (In fact, to argue in
this way would be to commit the logical fallacy of denying
the antecedent.) A second and related flaw in the argument
that there are different capacities for self-development is that
one cannot know that capacities differ on the basis of differences in achievement if the conditions for the exercise of
these capacities are unequal. For in that case, even if the
capacities were the same, they would be realized differently
or to different degrees. And as a matter of historical and

social fact, it is clear that conditions for the exercise of capacities have not in fact been equal for all individuals.

On the basis of these considerations, it follows that the inference to unequal capacities for self-development on grounds of unequal achievements does not go through. There may in fact be differences in capacities, but epistemologically we cannot know that there are. If this is the case, then we cannot use such purported differences as the basis for unequal rights to conditions. And in the absence of such grounds for unequal claims, we must conclude that equal rights are required. This is supplemented by the earlier argument I offered, which proposes positive grounds for equal rights to such conditions, namely, that these are the conditions for the exercise of human agency, which as an abstract capacity is equally present in all individuals.

There is of course a sense in which differences in self-development do in fact warrant different conditions, namely, where there are differences in kinds of self-development. Thus one's self-development as an artist requires different conditions from one's self-development as a doctor. In this respect, equal rights to the conditions for self-development do not entail equal rights to the *same* conditions, since the required conditions in each case are different. Rather, equality here would mean an equivalent claim to the various conditions that in each case are required for self-development.

The distinction drawn here between an equal distribution and a distribution of equivalent conditions is based on a related distinction, which runs through much of the rights literature. Ronald Dworkin characterizes it as a distinction between a right to equal treatment and a right to treatment as an equal (a distinction which I noted in the discussion of equality in Chapter 1). Equal treatment, it will be remembered, is a right that each person has to the same distribution of goods and opportunities, whereas right to treatment as an equal involves not an equal distribution but rather the right to equal concern and respect in the decision about the distribution of these goods and opportunities.[1] Gregory Vlastos makes a similar distinction. In arguing that the maxim of

165

distributive justice "To each according to his need," which "looks like a precept of unequal distribution . . . is in fact *the most perfect form of equal distribution,*"[2] he writes that equality of right means "That it is benefits to persons, not allocation of resources as such, that are meant to be made equal; unequal distribution of resources would be required to equalize benefits in cases of unequal need." The reason for this, he says, is that "the human worth of all persons is equal, however unequal may be their merit."[3] In these cases, as in mine, differential distribution of goods for the sake of an equal distribution of benefits is taken to be a requirement of justice, because of the fundamental equality of individuals.

In proposing a resolution of the paradox of self-development, I have argued that the principle of equal rights to the conditions, appropriately understood, does not entail contradictory conceptual claims and remains coherent. However, I have suggested that it needs to be qualified in a certain way, namely, with respect to considerations of merit or desert in recognition of particular achievements and with respect to contexts of social need. It is in this sense that I characterized this principle of equal positive freedom as one of *prima facie* equal rights to the conditions of self-development. It is a *prima facie* right in the sense I described earlier, namely, that in its strongest interpretation (that of Vlastos), any exceptions to it which are allowed have to be justified in terms of the same moral reasons on which the right itself is based or, again, as a necessary condition for the realization of the principle of equal rights itself, or else, in a somewhat weaker sense, by serious considerations of justice or morality, where the burden of proof in both cases always falls upon the claim being made against the *prima facie* right. This is to admit, however, that there are other principles of just distribution and just treatment that may come into play under certain circumstances.

In view of these various circumstances, I would now like to propose how the principle should be applied, though only in brief here. (These issues are also discussed in Chapter 7.) First, it is clear that the principle requires a strict interpretation of equal rights with respect to those conditions that are necessary for any activity of self-development whatever. Such conditions include the minimal means of subsistence, basic health care, civil and political liberties and protections, basic education, job opportunities, and participation in decision-making in contexts of common activity.[4] In each of these cases, the principle requires an equal distribution of these conditions to all individuals.

Beyond these universally necessary conditions, there are the conditions required for the different forms of development of different individuals. Here we may characterize the equal rights as rights to equivalent conditions rather than as rights to the same conditions, since different individuals obviously require different means in view of their various goals. Since every form of self-development is specific and differentiated in this way and requires more than the basic conditions noted above which are the same for everyone, it may be said that the equal right to self-development must minimally include some such specific conditions for each person. The most salient and appropriate conditions that would satisfy this requirement would be access to specialized or advanced training or education that is required for different paths of self-development. Such resources would be functionally equivalent despite their variety and different costs, in that they are equally necessary for alternative modes of development.

However, an equal right to the further conditions that would be necessary for everyone's *full* self-development is clearly not practically feasible, even in conditions of great abundance. Thus in some of the cases in which there are considerations of social need or value, the principle may require qualification or delimitation with respect to the specialized conditions that are necessary for individuals' self-development. In such contexts, as I suggested earlier, the criterion of achievement or performance sometimes plays a role as the ground for decisions about differential allocation of resources. For example, such a criterion would be appropriate in the selection of those who would be permitted to practice surgery and also in the differential allocation of resources to support such practice. For the social need for competence here would qualify the principle of equal rights to the extent that not everyone who would choose to become a surgeon would be competent to be one. Further, social need could also warrant the very large outlay of social resources which the practice of surgery entails (e.g., the support practices of anesthesiology and other medical specialties, nursing, testing laboratories, medical equipment, and hospital overhead). Such an outlay of resources would presuppose some standard of achievement or performance in surgery in order to justify it socially. Needless to say, where this criterion of achievement is applicable, the principle of equal rights to the conditions of self-development requires equal opportunities for such achievement. It may be seen in this example that a differential or unequal distribution of resources (in support of the practice of surgery) may be necessary to assure the facilities that are required for the equal right to the conditions (in this instance, basic health care). This may serve as an example of what Vlastos calls "an equitable inequity."

A similar qualification of the principle of equal rights to the conditions is relevant to the consideration of the second or practical paradox, namely, what I have called the paradox of distribution. Here, the condition of relative scarcity seems to make it impossible to satisfy the joint requirements of the principle, namely, equal rights and self-development. For under scarcity, equality seems to require the equal distribution of inadequate means and therefore the denial of necessary means of self-development to those whose requirements are greater than others. In answer to this, first, it seems clear that even in conditions of relative scarcity, at least some of the conditions of self-development can be made equally available to all, for example, civil and political liberties such as freedom of speech, and the right to participate in decision-making. Though the institutional provision and protection of such liberties do require an outlay of resources, this need not be an exorbitant one. Moreover, even in economies of scarcity, costs of the state apparatus, whether democratic or not, have always been a part of social expenditures; and

civil and political liberties would probably require less exorbitant expenditures than would nondemocratic institutions.
(However, this is obviously not intended as an argument for
civil and political liberties on the grounds that they are
cheaper than the alternatives!) Further, other basic conditions of self-development could be implemented equally if
the satisfaction of these conditions were given priority over
other social expenditures, and resources were allocated to
meet them. Such a basic condition would be that of minimal
means of subsistence. Beyond this, such other conditions as
basic education and health care could be assured as economies develop. Second, in the context of relative scarcity, it
remains plausible to suppose that some conditions of specific
and differential self-development can be provided equally,
though this would depend on the degree of scarcity in the
economy. (A bare subsistence economy, for example, would
have no surplus for such uses.) However, under conditions
of scarcity of resources, considerations of social need would
sometimes justify an unequal distribution of the means for
self-development in the face of the principle of equal rights,
since, in such practical circumstances, one would be especially concerned that the scarce resources be used effectively
and not wasted. To this end, it may be relevant to consider
past achievement or performance as evidence of the ability to
utilize resources fully and thus as warrant for their allocation. Whereas the scarce resource here may not be one that is
required to meet basic needs, nevertheless it must have important social utility in order to justify its unequal distribution. An example of this would be some resource, the careful
and competent use of which is required in order to provide
the members of society more generally with some of the
conditions for their self-development. The justification for
such a differential allocation on grounds of achievement or
talent thus remains tied to considerations of equal rights to
the conditions.

A further comment needs to be made concerning the implementation of the principle of equal rights under conditions of
relative scarcity, namely, that an adequate analysis of how

Chapter 6

Contemporary legal conceptions of property and their implications for democracy

Modern legal conceptions of property have been associated with theories of democracy in terms of the relation between property and freedom. Thus in liberal democratic theory, private property is seen as a condition for the freedom of individuals and thus as a basis for political democracy; alternatively, in socialist theories of democracy, social ownership of the means of production is seen as a condition for freedom from class domination and thus as a basis for democratic control of society. However, on the one hand, the liberal theory of property has tended to permit private property owners to exercise power over those who are propertyless, and these inequalities of power have undermined political democracy in practice. On the other hand, the socialist theory of property has been interpreted in ways that have led to bureaucratic and state domination of social life and thus has failed to produce democratic societies. The failures of these systems of property to provide the conditions for freedom and democracy are not simply aberrations of practice but are also based on theoretical misconceptions concerning the nature of property and its relation to human freedom. In this chapter I will give an analysis of the relation between property and freedom and will propose an alternative conception of property understood as a condition for democracy in social life. The normative basis for my analysis will be the concept of equal positive freedom, or the equal right of individuals to the conditions of self-development. I will argue that, when property is under-stood as a condition for such equal positive freedom, the legal conception of property as private property needs to be replaced by two other conceptions, namely, personal posses-sions and social property.[1] I want to develop these two latter conceptions and to clarify the distinction between them. Further, I will argue that this relation between prop-erty and freedom requires a revision in the conception of the alienability of property.

The philosophical basis of this analysis and critique of the legal conceptions of property is the theory of the nature of social reality, which I introduced earlier as *social ontology*. As suggested earlier about liberal political theory in general, lib-eral conceptions of property imply an ontology of isolated individuals in external relations; further, socialist theories of property tend to imply a holistic ontology of society within which there are internal relations. By contrast, the concep-tion of property that I propose is founded on the ontology of individuals-in-relations, or social individuals, where social wholes or structures are seen as entities constituted by these individuals.

CRITICISMS OF PREVAILING CONCEPTIONS OF PROPERTY

The criticism one may make of the prevailing legal concep-tions of property may be briefly summarized here. With respect to the liberal conception of property, A.M. Honoré has given a useful summary of the various rights that consti-tute its notion of ownership: These include the rights to possession, use, management, income, capital, security, and transmissibility, among others.[2] These rights define a conception of private property. Central to this conception is the notion of these rights as exclusive, namely, as rights to exclude others from possession, use, and management. Fur-ther, private property in this form permits unlimited accu-mulation through its recognition of the private right to the capital, which includes the right to alienate the thing for the sake of profit. These features of private property may be criticized for having permitted the development and perpetuation of economic and social domination and exploitation. Thus, as has been pointed out in socialist critiques, among others, private ownership of the means of production leads to the fact that the propertyless workers have to surrender control of their own production to the owners and cannot reap the full value of their own labor.

A further criticism of the liberal concept of property may be made from a theoretical point of view. One may argue that the philosophical justifications of the right to private property do not in fact justify the full liberal notion of property. Specifically, they do not justify a right of private property over social means of production, that is, those conditions required for social and not merely individual production, nor do they justify such features of property right as unlimited alienability and transmissibility, the absence of term, and unqualified exclusivity. Thus, for example, as Lawrence Becker points out in his book *Property Rights*, the theory that the entitlement to property derives from one's labor involves the condition that the acquisition of such property does not constitute a loss to others. However, private ownership of social means of production puts those who lack such property at a relative disadvantage at the very least or, if one accepts the labor theory of value, even deprives the wage workers of the full benefits of their work. In these cases, private property entails a loss to others, and thus, on this version of the labor theory of property, private property in social means of production is not justified.[3] As Becker also suggests, even where the labor theory of property is reinterpreted to claim that people deserve some benefit for their labor, this does not mean that such benefit need be in terms of private ownership of the things produced, or at least not in the full, liberal sense as involving, for example, the right to the capital or the absence of term. Rather, such benefit might be in terms of the use of the thing or some other type of benefit such as power or recognition.[4]

Likewise, the justification of private property in terms of its utility, where the acquisition, possession, and use of things is held to be useful or necessary for an individual's happiness, does not yet justify a right to unlimited alienability and transmissibility, an absence of term, or unqualified exclusivity, since these rights cannot plausibly be argued to be general requirements for an individual's happiness. An alternative utilitarian argument is that private property – including private ownership of social means of production – maximizes utility, in that it is the most efficient system for producing the greatest happiness for the greatest number. Here what is emphasized is its ability to maximize the production of goods and services. However, historically at least, such a system of private ownership of the social means of production resulted in great misery for masses of people and a sharp division between wealth and poverty, even though it increased economic productivity enormously. One may also argue in general that, if the system of private property involves the control by a minority over the conditions of activity of the majority, and thus social and economic domination, then it would be difficult to see how this could be consistent with the utilitarian principle of the greatest happiness of the greatest number. Moreover, even if one accepts the equation of utility (or the greatest happiness overall) with productivity, or the maximization of goods and services, one may raise the question, "Compared to what?" Although it may well be true that this system is more productive than what preceded it or than existing socialist systems of property, it does not follow that there are no alternatives that are more productive than it is. In this respect, the utilitarian argument is not conclusive. Indeed, the system of private property in the full sense has been widely modified and regulated to offset its nonproductive features (e.g., economic recessions and depressions, the abuse of natural and human resources). Moreover, I would argue that an economy of worker self-managed firms (based on a system of both social and personal property) would be more productive, even in the narrow economic sense, than existing alternatives.

Thus the major arguments that have been offered in support of private property fail to justify it in its full, liberal sense, nor do they justify the right of private ownership of social means of production. Yet these approaches – the labor theory of property and utilitarianism – may well establish a right to personal possessions, either because of the labor one has expended in producing them or because such possessions are necessary for one's happiness. This suggests that there is an important distinction to be made between personal property and social property. I will develop this distinction later and show how it is required by other considerations and in particular by the concept of equal positive freedom. Here, it should be stressed that it is specific features of the full, liberal legal conception of property – namely, private ownership of social means of production, unlimited alienability and transmissibility, absence of term and unqualified exclusivity – that sanction the use of property as a means of domination and exploitation. That is, they enable those who own property in the means of production to control the conditions of the activity of others who lack property.

It is just this use of private property as a means of social domination and economic exploitation that undermines democracy. First, it intrudes upon the political process itself by giving undue power to large property interests. Second, as a consequence of this, the relegation of the unpropertied or of small property owners to relatively ineffective participation in political governance leads to apathy and to cynicism about the political process. In addition, the inequalities and hierarchies of power that characterize a system of social and economic domination are antithetical to democratic processes not only in political life, but in social life more generally.

Insofar as this liberal legal conception of private property is understood as a condition for freedom, the concept of freedom with which it is associated is negative freedom or freedom from constraint. It signifies the freedom to choose to do as one pleases without external impediments. As I discussed it earlier, this conception of negative freedom is at the root of the liberal conception of political liberty. This political liberty has two aspects, namely, protection of the individual by the state from harm or constraint by other individuals and, further, protection from intrusion or control by the state in the free activity of individuals. As a condition for negative freedom, private property is a right against others, for example, insofar as it is a right to exclusive possession and use. Private property is thus seen as a right that protects one against the intrusion of others upon the exercise of one's will with respect to things owned. On the liberal view, individuals are regarded as having equal negative freedom and, thus, an equal right to the acquisition of private property. However, as we have seen, such equal freedom remains merely formal, because it is compatible with domination and exploitation, which lead to concrete inequalities in the freedom of individuals, and in this respect, the conception is insufficient. I have argued that it needs to be supplemented by a conception of equal positive freedom, which in turn requires a different conception of property as a condition for its realization.

One additional point may be made here concerning the liberal conception of private property. This concerns its ontological presuppositions about the nature of the entities that make up social life. These entities may be seen to be individuals understood as standing in external relations with one another, each pursuing his or her interest against the others. Thus the liberal conception of private property has historically characterized this relation among individuals as an adversarial relation and has taken property right as arising in a fundamentally competitive or conflictual context. Furthermore, in its full sense, the concept of private property rests upon the central notion of exclusivity, interpreted as an individual's right against others. This individualist ontology is evident also in the central justification for private property, namely, the labor theory of property. The labor that is the basis for the entitlement is always construed as that of an individual subject. This overlooks the fact of social production, which is the dominant form of labor in the modern period. To the degree that labor is social in this way, it may be seen that the labor theory of property gives rise to a different conception of property right, namely, social property. This conception will be elaborated later.

The alternative legal conception to that of private property has been the legal conception of socialist property. The model of property right I am addressing here is the model that has been developed primarily in the Soviet Union and Eastern Europe, and pertains to what I characterized in Chapter 2 as holistic socialism.[5] In brief, the features of this conception of property are that it is fundamentally social property in the sense of belonging to society as a whole and not to private individuals. This has been interpreted to mean that, in its fullest development, it is state property. This includes not only major national resources and land, but also the principal type of production organization, namely, the state enterprise. In addition to the state enterprises, there are collectives (primarily in agriculture) where the ownership is cooperative. Beyond these forms, individual property is recognized in objects of consumer use, but is not in general extended to ownership of the means of production.[6] Rather, the state is regarded as the owner of the means of production.[7]

The ontological presuppositions underlying holistic socialism, which I criticized in Chapter 2, also underlie this conception of property. They lead to the interpretation of social property as belonging to the whole. It will be remembered that my criticism of this ontology was that it does not give sufficient importance to the ontological status of individuals, seeing them instead as constituted by their relation to the whole. Thus this view fails to see that the whole is itself constituted by the social relations among these individuals. It regards the whole as primary and tends to reify it. Social property, therefore, does not belong directly to the associated producers in a given industry, but rather is taken to belong to the state as the legal embodiment of the whole (which may then apportion its possession, use, and management to state enterprises or to collectives). Thus, because the social whole is not regarded as constituted by the individuals in their relations, social property is identified with state property, and the state is seen as standing above the individuals. It is seen as the central authority that makes decisions for them, instead of as the instrument of their decisions. In these ways, social property is not under the democratic control of the producers. Rather, the control over property by the state becomes a means of domination by the state. Thus, contrary to the claims made for it, state control of social property fails to serve as a condition for freedom. This holistic socialist conception of property does not sufficiently see the intrinsic connection between social property and democracy. Such social property should instead be understood as a social relation among the producers in which they jointly control the conditions of production by democratic participation in decisions about it.[8]

A further criticism of this socialist concept concerns the inadequacy of its conception of individual property or personal possession. Although it makes the distinction between social property and individual property for consumer goods, it fails to give a fully principled grounding for such individual property and thus assigns it to a merely residual role or category. In what follows, I will propose a systematic view of property which encompasses both social property and personal possessions and which sees both as conditions for full freedom and democracy.

A PROPOSAL FOR AN ALTERNATIVE CONCEPTION OF PROPERTY

The need for an alternative legal conception of property arises from the deficiencies of the prevailing conceptions. On the one hand, they fail to provide the legal conditions for freedom insofar as they permit, or even generate, social domination. On the other hand, despite the stated intentions of each of these views to provide foundations for democracy (albeit differently understood), I have argued that each of them tends to undermine democracy, whether by undue power of large private property interests within the political process or, more thoroughly, by authoritarian control of political and social life based on state ownership of property. An alternative conception of property would have to overcome these defects.

In this alternative conception, property may be generally understood as the set of legal rights that specify the relations of social individuals to the conditions of their production or agency and to the products of this agency. This relation is one of control or disposition over these conditions or products. This conception of property is normative in the sense that the grounds for this right are the values of life and liberty. The value of property is thus derived and instrumental, since property serves as an indispensable condition for human existence and for the realization of human purposes.

However, since property connotes control over the conditions or means of production or agency, particular forms of property may make possible the control by some over the conditions that others require for their own agency. Such control, I have suggested, is the major means by which domination has proceeded. Thus property is closely connected with the possibility of either domination or freedom.

The alternative proposal differs from the two prevailing conceptions in grounding property right in the value of equal positive freedom. This positive freedom, as we have seen, addresses the need for the social and material conditions for self-development, and I have argued that all agents, by virtue of being agents, have a *prima facie* equal right to these conditions. Further, self-development was seen to require freedom from domination and thus control over the conditions of one's own activity. It is therefore not sufficient for these conditions to be available to one only under constraints or limitations imposed by others who control these necessary conditions, for in such a case the determination of the course of one's action would be subject to the will of these others rather than one's own. From the principle of equal positive freedom and from these considerations, it follows that agents have a *prima facie* equal right to control over the conditions of their activity. Since control over the conditions of agency is what we mean by property, these rights are property rights. The legal conception of property would thus express the institutional recognition and protection of these rights. It would specify particular forms of this property relation as rights, for example, as rights to possession, use, management, and income, though it would differ in certain important ways from the other conceptions, as will be discussed later.

There are both individual and social forms of agency, and it may be seen that each involves a distinctive mode of control over its conditions. That is, I want to argue that there are two distinct forms of property rights, each of which is appropriate to one of these types of activity. The first is personal property or possession, which is a right to control, or to have disposition over, those things that are required for the individual's own subsistence and self-development. The second is social property, which is a right to control those things that are required by individuals in common in order to realize their joint purposes. The argument for these two forms of property right stems both from the social ontology I have proposed and from the value of equal positive freedom.

On the basis of the social ontology, I have argued earlier that the distinction between individual and social activity is not merely the distinction between the activity of a single individual and the activity of an aggregate of single individuals. Rather, social activity or labor connotes a common purpose or goal and integrated activity toward that goal. In such social labor, the activity of a given individual is what it is only in relation to the activity of the others and in terms of some shared understanding of the common goal. Thus social or common activity is ontologically irreducible to the aggregate activity of individuals, each pursuing only his or her goals. On the other hand, individuals also set purposes of their own apart from common purposes and realize these through individual activity. Such individual activity cannot be reduced to being a part of a whole or regarded as being determined by social relations or social structures. This suggests that there is an ontological distinction between individual and social activity which is the basis for a distinction to be made between social property as what would properly belong to those engaged in a common activity and what would belong to individuals as personal property.

This distinction between personal and social property right and the nature of these rights may be established normatively on the basis of the principle of equal positive freedom and its corollary, equal rights to control over the conditions of agency. An individual's right to personal property or possession is a right to control those conditions that are necessary for the exercise of his or her agency, but subject to certain qualifications. It may be suggested that, in the first place, there is an individual property right to means of subsistence, insofar as this is a precondition for any human agency whatever. Beyond this, I would argue that personal property rights to the means of agency obtain, under the following three joint conditions: (1) that these means are necessary for the individual's activity in pursuing his or her own purposes (by contrast to common activity, in which the individual may be engaged with others in the realization of shared purposes); (2) that the unlimited possession and use of the things is either necessary or of decided advantage for their proper utilization in the realization of the agent's purposes; (3) that there are no prior claims that override the previous two conditions, specifically, such claims as (a) prior personal property rights of others in the things (except as these things may be acquired from these others as gift of by legitimate transfer), (b) social property rights in the things (to be discussed below), (c) rights of others to the things as necessary means of subsistence, and (d) *prima facie* equal right of others to control the means of their agency, except where, under conditions of scarcity of such means, it is sometimes desirable to determine rights to personal property on the basis of a principle of desert (as a corollary to the use of the principle of desert discussed earlier).

There is an additional condition that serves as the basis for a claim to personal property, namely, that the thing in question is the product of an individual's own labor or activity (but not the product of any social labor or activity in which he or she may have participated). This right to control the product of one's activity is justified here not only on the traditional grounds of the labor theory of property – generally stated, that one has a right to one's person and to control of one's activity,[9] and thereby to control over the products of such activity – but also in terms of the principle of equal positive freedom. For one may argue that control over the products of one's activity (as well as over the activity itself) is a condition for self-development, insofar as these products are the objective expression of one's activity and purposes through which one comes to recognize and develop one's capacities; and also insofar as the products of one's activity often serve as the conditions or means for one's own further activity, for example, in the production of tools or instruments for one's own use, or in the creation of goods for one's own consumption.

It should be noted that not all the conditions of individual agency have a claim to be regarded as personal property. Many of the social conditions for such activity – for example, educational institutions, cultural institutions (such as museums and libraries), parklands – require rights of access and use, but not of exclusive or unlimited possession and use. (See conditions 2 and 3b above.)

Equal positive freedom permits one to distinguish social property from personal property in a fundamental way. With respect to social means of production, that is, the conditions that are necessary for a common or joint activity, the principle of equal positive freedom requires control over these conditions by those engaged in the activity. For, as we have seen, if some who are not engaged in the activity, or only some of those who are so engaged, were to exercise such control, they would be controlling the conditions that the others need for their activity and would thus be dominating them. Such domination deprives the others of their equal right to self-development inasmuch as it excludes them from the social activity of making decisions about the projects in which they are jointly engaged. But as social individuals, such social activity is necessary for their self-development. Therefore, social means of production are social property in the sense that the right to these conditions or means inheres equally in all those who are engaged in this common activity. Such social property should be distinguished from personal property, since personal property connotes control over the conditions for the activity of an individual engaged in pursuit of his or her own purposes, and not in a common project.

Social property may be analyzed as involving two fundamental rights, again on the basis of equal positive freedom. The first is the right of all those engaged in a common activity to control the products of that activity, or to enjoy in common the benefits of their labor. This is, in effect, a labor theory of social property analogous to that offered in connection with personal property rights, and the grounds in the two cases are the same as well. In this case, however, these are social rather than individual activities, and therefore the right to control the product, which is required by equal positive freedom, is a condition for the development of the sociality of individuals as individuals-in-relations. Their control of the product as social property is one in which they share equally, on the basis of the corollary to the principle of equal positive freedom (namely that agents have *prima facie* equal rights to control over the conditions of their activity). This does not mean, however, that the value of the product need be divided equally among them, since the distribution of the value is one that they themselves have to determine (and they very well may decide to distribute it differentially on various grounds). It is clear, of course, that the income distributed among themselves in this way belongs to each individual as personal property to be expended as each sees fit (subject to the qualifications on personal property described earlier).

In addition to this equal right to control the product, there is a second, and related, right that social property connotes. This is the equal right to control the conditions of social activity. This signifies the right to participate in decisions concerning the uses of the conditions or means of social production in which one is engaged. It also connotes that one has a right to participate in decisions concerning the purposes and plans of the activity, since these are essentially involved in determining the uses of the conditions or means of activity. This suggests that in industry or the workplace, as well as in social activity more generally, decisions should be made through a democratic process in which there is an equal right of participation by those who engage in the activity.

In Chapter 1, I had derived this right of equal participation directly from the principle of equal positive freedom and the nature of agency. Here it has been suggested that this right of democratic participation may also be derived from the definition of social property, as I have discussed it. But since this social property right was also derived from equal positive freedom, it may be seen that both inferences to the requirement for democratic participation have a common premise. The second, however, arrives at this conclusion through the mediation of the concept of property right. As understood here, therefore, rights of democratic participation are not primarily justified by considerations of property right. Yet they are supported by the view of social property presented here.

There is another economic right that is closely related to the property rights I have analyzed here, and that is the right to work. Though it is not itself a property right, it is required as a condition for the exercise of property right and thus for the acquisition of property. For, on the basis of the preceding discussion, we may see that it is by engaging in social production that one earns a share in the control over the products and conditions of that activity, that is, an equal right to social property. Likewise, the right to personal property in the sense discussed earlier presupposes the right to work as the means for acquiring such property, either as the result of one's own labor or as a share in the income of social labor. The right to work is also implied by the principle of equal positive freedom, since the opportunity to engage in social activity is a condition for self-development, and typically, work is a fundamental form of such social activity.

Although the whole of the previous discussion has proceeded from the premise that there is a *prima facie* equal right to control the conditions of activity, that is, to property, this should not be misinterpreted to mean that there is a right to be provided with property, either by the state or by society at large. Rather, there is an equal right to the acquisition of personal property and to a share in social property, under the conditions described. In general, the right to own property is exercised through work. A further discussion of the application of these principles in an institutional model is given in Chapter 9.

Some of the features of the conception of property presented here are similar to those proposed by C.B. Macpherson in his book *Democratic Theory*. The most important similarity is that Macpherson emphasizes the view that property involves individuals' "access on equal terms to the means of labor."[10] Beyond this, he sees property right as developing into "the right to a share in the control of the massed productive resources."[11] In addition, he also sees property right as related to positive freedom, which he similarly interprets as individual self-development. Macpherson also briefly suggests that a developed view of property would include both a nonexclusionary form of common property and the protection of personal possession from intrusion.[12]

My view of property differs from Macpherson's in several important respects, however. First, Macpherson proposes that the developed concept of property should encompass the right to life and liberty.[13] This seems to me too global a view of property, including too much under this rubric, and it is also an inverted view, since property right should be seen as deriving from the value of liberty or freedom, rather than the other way around. (The property right to means of subsistence that I have proposed may be derived more directly from the value of life, as well as from the value of positive freedom. Its priority among property rights also derives from this. This right of subsistence is dealt with further in the following chapter.) Second, unlike Macpherson, I have made a distinction between rights to the conditions of self-development and right to control over these conditions, identifying property right only with the second. Macpherson seems to blend these two senses together in his conception of "access to the means of labor," seeing them both as property right. Third, Macpherson sees property right as undergoing an eventual transformation from being mainly a right of access to the means of labor to becoming mainly a right to share in political power, which will be exercised over mass productive resources. However, I would argue that "access to the means of labor" would remain an essential aspect of property right, even if necessary labor were to be eliminated by full automation as Macpherson speculates. It would remain as the right to control over the means of activity, both social and individual, which agents would require for their self-development. Furthermore, though the view I have presented also stresses the importance of participation in decisions concerning common resources as a property right, I would regard this not as primarily an exercise of political power, but rather as requiring democratic participation in decisions in economic and social life. It is possible that Macpherson intends to extend the conception of politics so that it includes the domains of social and economic activity. However, it seems to be more plausible to read him as saying that social and economic issues would become subject to political decisions that would be made democratically. If this is his view, then the presumptive difference between his view and my own is that his would lead to democratically exercised state power with respect to the social and economic domains, whereas mine would emphasize workers' self-management and participatory democracy at the community level, in addition to representative political democracy.[14] Finally, it seems to me that Macpherson's conception of property right remains too individualistic in his formulation of it as the individual's right to nonexclusion from access to the means of labor. I have argued that this right is grounded not only in the individual's right to self-development but also in the social nature of individuals and in the character of social labor.

The view of property I develop here may also be compared to that of the *Praxis* theorists (e.g., Mihailo Marković), especially with respect to the emphasis on the concept of social property. There are, however, important differences. The *Praxis* theorists' proposed conception of social ownership, which is intended to replace capitalist forms of private ownership of the means of production, interprets social property as the property of society as a whole, rather than either as state property or as the property of groups within society. Thus, although they strongly advocate workers' self-management, they do not see the self-managing units as owning the property of their enterprises. Apart from the vagueness of this notion of social property, it would seem to me that the authority of ownership of such "public" property, including the rights to dispose of it and control it, would tend to gravitate to the state, as the representative of the general social interest. In this way, such social property would seem to be indistinguishable from state property, and the institution of social property would thus seem to lead to an increase in the power of the state. But this runs counter to the values of participatory democracy and local control which the *Praxis* theorists themselves emphasize.

A similar criticism of the concept of social property, in the Yugoslav version, is made by Robert Dahl (though he addresses it more generally to the Yugoslav economy and not specifically at the *Praxis* theorists). Since the employees of worker self-managed firms, under the Yugoslav constitution, do not own its assets, but rather hold them in trust for society, Dahl writes that

> Because the structure, duties, and authority of the self-managed enterprises are determined by statutory and constitutional law, sovereign authority over the enterprises seems to rest de jure with the state and de facto with the leadership of Party and state. As a result, ownership of enterprises by "society" is almost entirely symbolic. Since even the prohibition against selling off assets is enforced by the state, here too the distinction between state and social ownership is shadowy.[15]

Finally, I would like to consider briefly how the general conception of property that I have presented here may be specified in terms of the traditional legal divisions of this concept. It will be seen that for the most part the same rights are important for both personal and social property. Furthermore, for both of these, some of the rights that have been traditionally associated with private property become problematic. On the proposed conception, it is clear that the rights of possession, use, and management are crucial for both personal property and social property. Thus, in the case of personal property, the individual has the right to possess the thing and to exclude others from its possession, to use it for personal enjoyment, or for his or her own purposes, and to decide how and by whom a thing should be used. Likewise, in the case of social property, the associated individuals as a group have these same rights, with the understanding that the decisions about use and management are to be taken democratically. In addition, another traditional aspect of property right, namely, the prohibition of harmful use, is clearly applicable to the new conceptions of property.

However, several of the traditional rights associated with property appear to present problems for the conception and need to be rethought or modified. First and most important is the right to the capital, taken to include the power to alienate the thing and to use it up or destroy it. Alienability is clearly an important aspect of property right that would have to be retained both for personal and social property. However, for both kinds of property, it would have to be taken to exclude the case in which alienation would result in gaining control over others through gaining control over the conditions that they need for their activity. Such control would violate the principle of equal positive freedom. (A similar restriction would seem to hold as well for the right to the income.) Further, the traditional power of transmissibility, the absence of term, and the right to security, that is, the immunity from expropriation, might have to be modified for the new form of social property.

The proposed conception of property is similar to the socialist legal conception in its introduction of the notion of social property. However, on the view proposed here, such social property would be understood not as state property, but rather as the property of the associated individuals engaged in a given common activity, whether in an industry or a social organization. Thus this model of property tends in the direction of what has been called "workers' self-management" and "worker control," as well as toward participatory control of social institutions and organizations. (However, where the scope of the common enterprise and the conditions for it are national, overall governmental coordination is required. In this case, as discussed in Chapter 9, the right of management would be entrusted to a national body or to the state, which would operate under democratic control and review.)

Obviously, such a view of social property differs from the liberal view of private property. Yet the conception developed here is similar to the liberal view in its emphasis on the importance of personal property as a condition for individual freedom. However, it excludes the use of such property to dominate others by controlling the means necessary for their activity and is thus distinguished from the traditional liberal conception. I would argue that these differences from the prevailing views enable this alternative conception of property to provide a firmer foundation for the development of democracy.

Chapter 7

What are the human rights?

There is considerable agreement among moral and political philosophers that there are rights that may be called human rights. There is considerably less agreement, however, as to what these human rights are, what the justification for them is, and what the priorities are among them. Thus for example, some human rights theorists, like Maurice Cranston and R.S. Downie, have argued that human rights should be limited to civil and political rights and should not include economic or welfare rights.[1] By contrast, others, like Alan Gewirth or Richard Wasserstrom, argue for the right to well-being as a human right, where such well-being includes economic or welfare considerations.[2] Similarly, Henry Shue and the English theorists Raymond Plant, Harry Lesser, and Peter Taylor-Gooby argue for subsistence or for survival as a basic human right.[3] There are also sharp differences concerning the question of priorities among rights, that is, concerning which rights may be sacrificed in order to preserve others, in cases where there are conflicts among them. Thus in addition to the traditional questions of priority between life and liberty, or between liberty and security, there is the question raised in contemporary discussion concerning the priority of political and civil liberties over economic and social rights, as for example in the discussion about Rawls's principles of justice. Likewise, there are divergent accounts of what justifies the human rights, with some theorists appealing to the nature of human beings or of human agency as the ground of human rights, others stressing a priori norms of human worth, dignity, and respect, and still others justifying human rights in terms of ideal agreements that would be made by rational choosers.

In this chapter, I will argue for a conception of human rights that emphasizes both economic rights and civil and political rights and sees them in relation to each other. Specifically, I will claim that the right to life (not to be confused with the views of the "right-to-lifers") includes rights to subsistence and health care, in addition to security, and that these must be taken together with civil liberties and political rights. Although a similar approach has been advanced by some other theorists, notably Shue and Gewirth, I will propose a somewhat different ground for this view. I will argue that in addition to the right to democracy, which is most often included among the protected political rights, there is yet another fundamental human right, namely, the right to participate in the making of decisions concerning social, economic, and cultural activities outside the political sphere. I have proposed earlier that every human being has an equal right to self-development and an equal right of access to the conditions required for it, and I have identified such self-development with a conception of positive freedom. These rights of participation and of self-development have not been included in other theories of what are the human rights. On the other hand, these themes have been discussed in some contemporary political and social theories (for example, by Macpherson and Pateman) but there they have not been explicitly considered in relation to a theory of human rights. Thus one of the aims of this paper is to show how these rights of participation and self-development are systematically related to each other and to the other human rights.

In the concluding part of this chapter, I will present a fuller account of what rights should be included among the human rights. However, I want to begin by considering a number of difficulties that have been raised concerning theories of human rights and particularly concerning the inclusion of economic and social rights among the human rights. In the course of dealing with such difficulties, I intend to develop my own arguments for what are the human rights and for what principles justify them.

There are, I think, four major difficulties that have been posed concerning those theories that include economic rights, rights to well-being, or rights to self-development. Some of these difficulties also bear on human rights theory more generally, for example, on whether any human rights theory is viable. These difficulties are as follows: (1) The question of scope–Should human rights go beyond negative rights, that is, rights that protect the individual against coercion or interference by the state or by others? (2) The question of priority–Do civil and political rights have priority over economic rights? (3) The problem of freedom versus equality–Is there a necessary conflict between these two and is one rather than the other the foundation of all human rights? (4) The problem of individuality versus sociality–Are human rights theories necessarily either individualistic or holistic in their approach or in their ontology? In this chapter, I will focus on the first question concerning the scope of rights theory. The other questions will be dealt with only briefly and in a subsidiary way, based on the analysis that I give of the first one.

THE QUESTION OF SCOPE

Must human rights be limited to negative rights, that is, to rights that protect the individual against coercion or interference by the state or by other individuals? Or may they also include the so-called positive rights to subsistence, economic and social benefits, and other means of self-development? There has been an extensive debate on this question in the literature. One well-established position holds that human rights should be limited to civil liberties and political rights on the grounds that human rights serve to protect individuals from coercion or interference in their actions by the state or other individuals. It is further argued that any rights that go beyond such protections would require the state to provide positive benefits and this would lead to increased state power and inevitable interference with an individual's liberty. A related objection to including economic and social rights among the human rights is that such economic and social claims do not meet such criteria for human rights as universality and feasibility.

The argument that human rights should be limited to negative rights that protect individuals against interference in their actions is made by such theorists as Cranston and Nozick. Thus Cranston writes,

> Since [the political and civil rights] are for the most part rights against government interference with a man's activities, a large part of the legislation needed has to do no more than restrain the government's own executive arm. This is no longer the case when we turn to the right to work, "the right to social security," and so forth.[4]

In a related way, Nozick maintains that welfare rights would involve redistribution by the state of property justly acquired and would thereby violate what he takes to be fundamental and inviolable individual rights.

Cranston argues that economic and social rights are not, properly speaking, human rights because they fail to meet the criteria for human rights. According to him, these criteria are practicability, paramount importance, and universality. He argues that such rights as the right to work and to social security cannot meet these criteria. Such economic and social rights are not practicable on his view since the correlative duties require resources that are beyond the capacities of states to provide. By contrast, he holds that the traditional rights to life and liberty require only forbearance from action on the part of states and thus are practicable. Likewise, he claims that social and economic rights are not universal since they pertain only to those occupying particular positions in society, such as employees or wage workers, with respect to the right to work, or the indigent, with respect to welfare rights. Finally, he claims that only the traditional rights to life and liberty are of paramount importance.

Against this view that social and economic rights are not practicable and that they go beyond the proper limits of the state, because they require the provision of positive benefits, the following argument has been made, and, to my mind, effectively: namely, that the traditional civil and political rights also require positive action and not merely forbearance on the part of the state and in this respect they are no different from the economic and social rights. Thus the positive actions undertaken and the expenditures incurred by the state in the provision of a judicial system, a police force, and a military, as well as the whole apparatus of representative government, for example, elections and legislatures – all of these designed to protect the traditional rights of life, liberty, and property – raise the question of practicability and of intervention in the lives of citizens just as much as do the social and economic rights. The problem of practicability is raised by the fact that the state in itself does not immediately possess the resources to provide the institutional protections for civil and political liberties and must therefore appropriate these resources in some way, normally by taxation, just as it would have to if it were to provide for social and economic rights. Similarly, the problem of intervention by the state arises for the traditional civil and political rights precisely on the ground that taxation or other appropriation of individuals' resources is required if these rights are to be protected.

Thus in their book, *Political Philosophy and Social Welfare*, Plant, Lesser, and Taylor-Gooby criticize Cranston's view by pointing out the extensive institutional forms which the government must support in order to secure the civil and political rights. Thus they say,

> Traditional rights – life, liberty, property, etc. clearly require forbearance on the part of others to be met. However, such forbearance cannot just be legislated into existence. . . .The securing of what Cranston is willing to regard as genuine

human rights therefore will require not just negative but also positive expenditure. In this case practicability is going to be a more serious test for traditional human rights than Cranston is prepared to admit. . . .It does not seem, therefore, that the stringent standard of practicability suggested by Cranston, which would allow it to be a human right if and only if it can be satisfied now, is appropriate.[5]

Similarly, Henry Shue argues,

. . .neither rights to physical security nor rights to subsistence fit neatly into their assigned sides of the simplisitc positive/ negative dichotomy.
   In the case of rights to physical security, it may be possible *to avoid violating* someone's rights to physical security yourself by merely refraining from acting in any of the ways that would constitute violations. But it is impossible *to protect* anyone's rights to physical security without taking, or making payments toward the taking of a wide range of positive actions. For example, at the very least, the protection of rights to physical security necessitates police forces; criminal courts; penitentiaries; schools for training police, lawyers, and guards; and taxes to support an enormous system for the prevention, detection, and punishment of violations of personal security.[6]

Similar arguments are offered by Susan Moller Okin in her article, "Liberty and Welfare: Some Issues in Human Rights Theory."[7]
   Yet a counterargument may be offered against this view that the traditional civil and political rights are just like the social and economic rights in the respect that both require positive action and expenditure for their satisfaction. It may be argued that although the civil and political rights require positive action by the state and not merely forbearance from acting, yet such positive action has as its aim the limitation of the power of the state and the prevention of its interference in the activity of individuals. Stanley Hoffman makes this point in his book *Duties Beyond Borders;* he writes,

Even though all human rights require the state to do certain things–that is, to act and not just to omit acting–this notion in itself is rather ambiguous, because many of the rights (particularly the political and civil ones) require the state to do things which will *limit* its powers, whereas many of the other rights, and particularly the economic and social ones, actually build up the state. It is true that the right to fair justice requires that the state provide an independent judiciary and adequate procedures, but the things which the state must thus do are actions for self-limitation and self-denial.[8]

I would agree that the limitation of the power of the state with respect to interference in the activities of individuals is a good thing and that the protection against such interference, which is ensured by the civil and political rights, is of great importance. I would also agree that there is a distinction to be made between those positive actions the aim of which is to limit state power and those actions that extend this power, as in the case of the provision by the state of benefits or of welfare. However, the purpose of the civil liberties and political rights is not only to protect individuals from interference by the state but is also to protect them from interference by other individuals or institutions. Thus the state cannot guarantee these liberties merely by forbearing from actions that would violate them, but must also act positively to prevent or to discourage such violations of these rights by others. Thus, the U.S. government has enacted and enforced a series of Civil Rights Acts to protect the civil and political rights of individuals from violation not only by the government itself but also by other individuals or social and economic institutions. But this very protection of civil and political rights may be seen to require a protection of rights that could be appropriately characterized as social and economic. For example, equal protection under the law, as a civil right, has been interpreted to prohibit discriminatory procedures in employment and education, which are economic and social domains. So too, the right to property, as a civil right, justifies laws against the restraint of trade by monopolistic practices, and this constitutes a limitation of interference with property rights by large-scale economic interests. In such cases, the state acts positively (through legislation, enforcement, and the courts) to limit the power of intervention or interference with the rights of individuals by either the government itself or by other institutions or individuals. Moreover, such action to limit power is not confined to the protection of civil and political rights, narrowly interpreted, as sharply distinct from the protection of social and economic rights. Rather, the civil and political rights themselves have been interpreted broadly to pertain to issues of social and economic interests. Thus, one cannot distinguish the sphere of civil and political rights from that of social and economic rights simply on the grounds that it is only in the case of civil and political rights that the role of the state is to limit its own power and to protect individuals from interference. Rather, we have seen that such limitations of interference operate with respect to both sorts of rights. Thus, Hoffman's attempt to retain the distinction between these two types of rights with respect to the role of the state does not go through. This is not to say that there is no distinction between those actions of the state that protect against interference—whether within the civil, political, or economic domains—and those actions of the state that require positive provision of social and economic benefits. However, what this distinction is, and the justification for the positive provision of benefits, will be discussed later when I consider social and economic rights as human rights.

We have so far seen that the protection of civil liberties and political rights has been interpreted to require protection of certain social and economic rights as well, as for example nondiscrimination in social and economic treatment and protection against restraint of trade or unfair competition. Such protections amount to a requirement of equality of opportunity as a negative requirement to refrain from acting in certain ways. However, these protections do not extend to the prevention of social domination and economic exploitation, which tend to undermine the civil and political liberties themselves. Thus economic deprivation leaves those who are deprived without efficacy in the exercise of the formal civil and political rights that they may have. For example, as I have already noted, powerful economic interests are able to exercise disproportionate political influence through well-financed lobbies, thus limiting or thwarting the effectiveness of voting rights. Or again, access to public media, which permits the expression of opinion to become influential, requires great amounts of money and this fact limits the efficacy of the freedom of speech of those who lack such access. Similarly, forms of social domination – for example, racism or sexism – tend to exclude those who are dominated from full participation in political and social life and thus from the full exercise of their political and civil rights. If the civil and political rights are to be fully exercised, the limitations or interferences with these rights imposed by social domination and economic exploitation must be eliminated. I would argue that freedom from such domination and exploitation should be recognized as a right that is necessary for the realization of the civil and political rights themselves. Such a right to be free from domination may be conceived as one that requires others to refrain from acting in certain ways. Moreover, if it is such a right, it would require the state to protect it. It may be seen from this that it is not only the civil and political rights that limit interference in individuals' actions by the state or by others. For here there is an instance of a social and economic right which is similarly characterized by the requirement to forbear from interfering. It requires not only that individuals and social and economic institutions refrain from interfering, but also that the state itself not engage in domination or exploitation.

Just as the exercise of civil and political rights requires freedom from domination, so too one may argue that the exercise of many of these rights requires positive conditions, for example, a minimal level of well-being, some education or training and access to information. Where such positive conditions are necessary for the effective exercise of civil and political rights, the simple absence of constraint would not count for anything. For it makes no sense to speak of protection from interference in an action that one has no means to undertake.

Freedom from domination and the availability of positive conditions for action are thus required for the exercise of the civil and political rights themselves. Beyond this, they are required for the realization of the fundamental human value of positive freedom. I would claim that this value provides the foundation for an adequate theory of human rights.

As I argued earlier, such positive freedom or self-development is a value grounded in the nature of human activity itself, an activity characterized by free choice as the capacity for self-development, but which requires concrete social and material conditions for its realization. Since all human beings are agents in this sense and thus equally have the capacity for self-development, I showed in Chapter 1 how, on this basis, there is an equal right to the conditions required for such self-development, that is, equal positive freedom. In subsequent chapters, I derived certain fundamental political, social, and economic rights from this principle. It may now be seen that such fundamental rights can be characterized as human rights since their basic justification is that they are required by the nature of human activity itself, and therefore they belong to every human being simply by virtue of being human.

I will discuss later in this chapter precisely which rights are to be included among the human rights. In the present context, however, it may be observed with respect to the requirements of positive freedom that civil and political liberties are indispensable protections for the exercise of freedom of choice. Thus negative freedom or freedom from constraint or interference is necessary for positive freedom. However, positive freedom as the fundamental value that grounds rights requires not only the recognition of civil and political rights but also the recognition of social and economic rights, which pertain to freedom from domination and exploitation and the positive availability of the social and material conditions for activity, as discussed in previous chapters. On this view, then, human rights would have to include not merely protection rights against interference with liberties, but what are sometimes called opportunity and benefit rights, which include *prima facie* equal rights to the means of activity as well as rights to the means of subsistence. Human rights would thus be extended to include certain social and economic rights.

I would like to return briefly to Cranston's original objection to such inclusion. It will be recalled that, in addition to practicability, Cranston proposed two further criteria for human rights which he claimed social and economic rights failed to meet. Specifically, he claimed that human rights had to be universal and of paramount importance. Cranston's arguments may be answered briefly here. Against the claim that social and economic rights fail to be universal because they apply to people only within a certain role or situation – for example, employees or the indigent – one may respond that this is equally true of many of the civil and political rights as well, as for example, the right to a fair trial or the right to vote, since these pertain to those in specific roles, namely those accused of a crime or those who are citizens. Universality clearly is an important criterion for human rights, but it needs to be interpreted as what would hold for anyone who finds him- or herself in the relevant role or situation. Likewise, paramount importance is a significant criterion for human rights, but here one may object to Cranston's application of it only to the civil and political rights of life and liberty. It seems clear that having means of subsistence is of paramount importance and in fact one may propose that having such means is required by the right to life, as is protection against being killed or tortured. Beyond this, one may argue that the right to exercise one's freedom in self-development is of paramount importance, even if the conditions for such self-development are rarely satisfied in the contemporary world.

An objection might be raised against the account I have given here, especially with respect to the proposal that an equal right to the conditions of self-development should be included among the human rights. It could be argued that such rights are not realizable and that no state could realistically undertake the duties that would be required to satisfy such claims. Further, it could be maintained that to include such extensive rights among the human rights weakens the entire project of establishing human rights as a practical set of international principles or guidelines.

Whether in response to these or other objections, many theorists claim that human rights should be restricted to a set of minimal or basic rights. This is the case even for those theorists, such as Henry Shue, who add subsistence or welfare rights to the civil and political rights. Thus Shue speaks of the central purpose of basic rights as "preventing or alleviating helplessness."[9] 'He writes, "Basic rights are the morality of the depths. They specify the line beneath which no one is to be allowed to sink."[10]

I would argue, instead, that an important function of a human rights theory is to provide a regulative ideal that specifies what is due to every human being. As such, the theory must include not only the minimal conditions for survival and civility that make human activity possible at all, but also the fuller conditions that are required for the free and self-developing activity that marks human beings as distinctively human. It should be obvious that such a right to the conditions of self-development is not an unlimited right to whatever one may want, since it is an equal right of all and therefore limited to what is compatible with such equality.

Such a regulative ideal is not limited merely to what can be effected in the present circumstances. Rather, it points to what is practicable or achievable, given commitment to the ideal, together with social changes designed to realize the ideal. From this perspective, a position that limits human rights to a set of minimum rights such as life and civil liberties appears as an accommodation to the prevailing limits of government and society.

Furthermore, as I indicated in the case of property rights considered earlier, many of the human rights do not require the provision of positive benefits (as the objection on the grounds of practicability seems to presuppose). Rather, they require the structuring of social institutions in such ways as to enable these rights to be realized. For example, the right to participate in social and economic decision-making does not require any provision of benefit but rather access to, and legitimation of, such participation in existing firms or institutions, or the founding of new firms or institutions on such principles. Moreover, even such a human right as a right to subsistence is not in the first instance a right to provision but rather to the economic opportunities by means of which subsistence may be earned. Only if this fails does the right to subsistence become a benefit right.

Despite these various considerations, it may nonetheless be observed that the conception of basic or minimal rights has merit, in that it properly recognizes that certain rights are preconditions for others and that some rights are necessary for the possibility of any human action whatever. This consideration raises the question of the priority among rights, which is the second of the four major problems concerning human rights that I noted at the outset. I will proceed now to a brief consideration of this and the remaining problems before proceeding to an account of what are the human rights.

THREE FURTHER PROBLEMS OF HUMAN RIGHTS THEORY

The question of priority among the human rights has been discussed in two main ways in the literature: first, as the question of whether one can distinguish between basic and nonbasic rights and what the distinction may be; and second, as the question of whether the civil and political rights have priority over the social and economic rights.

With respect to the first question, I would agree with those authors like Gewirth, Shue, and Plant, Lesser and Taylor-Gooby, who identify a set of basic rights (or "generic" or "minimal" rights), which are rights to the necessary conditions of any human action whatever.[11] Such rights are basic also in the sense that having these rights realized is a prerequisite for the possibility of realizing any other rights. Such a basic right would be the right to life as a right not to be killed. It is plain that if this right is violated then such other rights as a right to equal treatment or self-development have no purchase. However, the right to life or to survival clearly requires more than merely the negative right not to be killed. It also requires means of subsistence, as well as the provision of a level of health care adequate for viability. But the necessary conditions for any human action whatever include more than life. Since the action in question is human action, which on my view entails the exercise of free choice, the basic rights must include the protections for such action provided by civil liberties and political rights.

However, it may be seen that these basic rights do not stand in isolation from each other, but rather are mutually supportive of each other. Thus, for example, it is clear that being alive is a precondition for possessing civil liberties. Conversely, however, as Shue points out, rights of political participation may be regarded as means of assuring the security of life as well as the means of subsistence, since individuals acting in their interests through the exercise of these political rights are the best guarantors of their own security and subsistence. However, I would argue that this feature of mutual support among rights shows the need to extend the account of rights beyond the basic ones and in fact casts doubt on any hard and fast separation of basic from nonbasic rights. The distinction between basic and nonbasic rights still obtains inasmuch as the realization of certain rights is a precondition for the possession of others and inasmuch as certain rights are the necessary conditions for any action whatever, as we have seen. Yet, assurance or realization of the basic rights may require the exercise of rights that have been considered nonbasic. Thus, for example, the right to participate in economic decision-making concerning one's own interests, as in collective bargaining through labor unions, has historically been a major way of assuring that one's rights to subsistence and to a minimal level of health care be recognized. Similarly, one may argue that the protection of freedom of choice through civil liberties may remain ineffectual without the protection offered by rights to be free from exploitation or social domination. Such domination may severely constrain one's range of available choices or indeed prevent one in practice from exercising the formal rights of choice that one has. Thus what begins to appear is a network of interrelated rights that are mutually supporting. Further, the basic rights point toward extensions in terms of nonbasic rights, which serve as ways of realizing these basic rights themselves.

The notion of basic rights does not yet provide an adequate account of human rights. This is not only because the basic rights themselves require other rights as their guarantors. It also follows from the fact that basic rights do not provide an adequate account of the necessary conditions of human action in the following sense: We may distinguish between the minimal notion, alluded to above, of "any human action whatever" and human action in the fuller sense, as a process of self-development over time. The first case isolates analytically what one might call a discernible human act, whereas the second understands human life activity not simply as an aggregation of such acts but as a process of development which is marked by self-transcendence or self-development. Such self-transcendence involves the transformation of individuals and the development of their capacities through the realization of purposes which they themselves set. The conditions for such self-development, as necessary conditions for human actions in the fuller sense, are the foundations for human rights beyond the basic rights.

The second part of the question concerning priority – namely, the question of the priority of the civil and political rights over social and economic rights – may be considered in light of the previous remarks about basic rights. I claimed that such basic rights include subsistence rights as well as civil and political rights. As necessary conditions for any human action whatever, it seems clear that subsistence (as a social and economic right) has no lower priority than do civil and political rights, since subsistence is required for living and living is a precondition for human action, as are civil and political rights. This does not yet settle the question as to whether other social and economic rights beyond subsistence are basic or nonbasic rights.

This view of priority gains support from my earlier argument concerning the inclusion of social and economic rights among the human rights. The argument for the priority of civil and political rights over social and economic rights is often based on the view that the former are rights against interference rather than rights to positive benefits and therefore are more practicable and more universal than the latter. But as we saw, this argument fails on at least two grounds: first, that rights against interference also require positive action by the state no less than do the social and economic ones and, second, that social and economic rights may also be rights against interference. Thus this argument for the priority of the civil and political rights fails to distinguish them in the relevant respects from the social and economic ones.

A further important problem for human rights theory is whether there is a necessary conflict between the values of freedom and equality, such that rights based on these values are mutually exclusive. Thus it is argued that freedom of the individual as the right to determine the course of one's own activity and as the entitlement to the benefits of such activity, is necessarily violated by the requirement of equality, understood as a right of equal well-being or welfare. A right to equality of this sort is held to be an interference with the right to freedom, where this latter right is expressly defined as a right against interference. A form of this argument has been made by Nozick.[12] A different formulation of the presumed conflict between freedom and equality has been made by Charvet. He argues that the traditional conception of human rights is incoherent because it engenders contradictory requirements. On the one hand, it characterizes freedom as the determination by the individual of his or her own particular purposes and, on the other hand, it characterizes equality as the moral requirement to take the needs and purposes of others into account even when they conflict with one's own. According to Charvet, "the fundamental principle of equal rights also requires. . .that resources be distributed equally at all times. This thesis denies the freedom to make gains for oneself in which all do not share."[13] In such representations of the conflict between freedom and equality as those of Nozick and Charvet, freedom is understood as an individual right, whereas equality is held to introduce a social right or requirement. Thus the rights of the individual are held to be in conflict with the rights or requirements of society.

It seems to me that the argument concerning freedom and equality can be recast in another context which sheds light on its resolution, namely that of the traditional liberal theory of equal liberty. In its classic formulation, this theory states that each individual has the freedom to do as he or she pleases, provided that the exercise of this freedom does not interfere with or limit the like freedom on the part of the others. In this case, that freedom must be understood as equal freedom is not problematic since the right to freedom is regarded as a human right and therefore as a right that each individual has equally by virtue of being human. Thus it is part of the meaning of the concept of equal freedom that the freedom of any individual is limited by the requirement not to interfere with a like freedom on the part of any other. Such a conception of freedom is generally held to apply to the domain of civil and political rights, where it is customarily regarded as unproblematic. This seems to me to provide a model for the resolution of the presumed conflict between freedom and equality. For if freedom is taken not merely as an abstract capacity for free choice but also as the effecting of one's choices, which requires the availability of social and material conditions; that is, if freedom is taken as positive freedom or the freedom to develop oneself, then the equality of such positive freedom should also be unproblematic. For here, the right that each individual has to self-development is limited by the requirement not to interfere with a like right on the part of the others. Since the conditions for such equal freedom include economic conditions as well, equality of access to such conditions is required, and assuring such equality should be no more problematic than assuring the equality of liberty.

The counterargument to such an egalitarian view is that the requirement of economic equality as involving equal rights to the conditions of self-development violates the civil right to acquire and accumulate property; that is, it interferes with the freedom of property as a basic right. This counterargument may be answered in two ways. First of all, in terms of the argument that I just made, if freedom of the individual is understood as freedom of self-development that requires conditions, then the right to property cannot be interpreted in such a way as to violate equal freedom in this sense. Specifically, the acquisition and accumulation of property by one individual or by a group of individuals cannot be such as to prevent the self-development of the others. Accordingly, I argued earlier that property right needs to be reinterpreted such that the individual right to personal property is retained and, at the same time, that there is a social right of control over social property, that is, social means of production. The second and related argument is that the view that holds that the individual right to acquisition and accumulation of property extends to all property without differentiation is mistaken in that it fails to recognize that some labor is social labor. Thus the products of such labor are not the products of any one individual's activity, and therefore the claim to the benefits or control over such products as property rights cannot be made exclusively by any one individual. In such cases, it is wrong to view such property as an individual entitlement.

There is yet a further way of resolving the alleged conflict between freedom and equality as human rights. And this is to note that in some cases the equality among individuals does not in fact interfere with their freedom, but on the contrary enhances it. Thus the social and economic equality that precludes the domination of some individuals by others serves to increase the range of social interactions in which an

individual can engage and improves the quality of these relations. It also facilitates joint activity directed to common
goals, making it more effective, and producing a wider variety of material and social means for self-development than
could be produced without it.

The final problem of human rights theory that I noted at
the outset – namely, the question of the relation between
individuality and sociality – is closely related to the problem
just discussed. What is at issue here is whether a human
rights theory is to be formulated either in individualistic or
holistic ways. In the first case, human rights are seen as
grounded in the nature of individuals alone and not in any
social or systemic features of humanity, and they are regarded as borne by individuals alone. In the second case,
namely that of holism, human rights are grounded on what
are taken to be universal structures of society or on the
requirements of the common good. It should be clear from
what I have already said concerning the nature of positive
freedom and the relation between freedom and equality that
I would regard both of these views as mistaken and one-
sided. For although it is true that only individuals have
human rights and abstract entities like society or humanity
do not, yet such individuals are social beings or individuals-
in-relations. Similarly, human rights are not to be taken as
limitations on interference by one individual on another or
simply as establishing boundaries between individuals
which they may not cross, as they are on the individualist
view. Rather, rights also serve to establish modes of social
relations of cooperation or commonality among individuals
or groups of individuals. A clear case here is what I have
called the right to social property, that is, the right to joint
control over social means of activity. Yet, human rights are
grounded in the nature of individuals and not on society or
on the nature of social relations as such. Thus rights derive
from the character of these individuals as free and self-
developing agents, whose agency is fundamentally expressed through social relations.

THE HUMAN RIGHTS – A PROPOSED ENUMERATION

In this final section of the chapter, I would like to suggest an enumeration of the human rights, based on the principles and arguments that I presented earlier. It will be recalled that I proposed that human rights are grounded in the nature of human beings and that the fundamental characteristics of being human are free agency and social individuality. I advanced the conception of equal positive freedom as the fundamental value from which an adequate account of human rights may be derived. Further, in my discussion of major problems in human rights theory, I focused on the question of the scope of human rights and attempted to show that the arguments for the exclusion of social and economic rights from among the human rights fail to go through. I argued that the human rights should include social and economic rights as well as civil and political rights, and should also include benefit and opportunity rights as well as protection rights. I also claimed that though there is a distinction to be drawn between basic and nonbasic rights, the human rights should not be limited to basic or minimal rights alone.

I would like to begin my account of what the human rights are by introducing a right that follows from my earlier analysis but which has generally not been included in discussions of human rights. This is the right of participation in social and economic, as well as in political, decision-making, and it follows from the account I have given that it is properly to be included among the human rights. Although a right of democratic participation has been included in most accounts of human rights as a right of participation in the political process (at least in the form of voting rights), the right to democratic participation in social and economic decisions has been absent from any of them.

The argument for this right on the grounds of equal positive freedom was given earlier. Since the principle of equal positive freedom is itself grounded on the nature of human activity, and since it requires that one be free to determine the cause of one's activity, as a condition for self-development, and since common activity is one of the social conditions for this self-development, therefore every human being has an equal right to participate in decision-making concerning this activity, by virtue of being human. That is, it is a human right. In its political form, this right to participation is well-recognized as the requirement for democracy or political self-rule. However, if one acknowledges that the ground for such equal participation in decision-making is in fact the deeper principle of equal positive freedom, then there is no reason to limit its application to the domain of political life. Rather, the same requirement of democracy pertains to joint decision-making in social, economic and cultural life as well.

This human right to participation needs to be interpreted in terms of concrete institutional forms of decision-making, which would serve to realize it. Thus just as universal suffrage is the form that this right most generally takes in political life, in an analogous way workers' self-management and economic democracy more generally are forms for this right in economic life. Similar forms of democratic decision-making would be required in social and cultural life as well.

One may note here in passing that in the case of the other human rights to be enumerated, as well as in this one, it is important to interpret these rights concretely in terms of the various institutional forms that would serve to realize them. Some of these institutional forms are obvious, such as courts and police for the protection of life and property, or elections for the expression of the right of political participation. However, in other cases, the existing institutional forms may need to be changed in order to be adequate to the realization of these rights, or new forms may need to be devised.

What, then, are the human rights that follow from the analysis that I have given thus far? Without giving a full explication of each of them, and without establishing a strict order of priorities among them, one may nevertheless enumerate them as follows: First, there are what one may call the

two fundamental or basic rights of life and freedom or liberty. These rights are basic in the sense we discussed earlier;
that is, they are necessary conditions for any human action
whatever, and they are prerequisites for the possibility of
realizing any other rights. Further, since every human being
has these rights by virture of being human, and since in this
sense, no human has more of a claim to these rights than any
other, it follows that these rights are equal rights.

The right to life may be said to consist in the right not to be
killed (as a protection right) and also the right to the means of
subsistence (as a benefit right). Another benefit right, which
may be derived from the right to life, is the right to a level of
health care adequate to maintain viability. If one adds considerations here based on the right of freedom, then the right of
health care would require more than the maintenance of viability alone. It would require health care adequate to maintain the various life activities of individuals, for example,
work, education, and social activities. A related right is the
right against avoidable environmental harm or risk. Further,
one may say that the right not to be physically harmed or
tortured, that is, a right to one's bodily integrity and physical
security against violation by others, is based in part on the
right to life, because such harm may be life-threatening or
life-shortening. It also derives from the right to liberty or
freedom, in the sense that such violations of one's well-being
or diminution of one's physical or mental capacities by harms
are obviously constraints on one's right to freedom. Another
related right that has joint sources in the rights to life and
freedom is the right to peace, for the obvious reasons that
war violates the well-being of most people, if not indeed of
all, and in general violates the requirement of equal freedom,
involving, as it commonly does, aggression and domination.

The right of liberty encompasses rights of negative freedom and of positive freedom. These may be distinguished
roughly as those rights that serve to protect against interference with an individual's liberty and those that provide the
opportunities or conditions for the expression of this freedom as self-development. Among the rights of negative free-

dom, one may list the civil and political rights, such as freedom of speech, press, and association, the right to a fair trial, and the right to vote. As I have argued, these are not merely negative rights, since they involve positive action on the part of the state to secure them and since they are instrumental in the achievement of positive freedom. Another right that involves protection against interference with one's liberty, but that is also closely related to equal positive freedom, is the right to be free from domination and exploitation. As we said earlier, this right may be classified as a social and economic right, rather than a civil and political right, even though it is a right against interference, rather than a benefit right.

Another major right in the traditional account of human rights is the right to property. This is an essential right, but it is not an independent right as it has traditionally been conceived. Rather, I believe it can be derived from the right of positive freedom. As I suggested earlier, property is a right to control the means or conditions of one's activity in the maintenance of one's existence and the exercise of one's agency. As such, property is essential for generating the means of subsistence and provides the possibility for the expression of agency, which is essential for freedom understood as positive freedom. As I indicated earlier, property right takes two forms, namely personal property and social property. The first is a right to the conditions of one's own individual activity, including subsistence and individual means of self-development. The second – social property – is a right to the means of common activity or social production.

Among the rights required by positive freedom is the right of participation in decision-making in social, economic, cultural, and political life. Such a right, as noted earlier, is required by equal agency and is a condition for self-development. Another right grounded in freedom is the right to recognition as a person by others. It will be recalled that such reciprocal recognition was characterized earlier (in Chapter 1) as one of the main social conditions for self-development. Further, inasmuch as positive freedom involves the cultivation of character and intelligence, and requires rationality and informal action, it is the ground for a right to education.

There is a more general right than these others, which, because it is grounded in the very nature of human activity, may be classified as a human right. This is the right to the conditions of self-development, which is itself a basis for some of the other rights. Since it is in the nature of human beings to act to effect their purposes, and since the course of such actions through time is what constitutes the realization of freedom, therefore the recognition of someone as a human being involves the recognition of his or her right to the conditions necessary for such activity. A qualification here, however, which also obtains with several of the other human rights, is that this right to the conditions can be exercised only to the extent that it is compatible with a like right on the part of others, since all humans possess this right equally.

It is important to note that among the various rights related to the right to freedom, there are many that are necessary not only for the protection or exercise of an individual's freedom, but also for the protection and enhancement of social action. Thus, for example, freedom of speech is an obvious case of a right that protects communication and enhances the possibilities of group action. This is also the case with freedom of association and the press, as well as freedom from domination, and the rights of social property and of participation, among others. Further, in all of these cases, the modes of social interaction are themselves important contexts for the self-development of individuals.

There is an additional major right in the tradition of human rights, which we have not yet dealt with as a separate right, that is, the right to equality. As we saw, equality is built into the conception of human rights since they are equal rights by virtue of being human rights. Nevertheless, it is important to specify a right of equality which signifies a requirement of the equal consideration of the interests of any human being. This may be understood as a principle of fairness.

This enumeration of the human rights is not intended as an

exhaustive list nor as a full systematic account of all the interrelations among these rights. Rather, it is intended to show what the consequences are for a theory of human rights of the principles and arguments discussed previously in this book. If a list of the human rights is to be more than ad hoc, or an expression of particular preferences or changing political fashions, I would hold that it has to be grounded on a systematic account of the nature of individuals and of their social relations and on a critical analysis of the fundamental values and of the philosophical problems and principles involved.

Chapter 8

Making participation and authority compatible

The requirements for participation and for authority in political life appear to stand in contradiction with each other. Participation requires the full exercise of the agency of each of the participants in making decisions, whereas authority seems to connote that some individuals have the right to exercise power over others and to make decisions for them, to which these others are bound. This suggests that any democratic theory that takes participation as a central value would have to exclude any concept of authority; or alternatively, if some form of authority is seen to be indispensable to civil or political life, then the theory would have to recognize that limits on the freedom or agency of individuals can justifiably be imposed by an authority external to them.

This difficulty in democratic theory is more general than it may at first appear. It is not limited to arguments concerning only participatory forms of democracy. Rather, as some commentators have noted, a difficulty of this sort lies at the heart of liberal democratic theories and of their conceptions of political obligation.[1] For the fundamental difficulty in the relation of participation and authority really concerns the relation between agency and authority. The alleged incompatibility between the two has been posed sharply by Robert Paul Wolff in his book *In Defense of Anarchism*. Wolff argues that all forms of authority are incompatible with individual autonomy and therefore that no forms of authority

215

or political obligation can be justified.[2] More generally, the problem can be posed as follows: How can the free and equal individuals presupposed in democratic theory accept as legitimate the power of the state or of other individuals to constrain their actions or to make decisions for them with which they may not agree?

The complexities of this dilemma of authority and agency can be articulated further if one examines the institutional structures or forms of association within which authority may be thought to be required. Perhaps the least problematic case is that of a voluntary association in which all the members participate fully in making decisions. Here, the individuals freely associate with one another, make decisions, and share in the joint authority that these individuals have concerning their own association. However, this model of participatory, self-governing, and voluntary association is rare in the institutional contexts of contemporary society and is virtually nonexistent in those forms of political, economic, and social organization in which authority is most significantly exercised. With respect to these latter forms, the dilemma of authority asserts itself in ways that appear to be beyond resolution. Even in the best case of a democratic organization, where representatives are duly elected, there is the problem of how the authority of such representatives is compatible with the agency of those represented; for the representatives make decisions to which those whom they represent are bound. This is not only a theoretical difficulty. Even if representation is seen to be a practical necessity in certain contexts, there remains the question of the means by which the authority of representatives can in fact be made compatible with the freedom or autonomy of those they represent.

A still more problematic case where this dilemma asserts itself is that which concerns the authority of the state and the justification of political obligation. The problem arises because the state is not a voluntary association, and citizenship in the standard case is a matter of birth and geography, not of choice. Yet the theory of political obligation maintains that citizens are free and equal agents and at the same time they have political obligations to the state even though these have not been actively assumed. But it is apparent that there is a conflict here between the asserted freedom of the agents and the authority of the state.

In this chapter, I presuppose the theory concerning the freedom of agents and the nature of social relations that I have discussed earlier and upon which I will base a resolution of this problem. I also presuppose the view, argued for earlier, that participation is the most adequate means for the expression of agency in forms of association. I will offer an analysis of the concept of authority and propose a reformulation of it on normative grounds. This will be followed by a consideration of how the reformulated concept of authority may be seen to be compatible with representation in any form of democratic association. The relation between authority and participation in social and economic life will then briefly be considered. Finally, without attempting to elaborate a full theory of the nature of the state or the origins of its authority, I will consider the issues of political authority and political representation, particularly with respect to the problem of political obligation and the extension of participatory forms of governance within this domain. Though traditional democratic theory has focused on the politics of representation and governance in the state, my emphasis in this book is rather on the extension of democracy beyond the traditional domain of politics. Thus the discussion in this chapter will have as its primary focus the development of a general concept of authority and its relation to the theory of democratic participation advanced earlier.

THE CONCEPT OF AUTHORITY AND ITS NORMATIVE FOUNDATIONS

In general, concepts of authority, as well as historic and contemporary practices of authority, are in fact incompatible with participation and with the full exercise of agency in groups or associations. If authority is to be made compatible with participation, it will have to be reconceived and given an adequate normative foundation. In what follows, authority is to be taken as applying not only to political contexts but more widely to all forms of association, including economic, cultural, and social ones.

I will begin with a brief analysis of current conceptions of authority in the literature of political theory. For the most part, these approaches are descriptivist in the sense that they give an analysis of the concept based on current practices, or they compare various theories of authority, without attempting either a justification or a critique. In this sense, they are nonnormative, even where they describe authority as involving norms or rule-following behavior.

Among these conceptions, there are some that see authority as a type of power, in the sense of an ability that the authority has to command obedience or to effect one's will over others or through the actions of others. For example, Talcott Parsons speaks of authority as "institutionalized power."[3] Robert Dahl and Charles Lindblom, in an early work of theirs, refer to it in terms of commands backed by penalties,[4] and some writers in the Marxist tradition criticize authority as an ideological or political rationale for the exercise of class power. In views of this sort, authority is the power of some individuals or of an institution over other individuals.

A contrasting view sharply distinguishes power and authority and tends to identify power with the use of force, threat, or coercion, and authority with legitimacy in accordance with rules. Among those developing a view of this sort are Stanley Benn and R.S. Peters, Michael Oakeshott, Richard Friedman, and Peter Winch. This position is summarized by Richard Flathman in his book *The Practice of Political Authority* as involving the following two theses: "(1) 'Authority can be correctly predicated of A only if there are established rules by virtue of which A has authority.' . . . (2) 'If A has authority X, those persons (B's) who are in A's jurisdiction therefore have an obligation or obligations Y.' "[5] An additional clarification of this model is made by Richard Friedman, who holds that B's recognition of A's authority involves a judgment on the source of A's claim to authority , but not on the content of A's action.[6] This view of authority is called by Flathman the formal-procedure theory. It is associated with Max Weber's characterization of the legal-rational type of authority, which Weber contrasts with the traditional and charismatic types of authority. Whatever variations there are on this view, it nevertheless holds that in accordance with procedures or rules, some have the right to make decisions for others or to enact them, while these others have an obligation to abide by or carry out these decisions. Thus this view, as well as the first, sees authority as a vertical relation or a hierarchical one, in that authority is exercised *over* some, either by institutions or by others who stand in authority above them.

On both of these views, whether of authority as power or as legitimated by rules, the problem of the relation of authority and agency remains. In the first place, where authority is understood as power over others, the agency of these others is necessarily constrained by the will of the authority. For one of the defining characteristics of agency is the ability to decide for oneself what actions to take. This ability to choose freely to act is denied by any compulsion or coercion, such as is involved in power over one's actions by an external agent. In the second case, where authority is not understood as power over others in the sense of the use of force, threat, or coercion, but rather as legitimated by being in accordance with rules or procedures, nonetheless it is authority by some over others, where these others are required to obey whether or not they agree with the particular decision. In fact, on the second view, the practice of authority is held to be one in which the requirement of compliance with the authority is itself the reason for the action of the agent and other reasons are irrelevant.[7] Thus, for example, Joseph Raz writes that "accepting authority inevitably involves giving up one's right to act on one's judgment on the balance of reasons. It involves accepting an exclusionary reason."[8] However, it seems clear that agency requires just such freedom of judgment based on deliberation without prior exclusion of whatever the agent may deem relevant as a reason for action. Authority interpreted in these ways thus appears to be incompatible with agency.

From this, one may be tempted to conclude that if agency is to be taken as a central value, then all forms of authority must be rejected. Or, on the other hand, if compliance with some forms of authority is seen to be necessary, then such compliance cannot be construed as having any moral claim or as entailing any obligation, but at most only as a matter of expediency or obedience to superior force. When applied to the contexts of political authority, this constitutes one version of anarchism, and a philosophical defense of a view close to this (which we shall have occasion to discuss further below) has been proposed by Wolff in his book *In Defense of Anarchism*. However, this is not the direction of my own argument. Rather, what I would propose is that the concept of authority be reformulated so that it is compatible with agency and participation. This is then a proposal for redefinition on normative grounds, rather than an alternative description of present concepts or practices. Yet in this proposed reformulation, I will draw on many features of the existing analysis, and especially the conception of authority as involving legitimation by rules.

Before proceeding, one may note that there is an alternative attempt to reconcile authority with agency, which has been developed by one branch of liberal theory. This is consent theory, which is offered as a justification of political authority and political obligation. On this theory, although political authority and the laws of the state demand compliance from the citizens and these citizens are obliged to obey them, yet the force of this authority and the ground of this obligation is said to derive from consent. This consent theory has been subject to serious criticism in recent years[9] and I believe that in its present form it cannot solve the problem of agency and authority. I will consider this theory in greater detail later in connection with my discussion of political obligation.

In my view, authority derives from agency, and its legitimacy or its rightness consists in its being in accord with the requirement of equal agency. It will be recalled that equal agency is a presupposition of my argument and entails the equal right that all individuals have to make decisions for themselves and act on them. It follows from this that one agent cannot properly exercise authority over another or others and that therefore authority cannot be understood as a hierarchical relation. Rather, in any association of agents in a common project, the authority is shared or joint, in the sense that each agent participates in codetermining the decisions. Authority is therefore understood as constituted by the individuals in relations and therefore cannot have its legitimation in anything external to that constitution; nor can it be attributed to any abstract entity such as a rule, law, institution, or the state. The source of this authority is distributively in the agency of each of the individuals. Thus authority is connected with authorship or with the creation or production of actions and decisions.

This connection between agency and authority goes back to Hobbes's definition of authority in the *Leviathan*. There he writes,

That which in speaking of goods and possessions, is called an owner, . . . speaking of actions, is called author. And as the right of possession, is called dominion; so the right of doing any action, is called *Authority*. So that by authority is always understood a right of doing any act; and done by authority, done by commission, or license from him whose right it is.[10]

What is significant about this for my purposes is that authority is understood as the right to exercise the power to decide or to act and that this right has its source in the agency of individuals. However, I do not follow Hobbes beyond this. First of all, I do not accept his account of the transfer of this authority. For he sees this transfer as granting the right to act freely to the representative, while the original author retains only the responsibilities for these actions and the obligation to comply.[11] I will discuss this issue in greater detail later. Second, I do not follow Hobbes in his general characterization of individuals as fundamentally isolated, where each pursues his or her own self-interest, and whose forms of association consist of external relations. By contrast, the view I propose sees individuals as internally related in their pursuit of common aims and in their reciprocal recognition of each other's agency. This involves a shared understanding of these common aims as a condition for common action. Such a shared understanding implies an intentional relation both to the common purposes and to the rules or procedures that are followed in their joint activity.

The implications of this for a normative conception of authority are that the authority of a group or association with respect to their common actions is a shared authority among the members of a group. It is exercised by the agents over themselves as members of a group. It is therefore a reflexive relation and not an asymmetrical relation, as it is in the usual views of authority as a hierarchical relation. Where the members of a group make decisions by such shared authority, they obligate themselves to abide by these decisions. Such an obligation is horizontal and not vertical, in that the obligation is to themselves and to each other as members of the group. A model of this sort, in which obligation is self-assumed and horizontal among the members of an association, has been suggested for the case of political authority by Carole Pateman in her recent book *The Problem of Political Obligation*.[12]

It may be seen that the account given here of shared and reflexive authority as the rightful power to decide has the requirement of democracy built into it. On a view of democracy that sees it as that form of social decision-making in which the ruled rule themselves and in which they participate equally in decisions that affect them, a concept of authority of the sort proposed would seem to embody just those elements of self-rule and participation. Such a model of authority is most fully realizable of course in a voluntary association characterized by equality of its members and direct and participative practices of decision-making.

Thus this model sees authority as legitimate if it is in accordance with equal agency, in contrast to the major alternative model which grounds legitimacy in its being in accordance with established rules. Does this therefore mean that on the proposed model rules have no authority? In the strict sense, we must say that they do not, though this does not mean that rules are unnecessary. In fact, rules and procedures are most often necessary conditions for the exercise of authority. That is, some mutually understood and agreed upon way of making decisions and of enacting them is a prerequisite for any social organization.[13] In this sense, rules are the means by which the authority of the members of an association is made effective. They may therefore be called means of authority, and in a derived sense such rules may be called authoritative. The common usage in which rules are said to "have authority" seems to me to be misleading at least in the following sense: This usage tends to reify the rules, that is, to give them a status independent of their institution by the agents who are the authors of these rules. Such reification of the rules also tends to reify authority itself as a property that the rules confer upon actions or persons. This encourages the view that it is the rules that rule rather than those who have made them and are therefore able to change them. This general problem may be called *authority fetishism*, in which authority is thought to be a feature of some external agency independent of the members of an association and to which they are subordinated. Instead, rules and procedures are constituted and as such are subject to revision or replacement.

AUTHORITY AND REPRESENTATION

The concept of authority proposed above seems relatively unproblematic for small voluntary associations where decision-making by participation of all the members is feasible. And there surely are a wide variety of actual associations to which this conception does apply or could apply and I will consider these later. The difficulty with this conception of authority, however, emerges when one considers larger and more complex organizations in which decision-making requires some form of representation. The problem is this: If authority rests only with the agency of the members of an association, how can representatives have a right to make decisions for them? For if the representatives do have the right to make decisions for those whom they represent, which are binding upon them, then these representatives exercise authority over those whom they represent, which is the view of hierarchical authority rejected above. If, on the other hand, representatives do not have a right to make such decisions, then the representatives are reduced to instrumentalities of those whom they represent and are subordinated to the authority of those whom they represent. This dilemma of representation may also be formulated in terms of agency: For it would appear either that the agency of those represented is constrained by the authority of the representatives or that the agency of the representatives is constrained by the authority of those whom they represent. (Again, it is important to recall that I am treating the question of authority and representation here in general and not only in the context of political representation.)

The problem then is whether representation can be conceived in a way compatible with a nonhierarchical conception of authority such that this dilemma can be resolved. An approach to this question involves recognizing that representatives have no original or autonomous power or right to make decisions for those whom they represent. Rather, their very nature as representatives requires that they be authorized in some way to act in this capacity. Such authorization properly derives from the members of the association and not from any external source. Therefore, such authorization ought to be always subject to review and revocation.

This authorization of representatives has several dimensions: First, there is a formal aspect, which concerns the rules governing the choice of representatives and determining the range or domain of their functions. Such rules should be understood as either instituted or revisable by those represented. Second, this formal aspect of authorization (which is emphasized in Hobbes's view of representation, among others) needs to be supplemented with an additional sense of authorization, namely, that the representative is authorized to act in the interests of the members and under their guidance. Therefore, on the spectrum of types of representation, which ranges from that of explicit mandate, in which the representative simply carries out the instruction of the constituents, to that on the other extreme of totally independent judgment and action on the part of the representative, my own view is closer to the mandate end. In a general way, one can say that a representative needs to be responsive to the expressed wishes and instructions of those represented and to their interests and needs as they themselves perceive them. Procedurally, this means that the representative must consult frequently with the members. It also means that the fundamental authority of those represented needs to be assured by procedures for the election and recall of representatives as well as for referenda at the discretion of those represented. Additional procedures such as rotation of representatives or ratification by the whole membership of agreements or decisions made by the representatives may also be appropriate as ways of asserting the fundamental authority of the members. On the other hand, there is a need to recognize the agency of representatives, in that they must make decisions and exercise judgment. This is evident from one of the functions of representation, which is to substitute for direct forms of participation in decision-making where the latter are not feasible. In such contexts, the representative has to engage in discussions, the formulation of issues, debate, and compromise in the making of decisions, and all of these require the exercise of the representative's own agency.[14]

One may therefore distinguish the fundamental authority, which rests in the agents who constitute an association, from what we may call the derived authority or the authorized activity of their representatives. Such derived authority is instituted, delimited, and revocable by the members themselves, and is exercised in their interest. From these considerations, it is clear I think that both those represented and their representatives retain their agency. Yet with regard to the

225

functioning of the representatives *qua* representative, there are limitations on the scope of this agency. These limitations come with the role that the representative has presumably voluntarily chosen to play. In addition, the representative retains full agency beyond the limits of this role. Those represented likewise retain their agency insofar as the representative is a means for the effective expression of their agency in those contexts where participation is not feasible. Furthermore, it is they who authorize the representatives and to whom the representatives are accountable.

PARTICIPATION AND AUTHORITY IN SOCIAL AND ECONOMIC INSTITUTIONS

I have thus far indicated how one may conceive of the compatibility between authority and agency and between authority and participation, without regard to specific institutions and forms of association. I have also suggested earlier that the analysis was to apply not only to political contexts of authority but also to those of economic, social, and cultural life. I would like now to consider briefly these latter contexts and how we might suppose the normative concept of authority and of participation that I have described might be interpreted for them. One desideratum that applies to all these institutions and which I mentioned earlier in connection with the requirement for equal agency is that direct participation in decision-making is the most adequate expression of the agency of the members of an association and that it should be introduced or extended wherever feasible.

Considering first the domain of work or economic organizations, relations of authority are most often hierarchical and take the form of authority over workers by management. Thus managers have the right to make decisions about policy, production, and the work process to which the workers must comply as a condition for continued employment. Although unions may negotiate on behalf of the workers concerning wages, hours, conditions of work, and benefits, this does not yet touch on the structure of authority within the firm. The implications for this context of the alternative conception of authority, which I have proposed, may be summarized as a requirement for workers' self-management. If the principles of equal agency and shared authority are to be realized, then the right to participate in making decisions belongs equally to all those who work in a given firm. This shared authority concerns not only immediate conditions of work, but also questions of policy and planning. As I argued earlier (see Chapter 4), this does not mean that all questions have to be decided by all the workers, or that the function of management is dissolved or fully distributed among the workers. It does mean, however, that all those who work in a firm have a right to appoint the managers and also to remove them by procedures that they have adopted in common. In addition, the derived authority of the managers must be regarded as legitimate only to the degree that those over whom it is exercised have authorized it.

The alternative conception of authority may also be seen as relevant to decision-making in social and cultural contexts. The variety of such institutions suggests a need for a variety of models of who shall be included in the decision-making. Such institutions range from voluntary membership associations and professional societies to public and private service institutions such as schools, hospitals, and museums. In the case of voluntary membership associations, fundamental authority should be understood as shared equally among the members, who have a right to participate in decision-making concerning the association, for example, in such matters as the election of directors and representatives and the determination of rules and procedures. With respect to service institutions, participation in decision-making should include those who work there, as well as some representation of those whom the institution serves. An exception to this latter requirement would be in the case where the functioning of an institution is fundamentally subject to the operation of the market, such that consumers' views can be expressed through the market itself. (This is discussed in the following chapter.)

A final point concerning economic, social, and cultural institutions is that in order to make authority compatible with participation in the way proposed here, such institutions and associations need to become voluntary associations to the degree possible. That is, those who function in them should be regarded as freely associated members of the organization and not either as compelled to join or as subject to the authority of the few who serve as directors or managers. However, it is clear that such free association requires important social changes, such that choosing one's membership among alternative organizations is not merely a formal but a practical possibility, and further that participation and self-management become features of such organizations.

THE STATE AND THE PROBLEM OF
POLITICAL OBLIGATION

We come now to the final and perhaps most difficult problem concerning the compatibility of authority and agency. It is also the problem that has been most fully treated by philosophers and political theorists. In my view, it remains without a satisfactory solution. This is the problem of the justification of political obligation and political authority. The central question may be posed as follows: Is it possible for free agents to accept an obligation to comply with the authority of the state and its laws and still retain their agency? And what grounds can one give for such an obligation in the first place, if in fact it exists? On the usual view of political obligation, citizens yield their individual will and judgment and in place of it comply with the will and judgment of the political authorities. Moreover, they are obliged to obey the laws even if they disagree with their content or find them inconvenient or harmful. Yet the individuals are held to accept this authority not under constraint or coercion but by a voluntary act, which constitutes it as an obligation. The problems here are, therefore, several: What would justify free individuals in putting themselves under such authority? And what would

count as a sign that they have in fact assumed such an obligation? If, in fact, there is no evidence that such obligation has
been assumed, are there any other grounds for political authority and obedience to the laws that are compatible with
agency? Or if there are none, doesn't authority reduce to
sheer power?

Perhaps the sharpest presentation of the conflict between
authority and autonomy is that of Robert Paul Wolff in his
essay *In Defense of Anarchism*. Wolff's argument has been the
occasion of a wide discussion and debate in the decade and a
half since its appearance. It will be useful to isolate the main
issues that have been in dispute in order to situate my own
views in relation to those of Wolff and his critics. Wolff argues from two premises: The first is essentially a definition of
the state as "a group of persons who have supreme authority
within a given territory or over a certain population."[15] The
second is a Kantian definition of the moral autonomy of persons or agents as consisting in their freedom, and hence, in
their responsibility to be a law to themselves in their moral
decisions. "The autonomous man," Wolff writes, "insofar as
he is autonomous, is not subject to the will of another. He
may do what another tells him, but not *because* he has been
told to do it. He is therefore, in the political sense of the
word, *free*."[16] Since Wolff defines political authority as having a right to command (and a correlative right to be obeyed),
then those in authority demand obedience to their commands on the grounds of this right. This claim to obedience
as a right constitutes the state as a de jure state, and not as
one that exercises authority merely de facto. According to
Wolff, then, "Obedience is not a matter of doing what someone tells you to do. It is a matter of doing what he tells you to
do because he tells you to do it."[17] Further, he characterizes
the authority of the state as "the right of the state to command the individual and of his obligation to obey, whatever
may be commanded."[18]

From these two premises, it clearly follows that a moral
agent must forfeit autonomy to obey the law as the state
demands. Therefore, the conflict, according to Wolff, is unre-

solvable. "If all men have a continuing obligation to achieve the highest degree of autonomy possible, then there would appear to be no state whose subjects have a moral obligation to obey its commands."[19]

As Wolff notes, an obvious resolution of this conflict would seem to be the traditional democratic one: If those who rule are themselves those who are ruled, then those who command and those who obey are the same, that is, autonomy – literally, being "self-legislating" – is preserved. But the only case in which this would strictly be so, according to Wolff, is that of unanimous agreement, reached by direct participation of all the members of a state in arriving at such agreements. (Wolff originally held that this would be a case of perfect autonomy, compatible with political authority, but later changed his view in response to a criticism of it.[20]) And since any democratic alternative to unanimity and direct participation involves representation and/or majority rule, it follows that even in such a democratic state, some individuals would have to forfeit their autonomy, if they are to obey the laws enacted against their will by others.

The stark logic of Wolff's argument appears irrefutable, since once the premises are allowed, the conclusion follows. Critics have therefore focused on the premises, that is, on Wolff's concepts of the authority of the state and the moral autonomy of agents, in order to put his conclusion in doubt. Thus, for example, some critics have argued that Wolff's absolutist version of the sovereign authority of the state goes too far and that what citizens owe the state is no more than *prima facie* political obligation (subject to the reservations that conscience or morality demand)[21]; or that political authority is to be distinguished from moral authority, so that a state can never lay claim on moral grounds to the political obligation or the duties of its citizens to obey the law, but only on the grounds of the benefits that are the consequences of the state's system of laws (compared with other states)[22]; or that there is some gap left between the limits of the state's legitimation and the moral freedom of the citizens[23]; or that Wolff's conception of moral autonomy is too abstract and formal, and that there is "no very good reason to construe agency in this way."[24] In general, then, critics have tried to show that not every sort of political authority and not every sort of moral autonomy are incompatible.

Keith Graham, after offering a summary of the main criticisms of Wolff's view, suggests that Wolff's argument can withstand most of these criticisms, but that there remains an argument for democracy that would serve as a resolution of the conflict between authority and autonomy.[25] Graham bases this on a premise that he proposes that Wolff would accept, namely, that autonomy should be maximized (by inference from Wolff's view that one should forfeit autonomy as little as possible). Graham notes two openings that seem to exist in Wolff's own argument: first, Wolff's (later withdrawn) view that unanimous direct democracy preserves autonomy while admitting political authority; and second, Wolff's argument and example to the effect that sometimes it is rational to forfeit autonomy. On this basis, Graham develops the consequence – a strange one, from Wolffian premises – that majoritarian democracy is required by moral autonomy.[26] Thus, if the maximization of the individual's moral autonomy is an imperative from Wolff's point of view, and if Wolff, as a good Kantian, must universalize this so that the autonomy of all moral agents should be maximized, then it may be seen that a majoritarian system of democratic decision-making is just such a maximizer of moral autonomy. For if, as Graham has argued, all free rational agents are equally autonomous, then the maximization of autonomy is indifferent to the individuality of each agent. Therefore, rationality suggests "that a state of affairs should not be brought about if there are fewer rather than more decisions that it should. Conversely, if most decisions *favor* a particular state of affairs, less damage will be caused to the maximization of autonomy if that state of affairs is brought about rather than not. Or, to put it more simply, if you want to maximize autonomy where people disagree, accept majority votes."[27]

If the maximization of autonomy, then, is taken to mean

the widest realization of the choices of the most people – a sort of "greatest autonomy of the greatest number" principle – then the justification of authority compatible with this maximized autonomy would seem to have a strong utilitarian direction. The trouble with this is that it would seem to be difficult to derive a normative justification of the political authority of majority rule in the Kantian sense required by Wolff's principles, namely, in which there can be no obligation to yield to the will of others.

In the course of developing his argument for the maximization of autonomy, Graham adduces the fact that much of our activity is social interaction or joint action, in which conflicts are likely to arise that thwart the autonomy of some agents. It will be recalled that a conception of joint action is essential to the notion of freedom as self-development that has been central to my account. This conception of joint action suggests an analysis of the relation between autonomy and authority, which differs from Wolff's, and in which they may be seen to be compatible under certain conditions. Although this does not obviate the incompatibility alleged by Wolff under his definitions of the terms, yet it would do so under an alternative conception of the authority of the state and an alternative analysis of autonomy in this context. The logical form of this argument, then, is to alter Wolff's premises in order to avoid his conclusion which follows from them.

It will be remembered that, in my earlier discussion, common or joint activity was distinguished from individual action in that it involves not merely an aggregate of individual ends but rather an end shared by a number of individuals acting in common. In this context, I would suggest that the autonomy of each individual in such joint action requires a different analysis than would be given of that individual's autonomy exercised in pursuit of his or her own individual ends. For in the case of joint activity in which there are shared ends voluntarily chosen, the individual's autonomy can only be expressed in freely acting together with others in the codetermination of the joint activity. This may therefore be conceived of as a form of social agency, not in the sense that the collective as a body has any "agency" of its own, but in the sense that it is constituted by the joint agency of the individuals in a group. In this restricted sense, one may also talk of "social autonomy," but only as the expression of the autonomy of the individuals in their mutual decision to act together toward some shared end. Here, the individual does not "give up" his or her autonomy in the choice to cooperate. That would be the case only if individual autonomy were so narrowly defined as to mean exclusively the exercise of agency in pursuit of one's own separate or particularistic ends (as in a Hobbesian state of nature). But even the Kantian autonomy that Wolff endorses goes beyond this in its universalistic definition of a free will in the categorical imperative.

Thus I would argue that participation in joint decision-making remains an exercise of autonomy, inasmuch as the individuals have freely chosen to participate in the activity and in the determination of the shared ends, and since participation in common activity is itself a general condition for their freedom as self-development (as argued earlier), and finally, since the decisions to which they thus bind themselves freely have the authority of their own mutual self-determination and not an external or imposed one. However, a restriction on what individuals may bind themselves to in such collective decisions is that these decisions must not violate any of the basic rights of individuals (as discussed elsewhere in this book). In such a collective decision procedure, the equal agency of each individual is fully preserved since, on the model I have proposed, each has an equal right to participate. In this connection, it may be noted that it is the respect for the equal agency or dignity of each individual (following from the principle of equal positive freedom) that normatively requires a democratic decision procedure, rather than any principle of the maximization of autonomy. Further, it may be useful to add what may be an obvious point: The participation in joint activity that has been discussed here does not exhaust the range of an individual's activity, and the norm of individual autonomy continues to pertain as well to all those ends that individuals choose for themselves alone. Likewise, the autonomy of individuals is expressed in their having a right to participate (and therefore also not to participate) in joint action.

From the foregoing analysis of autonomy in the context of joint decision-making, it follows that the authority of such decisions with respect to those who participate in them is compatible with their autonomy. This conception of authority is in effect what I described earlier in the chapter as shared and reflexive authority, in which authority is legitimate if it is in accord with equal agency. If such a decision-making procedure were to constitute a body politic, then this would be a case of political self-determination, where political authority is compatible with autonomy. But whether a body politic or a state can be constituted in this way requires further consideration.

Now it seems that Wolff would accept some such joint decision-making procedure as a solution to the problem he poses, and he at first holds that a system of unanimous direct democracy is such a solution (at least theoretically, though he sees it as practically unfeasible). He writes, "Under unanimous direct democracy, every member of the society wills freely every law which is actually passed. Hence, he is only confronted as a citizen with laws to which he has consented. Since a man who is constrained only by the dictates of his own will is autonomous, it follows that under the directions of unanimous direct democracy, men can harmonize the duty of autonomy with the commands of authority."[28] He also sees such joint decision-making as constituting political (as against prepolitical or extrapolitical) self-determination, "for the authority to which each citizen submits is not that of himself simply, but that of the entire community taken collectively."[29] Yet, in response to criticism (as noted above), Wolff later rejects the idea that such an association and its authority could be considered political, that is, that it could constitute a state, insofar as such a form of collective self-determination does not create, as Wolff puts it, "the sort of political authority I was attempting to analyze."[30]

234

In a sense, then, Wolff is choosing a definition of political authority or of the legitimate authority of a state that requires by definition what is directly incompatible with what he chooses as a definition of autonomy. This is not an arbitrary choice on Wolff's part, in either case, since he relies on a Weberian notion of the authority of the state and a Kantian notion of autonomy. The result of such a choice of mutually exclusive definitions is, in logical form, the assertion of the propositions "If something is a case of political authority then it is not compatible with autonomy," and "If something is compatible with autonomy then it is not a case of political authority." By contrast, I have offered an analysis of autonomy in the context of joint decision-making in which the shared authority so constituted is compatible with autonomy; but Wolff appears to reject this sort of model because on his view it is not, properly speaking, "political," in the sense that it does not apply to the state. However, I have already suggested that there is a construal of this sort of shared authority which is, properly speaking, political, though it is not realized in any presently existing states. It may be considered as a normative ideal of the state and of political authority, in which such authority and individual autonomy are in principle compatible. In later discussion in this chapter, I will suggest how such an ideal may be applied in the context of arguments concerning political obligation. Here, however, I will only note the obvious point that the conception of political authority that I propose in this chapter necessarily differs from Wolff's. And while the conception of the legitimate authority of the state that he examines derives from traditional political theory and closely approximates to the claims of historical and existing states to such legitimate authority, nonetheless it remains a normative model or "a deduction of the concept of the state,"[31] in Kantian terms, as Wolff puts it. The alternative conception that I propose here is no less normative.

We have seen that on Wolff's conception, the absoluteness of the incompatibility between authority and autonomy may be mitigated only in the extreme case of unanimous direct democracy, though, as noted, he later rejects this as a case of political authority. Even in the original analysis which accepts such unanimous direct democracy as a solution, Wolff does not develop further the notion of collective self-determination that he sketches there, and does not see such self-determination as lending any support to majoritarian theories of decision-making as resolving the incompatibility problem. Indeed, a major portion of his work focuses on a critique and rejection of majoritarian theories of democracy as proffered solutions to this problem. On his view, in the case of majority decision or of anything short of unanimity, the minority, bound by the choice that is against their will, forfeit autonomy. Without getting into the complexities of the formal analysis of decision procedures, it may be useful to make two points here which suggest how a model of joint democratic decision-making is relevant to the achievement of autonomy.

The first concerns the way in which democracy by majority rule optimally preserves and enhances the autonomy of individuals. This may be seen to follow from the fairness of the majority rule procedure in making joint decisions concerning common activity. Any alternative decision rule – for example, two-thirds or three-quarters or unanimity – gives some members of the group a much larger say in the outcome than others. At the limit, a unanimity rule gives the single dissenting vote equal weight to the total of all the other votes in making the decision. Similarly, in the two-thirds rule, the minority position has twice as much say as does the majority in making the decision; and in the three-quarters rule, three times as much, etc. Therefore, if an equal right to participate also means having an equal say in the decisions, which fairness would seem to require, then majority rule is the decision procedure most compatible with this equality. But it is this very equality, or recognition of the equal agency of all the participants in the decision procedure, which guarantees that, in making such a joint decision, no one of them will be subject to a greater force of will – that is, the imposition of any other's will on him or her – than would be any of the others. Taken thus distributively, one may then say that each one's autonomy is both optimally exercised in such a majoritarian procedure and also protected against compulsion by any other.

However, the objection remains that, collectively, the will of the majority is imposed on that of the minority, so that in being obliged to accept the decision of the majority, each member of the minority is required to forfeit his or her autonomy in that case. Though it is impossible here to develop a full discussion of this traditional and difficult question, it may be useful to suggest at least how an argument *from autonomy* may be made in this context. First, the full exercise of an individual's autonomy requires the context of participation in common activity and in joint decision-making about it. This, as I argued at length earlier in the book, is a crucial factor in the conception of freedom as self-development. And since human beings are social individuals, to deprive them of the opportunity to exercise their autonomy in such ways is to deprive them of an essential aspect of their freedom. Second, since in a social process of this sort, it is inconceivable that every individual should always have his or her own way in all matters of decision, the very condition for the exercise of such autonomy is necessarily the acceptance of this fact. The optimal way in which this reality of social existence with others may be realized is in accordance with the principal of equal positive freedom, that is, with the recognition that no one has more of a right to effect his or her will in a joint decision than has any other and that each one is bound to respect the equal dignity of each of the others. But, as it was argued above, these conditions are optimally met by a majority rule system of democratic decision-making, in which the authority of the decision is not simply the authority of those who voted in the majority for it, but rather the shared and reflexive authority of all those who participated in the decision. It would then seem odd to adduce against this some abstract conception of autonomy, defined in a context-free way, as being forfeited in the majoritarian case. Such an abstract conception would be inappropriate for the context of joint decision-making in common activity as already argued. (Moreover, one might argue that it would be inappropriate in the case in which majority decision is understood only as an aggregate or as the vector-sum of the choices of individuals, each one acting only in his or her own particular interests, if such individual autonomy is defined within Kantian limits. For in that framework, on one interpretation at least, I cannot be said to rationally or freely will any action that would impinge on the autonomy of another individual. For then I would have to be able to will at the same time that every other individual should equally act to impinge on my autonomy. But since I cannot rationally will what would violate my own autonomy, I would not be able to universalize such a violation of another's autonomy as a maxim. It would then seem to follow that participation in joint decision-making in the context of an equal right to determine the outcome is not a violation of individual autonomy even in the case of an aggregative interpretation within a Kantian framework, since the majoritarian model, in equalizing each one's power to determine the outcome, thus protects the autonomy of each individual equally from being impinged on by the will of any other. This remains, however, a complex question, in interpreting Kantian autonomy for the context of social decision-making, and I do not pretend to resolve it here.)

Despite this justification of the authority of majority decisions with respect to the autonomy of individuals participating in the decision, there are limits to what a majority may legitimately decide – limits set by the principle of equal positive freedom itself – so that decisions that violate basic rights cannot have authority. A further condition is that all such associations for the pursuit of common aims be voluntary, in which individuals can enter and leave freely. It is clear that there are many difficulties that arise with such an argument and that the conditions under which such a decision procedure could be realized in the political domain would be difficult to achieve. Nevertheless, this suggests the direction of an argument in which autonomy may be seen to be compatible with majoritarian democracy. It should be added that a complicating aspect of this argument is that a group may want to determine that certain decisions are of such gravity that they require much more than a majority to ratify them, or may indeed require unanimity (as in jury trial). But I believe that such special cases may be seen to be compatible with a more general system of majority rule.

The second point to be made here about democratic decision procedures is that, on the model proposed here, the decision procedure is not exclusively nor necessarily even primarily concerned with a voting procedure. Rather, it involves participation in discussion, deliberation, and debate concerning actions to be taken or ends to be pursued. This has been a presupposition of the notion of participation, as I have discussed it earlier, both in self-management contexts and more generally, and I have argued earlier that such deliberative processes are also important contexts for the self-development of individuals and a fortiori for the exercise of their autonomy. This then differs from the characterization of decision-making simply as a voting procedure. In many cases, coming to agreement or to an agreement to disagree, or resolving a problem, or even deciding to suspend judgment, takes place without the formal resolution by means of a vote. A similar point has been made by Keith Graham in the context of considering the resolution of conflicts among individuals which would avoid possible threats to autonomy involved in majority voting.[32] Further, as discussed earlier, participation in decision-making through deliberation and debate constitutes a fundamental mode of the social interaction that characterizes individuals engaged in joint activity. It is through such interactive activity that the common authority of a group or polity expresses itself, and not simply through the instances of voting.

We may turn now to the questions posed earlier concerning political obligation. The previous discussion of Wolff's views and those of his critics focused on the general issue of the possibility of preserving moral autonomy in the context of the authority of the state. It remains to consider some of the major arguments that have been presented in justification of political obligation. They include the argument from the original social contract, which yields the natural authority of the individuals to the state by explicit consent; the argument from tacit consent, which founds political obligation on forms of implied consent such as ownership of property, or voting; the argument from the concept of a political society, which sees political obligation as entailed by this concept itself; the argument from the principle of fair play, which sees the receiving and accepting of benefits as obligating one on grounds of fairness within a system of cooperation; and the argument from gratitude, which holds that one owes an obligation to the state in gratitude for benefits received.[33]

These arguments have been subjected to serious criticism in two works, namely Carole Pateman's *The Problem of Political Obligation: A Critical Analysis of Liberal Theory* and A. John Simmons' *Moral Principles and Political Obligation*. I concur with many of their criticisms and will consider them in the following discussion.

The first, third, and fifth arguments may be easily dispensed with. With respect to the first, the original contract may have been binding on those who participated in it, but there is no good reason to believe that it binds later generations who have not explicitly agreed to assume this obligation. The third argument from the conception of political society simply builds the notion of political obligation or authority into the concept of society itself as a matter of the meaning of this concept and therefore begs the question as to what the grounds of this obligation are.[34] With respect to the fifth argument from gratitude, as Simmons notes, it is not clear why gratitude to the state should be the occasion for anything as strong as political obligation rather than some weaker response,[35] such as some form of payment or returned service.

There are serious difficulties with the second and fourth arguments as well – namely, tacit consent and fair play – however promising they may at first appear. The leading problem with arguments based on tacit consent is that it is not clear what would count as a sign or as evidence that such consent had been given or from what act one could infer such implicit consent. The idea of tacit consent is introduced in order to make obligation more general than explicit consent would allow. However, the difficulty with it is that it relies on reading the intentions of an agent by means other than the explicit expression of these intentions and this is at best a tenuous enterprise. Consent requires being aware that one is asked to consent and that a response to the question is called for and understood as such. Tacit consent theorists tend to rely on the act of voting as a sign of consent to the authority of the state and include those who fail to vote as obligated to the state simply because they have the right to vote. But against this one may argue that not voting may in fact be a sign of dissent or at least lack of interest, which can hardly be counted as tacit consent. And voting itself does not reveal the intentions of the voter. As Pateman notes, it may be the best he or she can do under the circumstances.[36] If residence in a political state is itself held to be a sign of tacit consent (as it is by Socrates and Locke), then the difficulty may be raised that such residence may hardly be counted a simple matter of free choice given the extraordinary difficulties of changing one's country, such as money, language, permission to emigrate or immigrate, and ties to family, friends, and job.

The argument from fairness similarly fails under criticism. If the claim is that simply receiving benefits is a source of obligation, then, as Pateman points out, since benefits are differential, this would lead to different degrees of political obligation, which is not what the concept requires.[37] Moreover, as Simmons observes, some of these benefits may be unasked for or even received without awareness, and therefore not accepted, in any voluntary act of obligation. If, on the other hand, one restricts the source of obligation to the receipt of *accepted* benefits, then the same problem arises as in the tacit consent argument as to what would count as a sign of such acceptance, since this is an intentional context.[38]

From these criticisms of the arguments that have been given for political obligation, Simmons, for one, concludes that "political theory cannot offer a convincing general account of our political bonds . . . . Most citizens have neither political *obligations* nor 'particularized' political *duties.*"[39] On this view, this does not mean that citizens should not obey the laws. Rather, he believes that there are other reasons for obeying the law which do not entail obligation. For example, some of the activities that laws prohibit are not morally permissible and other laws establish ways of doing things consistently. Pateman similarly concludes that there is no way to make obligation to the state compatible with the agency of free individuals. Instead, she proposes that all obligations must be freely and explicitly self-assumed, that they are always obligations to other individuals or citizens, and, perhaps most striking, that such obligations can only be forthcoming in participatory democratic associations. Thus she regards as illegitimate any general political obligation, and she holds that forms of representation do not generate obligations on the part of those represented.[40]

Since I believe that the criticisms of the grounds for political obligation are sound and that it is not clear that a case can be made for political obligation to the state, am I therefore committed to one or the other of the conclusions that Simmons or Pateman draws? More generally, is there an alternative account of political obligation and of political authority that follows from my proposed reformulation of authority and that is not vulnerable to the criticisms of the standard view?

As is clear from my earlier argument, the leading requirement for any account of political authority and political obligation is that it should be compatible with agency and more strongly with the equal agency of those who are constituents or members of the political community. One of the most vexing difficulties that threaten to render the problem of political obligation insoluble is that one is simply born into a state and into citizenship and only a few, namely naturalized citizens, have the occasion to choose their citizenship, and this under very constrained conditions. Therefore, the determination of one's citizenship is generally a matter of the accidents of birth and geography, over which one has no control. A related difficulty is that political obligation is generally construed as obligation to a particular state and its laws. It is therefore insufficient to ground such a particular obligation on general considerations of justice or morality, since then my obligation would extend to all just laws everywhere. The particularity of the obligation depends on the accidents of birth and geography. But since this is not voluntarily assumed, it cannot serve as a ground for such a specific obligation.

Since, on my view, no present state provides adequate conditions for the exercise of that authority which I described previously as shared authority freely constituted by the members, I would conclude that no present state has political authority in a fully legitimate sense. This does not mean, however, that all existing states constrain the agency of their members to the same degree. Clearly, there are better and worse states in this regard but none that measure up to the requirements of authority fully compatible with agency.

Under what conditions, if any, could such political authority and political obligation be realized? Beginning with the model of authority and participation in voluntary associations that I discussed earlier, there are several considerations that are useful for this context. The authority resides in the individuals who constitute the membership of the association and who have a right to participate in the making of the social decisions that affect that association. Since such members make and enact such decisions, they thereby assume an obligation to recognize the authority of their own actions. Thus, their obligations are essentially to themselves and to each other as agents acting in common. Since the decisions are freely reached and the association is voluntary, there is no question but that the obligation that follows from such exercise of self-authority is voluntarily assumed. Furthermore, if there is a right to participate, then even in the case where actual participation in a given decision is lacking, there is an obligation to accept the authority of the decision, because the member is always free to leave the association. Moreover, I have proposed that representation is not in principle incompatible with such a participatory conception, if both representatives and the procedures by which they are chosen are freely determined by the associated members and if there are adequate mechanisms for consultation, recall, and referendum.

I have suggested that such a model of participatory authority and voluntary association should be extended within the domain of economic, cultural, and social life. But we encounter difficulties in extending it to the domain of political authority. It can be extended to a very great degree and I would argue that it should be. Such an extension would require the introduction of direct and participatory deliberation and decision-making wherever possible and certainly at local levels. It could also easily involve the use of modern technologies of communication and information to permit both wider direct participation by citizens nationally, as well as fuller and more immediate means of consultation and mutual deliberation between representatives and those they represent. Correlatively, the model also suggests the need for greater accountability and responsibility of representatives to their constituents, as well as the elimination from the political process of the excessive influence of powerful lobbies and interest groups, which violate the requirement of equal agency.

The reformulated conception of authority and its correlative notion of reflexive obligation can be extended to the political sphere to the degree that the structure of political life can be made voluntary. This can be accomplished by recognizing that laws and procedures and the authority of representatives are constituted and changeable (as they are in some countries), and by ensuring a democratic right to participate in decisions. This requires, however, that the right to participate be substantive and not merely formal. That is, individuals must have access to social and economic conditions – such as education and freedom from poverty and from ideological coercion – which permit them equal agency in the political process. Were such circumstances to be achieved, I would hold that participation in the political process would create political obligation to the authority of the laws constituted in this way, as would also having the right to participate combined with some way of showing explicit

consent. However, even where such voluntary circumstances obtain, one still cannot say that there is an overriding
moral requirement to obey the laws. I would hold that the
primary requirement of agents is to uphold moral principles
and, if the laws violate these principles, they have a right to
disobey the laws. The development of the argument for this
is beyond the scope of this discussion. But one may note
further here that even with a fully democratic, participatory,
and voluntary association, unjust rules and laws may be decided upon and the obligation to comply with such laws is
overriden by one's moral obligation.

An important aspect of the proposed conception of political obligation is that the citizens of a state have no obligation
to the state as such, but only to their own common authority.
The state therefore becomes only a means for the exercise of
their own authority and therefore should not be reified as an
entity in its own right to which any obligation can be owed.

However, there remains a difficulty for this account that
may not be resolvable: namely, what to do with the individual who dissociates himself or herself from the political community and who does not either participate or voluntarily
consent to the rules? Can such total civil disobedience be
incorporated on the model of participatory authority? I believe that such a case reveals the limits of the state as a
voluntary association. As noted above, these limits follow
from the accidents of birth and geography that most often
determine citizenship. That is, someone born into a state
may not want to be a member, preferring either some other
state or no state at all. Emigration may sometimes resolve
this problem but does not completely eliminate it. (One essential requirement would be that individuals not only have
the formal right to leave a state or to emigrate, but also have
available to them the basic means to do so.) We may say that
the contingency involved in the relation of citizenship and
place of birth sets a barrier to transforming the entire domain
of political association into a fully voluntary one, at least as
states are presently constituted. However, my argument suggests that the attempt must be made to introduce as many of

the features of the voluntary as possible into political life and that this would serve to justify political authority in a particular sense.

A final point that can be made is that there are many reasons to obey the law apart from political obligation, as many commentators have noted, and that some of these are essentially related to agency. Here we may note that the rule of law itself and an ordered social life provides one of the main conditions for agency. Thus in addition to those laws that prevent harm, there are laws that, as publicly known and acknowledged, lend stability and coordination to activity. This in turn permits people to have reasonable expectations of the actions of others and to make plans for the future. This is to say that some modes of social agreement and common understanding are necessary conditions for the actions of individuals. But it should be clear from my previous argument that this does not sanction bad laws as necessary evils, nor does it place the laws above the agents who introduce them and can change them.

Chapter 9

Participation and self-management: a model of democracy

How are the normative principles that were developed in the preceding chapters to be applied in the practical contexts of social, political, and economic life? What would a model of democracy based on these philosophical foundations look like? In this chapter, I will present one such model. It will in effect be an interpretation of these principles, using them as guidelines, but will not presume to specify the detailed structures and practices that the proposed democratic institutions would require. These would depend on the particular historical, social, or national circumstances of the application, and on the choices of the individuals involved.

The model attempts to provide an alternative to the two conflicting forms of society that are currently dominant, namely, Western democratic societies and contemporary socialist societies. In part, this alternative is intended to overcome the defects and failures in the practices of these two social forms, just as the conceptual framework on which it is based was intended to overcome the deficiencies and inconsistencies of the two alternative theories of liberal individualism and holistic socialism. In part, however, the model, like the theory it interprets, is intended to stand on its own as a normatively valid and practically feasible proposal.

As discussed in the Introduction to this book, a major problem in contemporary political practice is that both Western democratic societies and existing socialist societies fail in different ways to provide the conditions for full individual freedom and for equality and social cooperation. Thus existing socialist societies, both in Eastern Europe and in the Third World, are undemocratic in that they fail to protect individual civil liberties, such as freedom of expression and association, and political rights, such as the right to choose one's political representatives freely and the equal right to stand for office. Furthermore, while such societies attempt to introduce equality and cooperation as principles of economic and social life, yet they exhibit serious domination in the form of extensive bureaucracy, state control, the repression of individual differences, and personal and psychological domination. On the other hand, Western democratic societies, while they protect individual civil liberties and political rights to a significant degree and espouse principles of equality in political and social life, nonetheless are not fully democratic in that they do not permit effective political participation by the poor, disadvantaged minorities, and even by the working people who comprise the large majority of the population. This results from the distortion of the political process by the power of wealth, and lobbying by special interest groups. Such societies are also not fully democratic in that social and economic life outside the political sphere are often characterized by economic exploitation, special privilege, and forms of social or personal domination. Furthermore, Western democratic societies fail to take seriously the principle of social cooperation as a condition for full human freedom.

My earlier analysis proposed a theoretical mediation between what appeared to be the conflicting values of individual freedom, on the one hand, and equality and social cooperation, on the other. The model to be presented proposes the practical compatibility of these values and, indeed, their interdependence, such that the full realization of each value requires the others. However, the question arises whether such a model of democracy is feasible in practice or whether it is purely a normative ideal. It is often argued with respect to the apparently conflicting values of individual freedom, on the one hand, and sociality and equality, on the other, that in practice one is compelled to choose between them, in the form of either Western democratic capitalism or Soviet and East European socialism. I believe that this is false. Furthermore, within the framework of the theory of democracy I propose, questions arise concerning the feasibility of implementing equal rights to the conditions of self-development (as discussed in Chapter 5) and of extending democracy to the economy in the form of workers' self-management (as discussed in Chapter 4). A particular problem would also seem to arise concerning the applicability of the principle of participatory decision-making to large, complex, and advanced industrial-technical societies. I hope to show in the present chapter that a model based on the normative principles I have proposed is feasible; that it is applicable to complex and advanced societies and is not merely a suggestion for small, social experiments; and that it builds upon many existing institutions and practices. But of course it goes beyond them in crucial ways that characterize it as the new democracy.

There are several general remarks which may be made before turning to the specific proposals. First, it follows from the theory that all the institutions of society – social, economic, political, and cultural – should be democratized. Furthermore, the legitimation of the functioning of such institutions on the grounds of equal positive freedom requires the fullest degree of participatory decision-making feasible. Also, the institutions should be designed so that the political, economic, and sociocultural spheres each function separately, although they bear on each other. Such a separation contributes to the preservation of balance among these spheres, and to the prevention of any monolithic control of the society as a whole. It also contributes to diversity in the options for democratic participation and individual self-development. Finally, democracy in these institutional contexts has to be founded on reciprocity in interpersonal relations. It is not sufficient to propose changes in objective institutional structures without at the same time recognizing the importance of changes in relations among people. It will become clear that some of the specific proposals in this chapter have been anticipated in the earlier discussion of the principles and are simply brought together and made more explicit here.

The first set of concrete proposals concerns the economic sphere. The four points I will deal with here are workers' self-management, the market, planning and regulatory functions, and the distribution of income. One of the most decisive features of the proposed social structure is the democratic management of economic activity by the workers themselves. This would be in the form of ownership, control, and management of each firm by those who work there.[1] Such workers' self-management means that the workers in a given firm, that is, all the members of the firm, jointly determine the planning and production for the firm and the work process (including allocation of work, rates of production, hours of work, and work discipline). They also decide on the distribution of the firm's income, including reinvestment in production, depreciation costs, and the division of "wages" to be paid among themselves, as shares of the net revenue. In addition, the workers control the sale of their firm's products. The capital of the firm is the workers' joint or social property, which is to say that they have the legal rights to possess, use, manage, or alienate this property.

By including all the members of the firm as part of the worker self-management structure, I am suggesting that this would encompass those workers who are now regarded as managerial personnel, such as supervisors and engineers. Further, since this model takes the firm to be the shared property of the workers, "self-management" here encompasses not only managerial but also ownership functions. This is not to say, however, that there is necessarily a carry-over into the worker-controlled firm of exactly the same managerial or ownership functions that are found in present privately owned firms; for the social relations between workers and managers and between workers and employers, which are characteristic of the present form and which often represent conflicts of economic and social interest, would no longer obtain,[2] though new sorts of difficulties in the social relations among workers in self-managed firms may well arise.

Such workers' self-management does not entail that all the workers decide on every feature of the production and sale of their products. They may well decide to appoint directors or managers of various aspects of the firm's activities. However, such delegation of powers and functions rests entirely upon the democratic decision of all those who work in the firm. This democratic decision-making should involve direct and immediate participation up through as many levels of the firm's activities as is feasible. What is intended here, of course, is that all those who work in the firm have an equal *right* to participate in decisions, not that they are required or obliged to do so.

The second major feature of the proposed economic structure is the market. Firms are free to buy and sell to other firms, institutions, or to individual consumers. The market therefore determines prices and serves as an instrument for adjusting supply and demand. Thus, the market functions as the locus for the exchange of commodities. However, unlike the capitalist market, what is excluded here is the market between capital and labor. Rather, the workers' incomes are determined by their own division of the net revenue of the firm among themselves.

In terms of the values and principles discussed earlier, the virtues of such a market scheme are three: First, it preserves the freedom of workers to determine what to produce and the freedom of consumers to determine what and from whom to buy. In the ideal market, the firms relate to each other and to individual consumers as free and equal exchangers. Second, the market is an efficient means of reflecting the needs and wants of consumers and of adjusting supply to meet the effective demand. Third, the market fosters variety in what is produced because it expresses the multiplicity of wants and it leaves producers free to satisfy them. In all these respects, the market is superior to a centralized planning scheme in which decisions are made from the top down, as they are in many existing socialist economies. Such centralized planning removes the autonomy of the workers in determining production, is often inefficient, and fails to provide variety because the planning bureaucracies tend to be insensitive to differentiated demands and cumbersome in adjusting supply to demand.[3] However, in claiming that the market is suited to realize the principles, I do not mean to imply that it is the only system that could satisfy these principles. But the market form is already available and well-developed and requires no third party to intervene between producers and consumers, or to validate their choices.

Against this, it may be argued that the introduction of a market economy, even in the democratic contexts of worker self-management with its egalitarian tendencies, would simply reproduce the worst features of existing corporate market economies, namely, class polarization with gross inequalities of wealth, domination over and exploitation of labor, and the relentless pursuit of profit without any consideration of social need. But this argument, which attributes these ills to the systemic tendencies of market economies as such, seems to me specious. For it is not the market as such that produces these outcomes, but rather the social relations of property, in which control by some over the conditions of productive activity of others leads to domination and exploitation. This requires a market in labor, which the model here explicitly excludes.[4] Further, the democratic structure of self-management proposed here would eliminate such property-based power of some over others.

There are also other ways in which the economic model proposed here could avoid some of these consequences of present market economies. The application of the principles described earlier could be expected to mitigate some of the extreme inequities that an unbridled market economy may produce. Further, the habits of cooperation induced by the participatory practices of self-managing firms would likely generate a more cooperative and less cutthroat ambience for market competition as well. Again, since there would be no labor market, workers would not be totally dependent on the market as wage-labor since they would also share in the proprietorship of the firms of which they are members (though it is true that these firms would be engaged in market competition with others, and the workers' livelihood would fluctuate with market conditions in this sense). The unrestricted pursuit of profit without regard for social need would have to be regulated (see below), but among worker self-managed firms the pursuit of profit may be justified insofar as it produces the goods and provides the widest conditions of material well-being and choice for the self-development of the individuals of a society.

There are other problems arising in a market-oriented economy, which have been widely observed and criticized, but which do not stem from the nature of the market economy itself and are rather attributed to abuses of it. These would have to be considered in a worker self-managed economy as well, insofar as they may still arise. These include attempts to control the market by means of collusion among firms or by monopolistic practices such as price-fixing; attempts to manipulate consumer demand by deceptive advertising; and the pursuit of profit without regard to larger social needs or public welfare, for example by disregarding consumer safety or environmental hazards. (However, it may be suggested that worker self-managed firms would be less likely than traditional capitalist firms to permit violations of the occupational safety of the workers themselves in the pursuit of profits.) Problems arising from market practices would be the province of market-regulatory and planning commissions in the proposed model.

Such commissions constitute the third feature of the proposed economic structure. The planning commissions would affect the direction of production in the economy indirectly, by making funds available for new investment to existing or prospective worker-managed firms. The commissions would derive these funds from taxation of the social capital of firms. They would operate regionally where possible, though some national planning would be necessary.

These commissions would be political bodies in the sense that they would be made up of elected representatives of the people. They would not be chosen as representatives of the workers in the firms, but rather by the workers in general, in their capacity as citizens, who would presumably be in a better position to make decisions in the interests of society as a whole. The unit to be represented on the planning commissions will, therefore, be a political unit at the most local levels possible, rather than an economic unit (e.g., a firm or an industry).

The market-regulatory commissions will function to see to it that the market is free of abuses, such as price-fixing, monopolistic practices, violations of contract, or deceptive advertising or merchandising practices. These commissions are not intended to control the market, but to permit it to operate fairly and effectively. Like the planning commissions, the market-regulatory commissions will also be democratically elected entities representing the public.

Both the planning commissions and the market-regulatory commissions are necessary to correct malfunctions of the economy and to help it to meet social needs. Thus, although worker self-managed firms together with the market are seen as the principal moving force and adjustment mechanism, respectively, of the economy, nonetheless, these cannot be expected to meet all the needs optimally, or may sometimes meet them in a haphazard or distorted way. The commissions, in representing the general social interest, are thus balancing and corrective mechanisms, and can also foster innovation to meet important social and economic needs.

The fourth feature of the proposed scheme concerns the principles and mode of distribution of income. It combines elements of the two well-known principles of distribution according to work and distribution according to needs. The scheme excludes deriving income from investment or from exploitation of the work of others.

Most generally, income will be distributed by the workers in each firm, by a process of participatory democratic decision-making in which they determine the allocation of the net revenue of that firm among themselves. Since this is an autonomous democratic procedure, the principle that they use for distributing income is up to them. However, since the amount of net revenue to be distributed among the workers in a firm depends in part on their work, the principle of distribution of income is to this degree a principle of distribution according to work.

This principle is complemented by the principle of distribution according to need in important areas of social and economic life. Thus, individuals are assured of basic education and health care according to their needs. A principle of need should also be in effect with regard to means of subsistence, which should be available to those who are unable to work because of age or illness, or those who are unemployed. A system of social insurance, like those currently available in advanced societies, would be able to provide not only such basic means of subsistence but also the conditions of self-development to some degree.

Just as democracy is necessary in the economic sphere, so too is it necessary in the organization and relations of social and cultural life. Just how this democratization applies in these contexts would vary with the specific nature of the social and cultural institutions and activities. These include educational institutions, such as schools and universities; cultural institutions, such as museums and arts organizations; health services, that is, hospitals, community health organizations, etc.; welfare and social service agencies; scientific research centers; the media; sports; religious organizations; charitable organizations; and the wide variety of voluntary associations through which people pursue their social and cultural interests. One may also include under the general heading of social and cultural life, the family and other child-raising and living arrangements.

Here, as in the economic sphere, the institutions should be self-managing, and for the same reason: namely, to provide the conditions for the individuals' self-development by participating in the control of their own social activity. Thus, each such institution would be managed directly by all those who work in it if it is small enough, or would have a managing board made up of representatives of those who work there or those who are involved in the range of that institution's activities. More specifically, where the social or cultural institutions operate in the market and are therefore subject directly to considerations of what consumers want, it is sufficient to have the board made up of the workers in the institution, who together decide upon the policy and activities of that institution. Where the institutions are partly or wholly exempt from market function, and depend largely on public funds, it would seem appropriate to include on the board not only those who work in the institution but also representatives of those who benefit from or use the institution, as well as representatives from the public at large, or the state.[5] In addition, there are those institutions that have to take into account the needs of consumers in a way that is more direct than a market permits, even though such institutions may function in the market. In such cases, the managing boards should have representatives of the users, in addition to those who work in the institution. Examples of this latter type of institution would be privately funded universities or hospitals, which would operate in addition to those publicly funded ones that provide free or low-cost education and health benefits.

In social and cultural institutions, as in economic ones, self-management signifies that workers in such institutions, and (where relevant) representatives of those who use them or take part in their activities, have a right to participate in formulating policy and procedures. This is not to say that all members should participate in deciding on all aspects of the institution's operation.[6] Rather, all have a right to decide general matters of policy as well as to make decisions concerning those areas directly related to their functions. Furthermore, decisions that require special expertise in order to make competent judgments should be reserved to those who are certifiably competent to make such judgments. An example of this requirement of expertise would obviously be medical or surgical judgments.

Clearly, the requirement for the democratization of such social and cultural institutions does not mean the imposition of majority rule by the whole society upon these institutions or the intrusion of extrainstitutional constituencies upon

A model of democracy

their decision-making process. Such institutions retain their autonomy and adopt such democratization as an internal decision procedure.

With respect to the funding of these institutions, one would expect that some would operate wholly within the market, some would be publicly funded, some funded by firms, some privately funded, and many, perhaps most, would derive their funds from a mixture of these sources. It seems to me that in social and cultural affairs, such a proliferation of funding sources is important. Thus, for example, it would be good if the arts were funded from a multiplicity of sources in order to preserve diversity and to prevent any control by the state, as well as to prevent the subservience of the arts to market fashions or requirements.

The democratization of social and cultural institutions, as well as economic ones, can be fully effective only if there is reciprocity in interpersonal relations, that is, only if people generally relate to each other as equals and with respect for each other's individual differences and interests. For the very process of participatory democratic decision-making entails such reciprocal recognition. Conversely, the achievement of such reciprocity in personal relations generally requires certain institutional forms to support and encourage it.

Such recognition of equality in interpersonal relations, as a condition for democratization in social, economic, and political life, would have important consequences for relations between men and women. This equality would in practice require not only the elimination of discrimination and domination, and positively, equality of opportunity and equal pay for equivalent work, but also equal opportunities for self-development and men's equal responsibility for housework and childraising. It would also afford greater freedom to consider alternative forms of living arrangements and of childraising. In addition, extensive day-care facilities would be a prerequisite for the equal participation of women both in economic life and in social, cultural, and political activities. Conversely, the development of democracy in all these spheres would help effect a radical change in the status of women, for it would undermine the basis of domination by the few, predominantly men, who have the decision-making power over the conditions of the activity of women.

These proposals for the democratization of social and cultural life, together with economic democracy, bear upon the democratization of the political sphere to which I now turn.

Political life has traditionally been the domain in which democracy has been thought to apply. Democracy here has connoted forms of political representation, popular elections, and the protection of civil and political rights of individuals. Many of the features of existing political democracies would be carried over in the proposed model. This follows from the fact that, traditionally, political democracy has been based on the principle of equal negative freedom, which as we have seen is a precondition for equal positive freedom as the central principle of the view I have developed. Further, since a main thrust of my argument is the extension of democracy beyond the political sphere to the domains of economic and social life, it is apparent that my model of political democracy will incorporate many of the basic features of existing democratic practice. Thus, for example, one crucial aspect of democracy which I would adopt in my model is the constitutional protection of equal civil liberties or basic freedoms (such as freedom of speech, press, association) as well as equal political rights (such as the right vote, to be elected). In addition, such established practices of modern democratic states as the universal right to vote, periodic free elections, and a system of representation are basic features of the proposed model. The principle of the separation and balance of powers, characteristic of some contemporary democracies, is also of great importance, both with respect to the various functions of government, as well as the levels of government. Thus, the division of powers among the legislative, executive, and judicial functions of government, together with a system of checks and balances, helps to prevent any one of these branches of government from dominating the others. A similar check on the over-centralization of power is provided by the division of political decision-making into various levels, for example, local, state, regional, national. In addition, the separation of the political sphere itself from the economic sphere is also important in preventing the excessive concentration of power in either of these spheres. In this respect, this model differs from that of the Yugoslav *Praxis* theorists, specifically, that of Marković, who proposes the integration of the social, economic, and political spheres within the framework of political decision-making, such that the interests of these various spheres would be represented in some multicameral political body.[7] It seems to me that this would in effect lead to the subordination of the economic and social spheres to political decision-making and to the intrusion of the political into these other domains. The dangers of such supervening political power are well known.

Yet, even where modern political democracies possess all these features, these states are not fully democratic. This is in part because their political democracy is undermined by the lack of democracy in the economic and social spheres. Thus, the power of concentrated wealth can be used to influence the political process in its own interests. Or again, economic and social alienation may lead to feelings of political power-lessness and to voter apathy, leaving the process of govern-ing without genuine popular support. The democratization of economic and social life in the structure proposed here should contribute to the elimination of alienation and of the distortion of the political process by the power of money. The proposed structure would therefore permit the fuller realization of these forms of political democracy.

However, the achievement of political democracy in these senses is not yet sufficient for the full democratization of the political sphere. The crucial feature that is necessary is the addition of participatory forms in political life. Such participa-tory decision-making is characterized by direct and immedi-ate involvement in the process of decision-making by the individuals concerned. Thus, in this process, the authority of the individuals is not delegated to some representative but is exercised directly by them. Further, all the individuals have a right to engage in the discussion of matters for decision, and they codetermine the outcome by their vote, according to appropriate rules that they have adopted.

Such participation would require, first of all, local political institutions that have the power to decide local issues. This means the introduction of nonparty political organizations at the neighborhood or community level, which would themselves be part of the structure of government. These local political units would not merely delegate authority or choose representatives to higher bodies, but would themselves make decisions on a wide range of community issues.

Second, though a system of representation is necessary at higher levels of government, it is possible to introduce a greater degree of participation at those levels than exists in present forms of representative democracy, where participation is usually limited to voting for representatives. The process by which candidates for political office are nominated or selected can itself be democratized by being removed from the control of small political cliques or powerful economic interests. Where such electoral processes take place, as they most often do, within political parties, this requires that the party structures themselves be made more participatory. Beyond this, increased participation could be effected by the availability of well-structured and feasible mechanisms of referendum and recall. In the case of recall, a political constituency can choose to remove its representative from office outside of the ordinary electoral procedures, if its members judge that such a representative has failed in his or her function or has betrayed their trust. In a referendum, the possibility exists for a direct decision by the electorate, bypassing the usual means of decision-making by representatives.

Other means of involving the larger public in political decision-making at higher levels are the use of new electronic technology to make possible two-way consultations of constituents with their representatives and to permit the public to play an active role in formulating some of the issues to be considered by the legislature. Moreover, efforts can be made to involve a greater number of people in actively testifying at or participating in committee hearings, which may be made accessible to a larger public either by electronic means or by being held regionally. The new information technologies would also make feasible wide access to the background information necessary for effective participation in the political process. Thus, for example, immediate access to information about existing and pending legislation as well as other pertinent data can be made available to geographically disparate constituencies through telecommunications networks. However, the increased availability and accessibility of such information would not guarantee that it would be widely utilized. This would require an electorate confident that its response would be effective and that therefore it made a difference to be politically well-informed.

These proposals concerning the concrete structures and practices of economic, social, and political life are intended as realizations of the values and principles discussed earlier in the book and, in particular, those of equal positive freedom and of democracy. In the model I have presented here, the freedom of individuals may be seen to be compatible with their equality and sociality. Though this model draws on some existing social forms, I would propose that it constitutes a distinctive and coherent alternative to the prevailing systems.

Chapter 10

Technology and ethics: should technology be left to the experts?

INTRODUCTION

Contemporary advanced technology seems to be beyond the control and understanding of the vast majority of people. Like advanced science, it is the province of the experts. Such technology is esoteric in its theory and design; yet its impact on everyday political, economic, and social life is pervasive. The question arises whether all those who use the technology as well as, more generally, those whose lives and futures are affected by it have the right to a say in controlling it, or alternatively, whether control of technology should be left to the experts. This question may be posed as one of democracy versus technocracy. That is, in this domain of technology should there be rule by the people or rule by the experts? Furthermore, even if one argues that there is a moral and political requirement for democratic control of technology, it is unclear whether such control is feasible given the specialized and expert knowledge and training that contemporary advanced technology demands. Would not control of technology by an uninformed and untrained public threaten technological progress or lead to dangerous misuse of the technology? And further, would such democratization of technology require the dismantling of high technology and a return to simpler and less advanced forms?

It is clear that at present technology is not democratically controlled either by those who produce it and run it or by the consumers who use it or by the public that is affected by it more generally. This holds not only for research, design, and development of technologies, but also for planning and policy decisions concerning their use or application. Indeed, it is not evident who does in fact control technology, whether it is the designers, engineers, and technicians or instead the managers and owners of industry or the government and military who fund these technologies. In any case, technology seems to be controlled by only a small minority, whereas it affects everyone. The question therefore arises whether there should be democratic determination of the development and uses of technology and, if so, by whom – whether by the voters in a political process or by those more directly involved in the production and use of the technology. But this question of who should control technology suggests that there is a prior question that requires conceptual clarification, namely, what does "control of technology" mean? It will be seen that there are several senses of control here that need to be distinguished. Further, the resolution of the normative issue of who ought to control technology depends in part on an analysis of what the relation is between technology and those who design it, produce it, or use it, or more generally, are affected by it positively or negatively.

ETHICAL NORMS AND THE REQUIREMENT
FOR DEMOCRATIC CONTROL OF
TECHNOLOGY

Technology is essentially a means and not an end in itself. As an instrumentality for the realization of human purposes, it derives its value from the purposes that it serves and from how well it satisfies these ends. The normative question here is what are the ends which technology ought to serve and what are the values that determine the appropriate forms and uses of this technology. Any evaluation or critique of technology in ethical terms as well as any consideration of its appropriate organization and control must therefore derive from an account of what are the fundamental ethical values. These values, which I have discussed in previous chapters, are life, freedom, equality, and reciprocity. Further, I have argued that democracy as a principle of the organization of social life is a central value that is required by these others.

These normative considerations seem to lead to the requirement for democratic control of technology. For if only a small minority are able to control the technology that a large majority require as a means for their activity or as a condition for their well-being, or if a minority controls a technology that is harmful or dangerous to the majority, they are effectively denying to these others the equal right to control the conditions of their activity, which the principle of equal positive freedom demands. By contrast, what is required by the fundamental ethical values is an equal right to codetermine the uses to which the technology is put and the course of its development. With respect to the economy, this suggests that there ought to be rights of participation by all those in a firm—workers, as well as engineers or managers—in decisions concerning the uses of technology in that firm. It would also seem to require that the public at large, as consumers of technology, have a right to participate in decisions about its use and development. However, these conclusions from the ethical principles stand in apparent conflict with the practical and overriding need for expertise in matters concerning high technology.

Before turning to this central problem, I would like to consider the implications of the ethical framework I have proposed for a critique and evaluation of contemporary technology. Such a critical analysis will reveal whether technology serves the ends or values that it ought to serve or whether it in fact subverts these ends. It will also show how people are affected by this technology positively or negatively, which will provide a basis for the subsequent consideration of who ought to have the authority or responsibility for controlling this technology.

CONTEMPORARY TECHNOLOGY – SOME
POSITIVE AND NEGATIVE DIMENSIONS

The critique of contemporary technology is already well developed, for example, in the works of Marcuse, Ellul, Winner, Gendron, and Barbour.[1] Thus my own discussion will
focus only on those criticisms of technology and of the control of technology that may be made from the standpoint of
the fundamental ethical values presented earlier. I will also
consider the question of how technology is controlled and by
whom, and will offer an analysis of the several different
senses of control. But before proceeding with this criticism
and analysis, it may be helpful to review briefly some of the
positive features of technology in terms of the fundamental
ethical values discussed earlier. For otherwise, it might appear wrongly that technology, on the view presented here, is
inherently bad and that it has unmitigatedly harmful effects.

The positive evaluation of technology encompasses some
obvious and well-known features. Technological advances in
agriculture and industrial production have raised the level of
material welfare, at least in the advanced industrial nations.
Likewise, dramatic advances in medical and pharmaceutical
technology have led to the elimination and control of many
diseases, to decreased rates of infant mortality, and to greater life expectancy. In these ways, technology has contributed
to the provision of greater means of subsistence and to im-
proved health and thus has helped to realize the value of life.

Similarly, the value of freedom has been served by the
many ways in which technology creates new options for action. Thus in material and cultural life, in forms of transportation and communication and in many other ways, modern
technology has multiplied the opportunities for the development of individuals and of their social relations. Moreover,
technology itself has provided a domain for the expression of
human inventiveness and creativity. With respect to the
value of equality, the material abundance that technology
can produce provides the possibility for a wider and more

265

equal distribution of wealth. Further, the technologies for the mass reproduction and distribution of educational, cultural, and artistic products creates the opportunity for greater equality in these domains. Likewise, communication and transportation technologies widen and universalize the network of social interaction and make possible a fuller development of reciprocal social relations and social cooperation on a world scale.

Less obviously perhaps, technology may also be said to introduce the means of greater democratization, not only of political, but of economic, social, and cultural life. Thus, electronic technology is already capable of effecting more direct and immediate exchanges between people and their political representatives and could also be used to facilitate more participatory decision procedures, both in political and other contexts, as noted earlier. Furthermore, technology can provide some of the means for democratic control of technology itself. Such control no longer requires major centers or concentrations of power, but can be exercised in a decentralized way from any number of points with the help of information and communications technologies.

For all this, one may seriously criticize the effects of technology with respect to these same fundamental ethical values. With respect to life as such a basic ethical value, there are some obvious criticisms of the effects of technology, which need to be stated only summarily here. Clearly, contemporary military and industrial technology constitutes a major threat. This is most directly evident in military technology, which is deliberately designed to destroy life, most notably in the technology of nuclear warfare in which total destruction of human life and of the environment is threatened. Industrial technology, though it is not deliberately aimed at the destruction of life or of health, yet has caused death, injury, and disease, particularly in the working population. Such effects have occurred as a result of occupational hazards and associated diseases, as well as environmental pollution, among other causes.

With respect to the fundamental value of freedom, contemporary technologies make possible the intensification of control by few over the work activity of large numbers who require this technology as a means of their labor. Other effects of modern industrial technology on the work process include limitations on freedom of action and freedom of choice, which follow from the fragmentation and routinization of the work process, for example in Taylorism or in the so-called rationalization of work. At the same time, the introduction of new labor-saving technologies also leads to technological unemployment, with its deleterious consequences for the economic and psychological well-being of the workers. These various constraints on freedom that are associated with modern industrial technology have been extensively studied and criticized in terms of the concept of alienation.

In the domains of consumption, leisure, and cultural activities, the use of modern technologies of production and communication can lead to limitations of freedom of choice through the creation and manipulation of artificial needs and the control over the options available to the public, for example, by marketing and advertising techniques. Likewise, in the cultural media such as TV and newspapers, increasingly centralized control of technology restricts the options that are available to people.

Yet another limitation on freedom that is especially important in view of the sophisticated nature of high technology results from the lack of knowledge and understanding of such technology on the part of the public. High technology, which is based on advanced scientific and mathematical theories, is regarded as inaccessible and thus beyond the control of the public. Such control is thus presumed to be the province of experts. In this way, technological ignorance delimits the freedom of people to engage in rational decisions about technology.

Because of these and similar considerations, it has been argued by some critics that technology itself dominates people and that it is an "autonomous" force. However, such a view seems to me to be a case of technology fetishism or the reification of technology, in which it is treated as if it were itself an agent.² But technology, as I have suggested, is only an instrument and domination is exercised by people through it. That is, the technology itself makes no decisions about how it is to be used or which of its requirements are to be met, nor does it invent or design itself. At the same time, however, this is not to say that the forms of technology are simply neutral and completely open to either good or bad uses depending on the social relations in which they are used. Rather, some major forms of technology already embody social relations of domination and control, and lend themselves to such uses. Most notable here is military nuclear technology. But this is also evident in those modes of industrial technology that impose fragmented and unsatisfying tasks on the worker and that organize the work in such a way that it is subject entirely to supervision and control by others, with no autonomy for the worker.

Technology, used in these ways, violates not only the value of freedom, but also the values of equality and reciprocity. For domination is obviously an unequal and nonreciprocal social relation among individuals. Further, some of the forms of contemporary technological organization of work and of social life lead to the isolation of individuals from each other and to fragmented and anomic social relations. In these respects, reciprocity as the mutual recognition and cooperation among individuals is rendered difficult.

These criticisms of technology in terms of the violations of the ethical principles of life, freedom, equality, and reciprocity come together in the issue of democratic control of technology. In contrast to the forms of craft technology of an earlier period, contemporary forms of high technology involve very little control by those who use them or are affected by them. First, contemporary technology is largely mass technology, designed not for individual control but rather as a system in which in principle any individual user of the technology can be replaced by any other. Second, such mass systems lend themselves to direction from the top by a few individuals. In fact, large-scale technologies are owned or directed by private corporations, government agencies, or the military, in which decision-making power is often vested in top-level managers or policy makers. (However, some significant large-scale technologies like computer systems and networks lend themselves also to decentralized and relatively autonomous uses.) Third, design and technical control of complex systems depends on a relatively small core of technical experts who understand the functioning of such technologies. Fourth, decisions about which technologies are to be developed, expanded, or abandoned are not in general open to the participation of the consuming public, except to the extent that the market plays some role in determining the acceptability or use of certain products or procedures. Fifth, there is lack of control insofar as, in many cases, it cannot be predicted with any confidence what the long-range environmental effects of some new technologies may be, for example, space technology, use of chemical sprays and agents, or genetic engineering technologies. And sixth, there is little effective public participation in the planning and decision-making concerning the environmental effects of new technologies, either in the political sphere or in industry. In all of these ways, contemporary technology in general remains outside the domain of democratic participation and control, contrary to the normative requirement of democracy.

CONTROL OF TECHNOLOGY: AN ANALYSIS
OF THE CONCEPT

Although it is clear that technology is not democratically controlled, there remains the problem of determining who in fact does control it. The central question is whether technology is under the direction of corporate owners and managers, on the one hand, or of the technical experts whom they employ, on the other. Although managers or boards of directors have the authority and the power to make policy decisions, they often lack the technical training that would permit them to control high technology at the point of its design or use. Because of this, a certain and sometimes very

Rethinking democracy

large degree of de facto control of policy decisions concerning technology is in the hands of engineers or technicians, or is strongly influenced by their judgments. Of course, engineers are central in the design of technology and in its application in particular contexts; and in these respects, they may be said to control the technology. On the other hand, owners and managers remain central in determining policy, which has to take into account considerations of corporate profit or competitive advantage, and such policy may constrain the engineers' design and development of technology in these directions. One might mention in passing the additional complication that ownership and management are most often separate in large corporations and this leads to further questions about who controls technology. Further, in the increasingly large sphere of those technologies sponsored and used by the government, there is also the problem of who controls it, whether the representatively elected policy makers, or the appointed officials and bureaucracy, or again the technocrats who run the government technologies. There is the further question of possible control or major influence over government policies concerning technology by private corporations in the interest of their profit, or by the military in the interest of increasingly sophisticated war technology. A similar problem of determining who is in control arises concerning military technology itself. In this sphere, the contenders for control would seem to be government policy makers (since the military is an arm of the civilian government), the different military services vying for the most powerful military technologies, the military technicians and engineers who actually develop and operate the systems, and finally those private corporations whose production is largely aimed at military supply. Within this complicated framework of alternative sources of control, whether in corporate, governmental, or military contexts, one thing is clear: Control remains largely out of the hands of the vast majority of the workers who are involved in the use of the technology and of the people who are affected by it, either as consumers or in terms of its effects on their environment (with the exception, perhaps, of those policy decisions concerning technology that remain within the purview of elected representatives).

However, the foregoing considerations of who controls technology and of the issue of democratic control of technology presuppose some clear sense of what precisely it would mean to exercise such control. The control that an engineer or technician exercises in a missile launching is clearly different from the control that Pentagon planners have in deploying this technology. Or again, the control that a Detroit automotive design engineer has in modifying an exhaust system surely differs from the control that the Environmental Protection Agency exercises in regulating auto emissions. There are obviously several senses of "control of technology" that need to be distinguished.

In the case of the control by a technician or an operator of a specific piece of technological apparatus, where control means the ability to use that technology, and requires skill or know-how, we may speak of *technical* control. This would apply not only to highly skilled technicians but also to ordinary users of popular technology, for example, automobile drivers, typists, and users of household equipment. By contrast, the power to determine how and where a given technology will be used, and the assignment of its use to specific persons, is a form of managerial control which we may characterize as *tactical* control. It is tactical in the sense that it carries out in specific applications a more general policy or plan. Such policy making and planning concerning the direction of the development of a technology and decisions as to whether or not to deploy it constitute a higher level of managerial control which we may call *strategic*. Such strategic control functionally describes policy and planning practice in firms or in the economy as well as in government contexts. Technology assessment is relevant here as the evaluation that informs such strategic policy and planning decisions.

A different sense of control applies to the design of technology. Any given design determines a range of possibilities, within which the technology can be used. However, though a design may be intended to effect a specific purpose, the means that the design affords may be applied to very different purposes unintended by the designer. Yet, the formal and technical possibilities for any of these applications is limited by the design itself. This may be characterized as *design* control. It is distinct from strategic control, which is concerned with the choice of purposes for which the technology will be used. Where design controls the range of possibilities of utilization of technology, *regulatory* control determines what is permitted and prohibited in the design and use of technology. Such regulatory control can affect all the previously defined modes of control. There is one other distinction that may be made and that concerns the actual production of the technological means or apparatus. Those who produce the technology exercise a kind of control, with respect to their control both over the quality of the product[3] and over the actual act of production, including the power to cease production. This may be designated as *production* control.

Beyond these different senses of control, there are different ways in which the decisions about control may be reached in each case. For example, technical control is most typically a matter of individual judgment and skill, and thus of individual decision. Even where a complex technology demands many operatives working together, each one makes his or her own decision in applying judgment or skill to the operation. So too, tactical and strategic decisions about technology are usually made by middle and top management in firms, and by executive or appointed officials in government, though here elected representatives may play a role in both tactical and strategic decision-making (e.g., in approving legislation funding, and executive policy proposals). This suggests distinctions among different forms of decision-making, and we may see that these cut across the different types of control. Four such forms of decision-making suggest themselves: (1) individual, (2) hierarchical, (3) democratic, and (4) market. Whereas the senses of control discussed above characterize various functions, these four forms of control describe how and by whom decisions about the technology are made. Individual control in decision-making would seem to apply necessarily in the case of technical control and often in the case of design control. In hierarchical forms of technological control, the power or authority to make decisions is top-down, that is, the higher authority makes decisions of more general scope and may override the decisions of the lower authority. The authority at any level may be an individual or a group, for example, a committee or a board. The managerial (tactical and strategic) and regulatory control functions described above are most often of this type.

Democratic control of technology means, in the most general sense, that there is a right to participate in decision-making by all those engaged in the enterprise to which the decision refers. Such participation is usually by equal vote and decision is by majority, though a group may collectively decide to adopt a different decision rule. (Such cooperative decision-making, however, may be distinguished from forms of cooperative activity, which are not necessarily determined by democratic decision procedures, for example, cooperation in military or in surgical practice, where the decision-making is hierarchical.) At present, one may say that the only senses of control that are even partially democratic in this way are the forms of tactical and strategic control exercised by elected representatives in government policy making about technology and, very indirectly, regulatory control where it is sensitive to popular democratic influence. One may also include here the case of production control in which the decision to proceed with, or refrain from, the actual production of a technology is collectively and democratically made by the workers in a firm, for example, in a strike vote or in a decision not to produce a certain technology on the grounds that it is harmful or morally wrong.

Democratic control is obviously the kind that is of greatest importance for the discussion here of technology and democracy. The question is whether such a mode of democratic control is viable in the contexts of managerial and regulatory decision-making, whether in industry or government. That is, is workers' self-management a feasible and normatively desirable mode of control of technology? Likewise, is a more fully participative form of political democracy an improvement over current relatively indirect modes of democratic control of technology in government? On the basis of my previous arguments concerning the normative requirement for democracy, it is clear that the answer to these questions is affirmative. However, I will limit my analysis (later in this chapter) to the question of the democratization of technology in economic contexts.

Beyond the contexts of managerial and regulatory control, the question of democratic decision-making is simply not relevant in the case of technical control, which is exercised by an individual alone. And such democratic decision-making would seem to be less than optimal in design control, where design by committee is generally infelicitous. However, design teams in complex engineering projects often engage in successful cooperative activity, though usually not by any democratic decision procedure.

Finally, there is a form of social decision-making that indirectly operates to control technology, and that is the market. In a market economy, consumers of technology provide feedback to the designers and managers of technology by their economic choices. The market therefore has an influence upon decision-making – whether in individual, hierarchical, or democratic modes – in the contexts of management and design. In a certain sense, this feedback is like that provided by technology assessment: Both are tests of how well the means provided by certain technologies serve the ends of the users.

THE DEMOCRATIZATION OF TECHNOLOGY
AND THE PROBLEM OF EXPERTISE

One of the central problems for the democratization of technology is the requirement for specialized scientific and technical knowledge and training, which is posed by contemporary high technology. It was one of the main inferences of my argument earlier that technology in general should be democratized in order to realize the fundamental ethical values I proposed. In the case of low technology, such democratization poses no major problem of feasibility. Such low technology includes craft and industrial techniques, which are already accessible to and well understood in their function by the majority of those who utilize them in their work and social activity. Examples of such technology are the standard machines of industrial production, for example, lathes, drills, and presses, which skilled or semiskilled workers understand. Similarly, common mechanical and electronic devices such as the automobile, telephone, typewriter, and even such more sophisticated devices as personal computers and word processors may be regarded as relatively low technology, though recently developed. The claim here is that those involved in the production and use of such technologies in work contexts should contribute to decisions concerning such production and use. Furthermore, in the case of large-scale public technologies (e.g., transportation, energy, and communication), the consumers should have a say in decisions concerning their use or development. In these cases of low technology, the technical expertise required for rational judgments about production and use is within the comprehension of the skilled and semiskilled workers in the industries that produce or use them. Such technical expertise is also accessible to the public at large as part of the culture.

However, with high technologies, the case appears on the face of it to be different. Such high technologies as electronic engineering, computer design, genetic engineering, space technology, and aerodynamics are not generally accessible to either the workers in these fields or to the public. The understanding of these technologies is the province of scientists and engineers and requires expertise and specialized training. If the knowledge of such technology is one of the main prerequisites for the ability to control or direct it, then how can one speak of democratizing such control? The choices seem to be either turning everyone into scientists and engineers or abandoning expertise and permitting everyone, whether knowledgeable or not, to make decisions, thereby losing the benefits of technological development. This poses the apparent dilemma of technocratic versus democratic control of technology.

A resolution of this dilemma can only be found if in fact there is a way of introducing democratic participation in the control of technology while at the same time preserving the essential role of expertise. In economic contexts, the issue of democratization of technology would concretely arise with respect to such major functions of firms as planning, production, and marketing, and (where applicable) research and development. Each of these functions involves the use of different technologies, and therefore the specific form of democratization and the degree to which it is practically feasible would vary in each case. Thus, for example, production involves machine technology, information technology, and the techniques of quality control. Planning and marketing involve the use of statistical and forecasting technologies, and systems analysis; while research and development centrally involves design and engineering technologies. It may be seen that the form of democratic decision-making has to be interpreted differently for each of the senses of control analyzed earlier where such democratization is relevant, namely, managerial control (tactical and strategic), which includes policy and planning; regulatory control; production control; and within the limits to be discussed, even design control, which includes research and development. (It will be recalled that technical control is a matter of individual decision-making, and therefore the question of democratization is irrelevant here.)

In general, democratic decision-making concerning technology in the contexts of economic life would be an aspect of that democratization earlier discussed as workers' self-management. In a worker self-managed firm, the purposes for which technologies are to be used should be determined by all those who work in the firm, in consultation with those members of the firm who are experts (or with external ones). The experts could determine the feasibility of these goals, perhaps proposing various models for their realization, from which the members of the firm would choose the one to be implemented. In this way, the members of the worker self-managed firm all have a right to an input into discussions about the policy of the firm and also into the decision of how these should be put into practice in terms of the requisite technology. This would constitute democratization at the level of managerial control involving policy and planning decisions, as well as the ways in which these decisions are to be implemented. Furthermore, such worker participation in decisions on technology would add an emphasis on important parameters of work activity that are presently often neglected by management. For in addition to being interested in efficiency, productivity, and profitability, as is the usual case with management, members of a worker self-managed firm would be prone to be more sensitive to the impact that the use of given technologies would have on their conditions of work and the quality of work life. They might well also be responsive to issues of consumer need and environmental effect, since they are themselves also consumers and residents of the local area.

The function of the experts on this model remains largely what it is at present, that is, to provide the best design and the most efficient, appropriate, and cost-effective methods for attaining the goals of the firm. Beyond this, technical experts or engineers could facilitate the democratic decision-making process by interpreting the engineering options for the other workers and informing them of the implications or side effects of these various alternatives. Furthermore, the cost–benefit analysis that is used to assess potential new products or methods would involve the technical experts in considering parameters that are not ordinarily included at present. For example, in the context of planning and decision-making with the other workers, the engineers might be more prone to include such factors as quality of work life, health, and well-being of the workers, as well as the workers' own recommendations as to how the work process might best be organized. Additional cost–benefit considerations would also include the social costs of environmental pollution in their locale.

Such changes in the experts' relation to the work process and the changes in the approach to cost–benefit analysis would derive from the fact that the ultimate decision-making authority in the firm now would rest with all the members of the firm, and the experts could be expected to take the needs of their co-workers more seriously into account than is the case at present. Moreover, since the technicians and engineers in such worker self-managed firms would themselves be members of the firm and comanagers with the others, such technical experts would have interests beyond their narrow specialities, since they would now be involved with the others in general policy and planning decisions. They would thus be concerned with the determination of goals and not merely with providing the technological means for goals determined by others.

The preceding forms of democratization, considered here initially in the context of managerial control, and the establishment of institutionalized cooperation between technological experts and other workers in a firm, may also be seen to apply in the contexts of regulatory, and of production control. Insofar as a firm or an entire industry may institute its own regulations concerning conditions of work, product design, and safety, etc., such regulations function as modes of self-governance in the cases where the decisions are made jointly by the very same people who are affected by them. Thus economic self-regulation by worker self-managed firms with respect to the uses of technology is analogous to government regulation of such technology – for example, in emission standards and other pollution controls and safety regulations – when such government regulation is determined by a democratic process. Just as in managerial control, expertise in the areas of regulatory control at the level of a firm would be put at the disposal of all the members of a firm who would then jointly decide which regulations are necessary.

In the ordinary firm, where workers have no role in management, production control is the power that workers can exercise over whether or not to carry on production. This power may be exercised by an individual worker alone or may be exercised democratically, as in a decision to strike by a union. In a worker self-managed firm, control over the actual production of a technology becomes identical with managerial decisions about production, since the workers ultimately have the power in managerial decisions to proceed with or refrain from producing a certain technological item. (Although, on the model I present, the workers may delegate managerial decision-making to managers whom they appoint, they retain ultimate decision power and may choose to exercise it in matters of policy and planning.) Further, quality control in the ordinary firm is traditionally an engineering function, separated from the workers' activity in production, and serving as a means of screening and eliminating defective items. In democratic control of technology, such quality control would become integral to the work process itself and would be the collective responsibility of all the workers.

I suggested earlier that design control may suffer if democratic forms of decision-making were applied to it, for the obvious reason that majority votes do not conduce to, much less guarantee, optimal engineering design. Here, the judgment of the experts would seem to be best. Nevertheless, there are two elements of democratic participation in design that remain feasible and which do not compromise expertise. First, there is the input that the workers in a firm may provide to the design engineers, on the basis of the workers' own knowledge of the production process and of the technology that they are using or producing. Second, as suggested, since the goals of a firm are determined democratically by all the members of it (including production workers and design engineers among others in the firm, in consultation with each other), these goals provide parameters for the design process.

The feasibility of such a model for the democratization of technology may seem problematic at first glance, for it may be taken to suggest that the technical experts who are now presumed to be in authority would be subordinated to the popular will of nonexpert workers to whom the experts would then be accountable. However, the fact is that at present, technological experts do not function in the fully autonomous way that this view supposes, but are often subject to the external authority of owners and managers of the corporations that employ them. Moreover, on the proposed model, these experts would not be accountable to the workers as their new authorities but would rather constitute, together with them and with the other members of the firm, a self-governing body. Furthermore, there is no reason to suppose that the role of expertise would be diminished in any way, or less highly valued, in worker self-managed firms than it is in corporations at present. For the members of the firm would all be vitally interested in the success of the enterprise and therefore in the most thorough utilization of the technological expertise available to it. Yet, because of the distinctive and new features of the social relations between workers and experts on this model, its full implementation would require changes in the education and orientation of both workers and technical experts. The workers would have to attain a higher level of understanding of technology so that they could participate rationally and effectively in making general policy decisions concerning it. Similarly, the engineers and technicians should be educated about the relations of technology to ethics and of technology to society, so that such concerns would play a role in their technological thinking itself.

POSSIBLE CONFLICTS BETWEEN
DEMOCRACY AND THE FUNDAMENTAL
ETHICAL VALUES

It is conceivable that a democratically taken decision concerning technology could be in violation of one of the fundamental ethical values such as life or freedom. For although the people are in general the best judges of their own interest, yet because of imperfect knowledge or fear, they may be led to decisions that either are against their own best interest or contravene fundamental values. This is a general problem of democracy, which is not peculiar to the question of technology. However, there is perhaps a special difficulty with respect to contemporary advanced technology, whether in worker self-managed firms or in the context of political democracy. For the extensive public ignorance and fear of high technology may lead to decisions that are irrational or which threaten life or liberty. In such cases, the question arises whether it is ever right to override democratically made decisions if fundamental values are violated by them. In short, should the public be overruled when it is wrong, and if so, by whom? This concerns the issue of the ordering of values, and specifically, how the value of democracy stands with respect to the other fundamental values.

Without going into the deep philosophical issues here, I would claim first that democracy is more than a mere means for the achievement of the basic values. Rather, it is the best and proper institutional embodiment that gives expression to the values of life and of equal positive freedom. Therefore, democratic decisions have an ethical status which must be taken very seriously and questioned only in extraordinary contexts. However, the values of life and freedom are ethically prior even to democracy. The priority of these values, expressed in the basic rights of individuals to the protection of life and freedom, supports ethical acts of conscience against democratic decisions that violate these rights. Such rights also provide the basis for a system of judicial appeal in order to protect them, even against a democratically taken decision. In both of these cases – of conscience and of appeal to the courts – the normative force of the fundamental ethical values is affirmed and they serve as criteria of judgment.

Further, because of the centrality of these values, democratic decisions about technology ought to take them as a guide. That is, these decisions should strive to enhance life and equal positive freedom by means of the uses to which technology is put.

Even though I have posed the problematic case in which

Chapter 11

The democratic personality: self-development, character, and political participation

INTRODUCTION

Authoritarianism and the authoritarian personality have been central themes in the political philosophy and political psychology of the last several decades. Thus there have been such noteworthy studies as that of the authoritarian personality by Theodor Adorno, Max Horkheimer, and other members of the Frankfurt School, as well as studies of the nature of authority and authoritarianism by Hannah Arendt. The emphasis on these themes within political theory was not surprising given the prevalence of the phenomenon of authoritarian regimes in this century. The authoritarian personality in these contexts is an ambiguous concept, since it connotes both the personality of an authoritarian or dominating leader with its various psychological and political implications, and the personality of those who crave domination and authority and who are "born followers." However, there has not been comparable attention paid to what we may call the democratic personality, or to the social and political environment that fosters it. This may be because the democratic personality has not presented itself in such historically singular and traumatic paradigms as those of the authoritarian personality as leader, such as Napoleon, Bismarck, Hitler, and Stalin, among others, and its complement, the authoritarian character as led. Another reason for this relative neglect may be that traditional democratic theory holds that democracy is essentially a government of laws, not of men, and that therefore personality is consigned to the sphere of private life, rather than political life. Yet, historically, there have been notable treatments of the democratic character of individuals as a condition for democracy, for example by Alexis de Tocqueville, Walt Whitman, John Stuart Mill, and John Dewey, as well as by such socialist theorists as Kropotkin and Robert Owen. Recently, as well, with the upsurge of interest in participatory democracy in the late sixties, there have been some initial studies of the relation between character and democratic politics, for example, by C.B. Macpherson and Carole Pateman.

In this chapter, I want to raise the question of what general features of character conduce to a form of democracy that emphasizes participation and which extends not only to the political realm but to the economic and social realms as well. Thus one may ask: What specific traits of character lead to political participation by the individual or to the assumption of responsibility in the making of social or collective decisions? Are character traits like tolerance for the views of others, altruism, and a sense of justice requisite for the functioning of democracy? Such an approach implies that certain traits of character are politically relevant and that one can reconstruct what may be called a democratic personality. However, as we shall see, it would be a mistake to think of such a democratic character as having some fixed set of essential traits. In this chapter, I shall also consider to some degree a question which is the converse of the first. Whereas the first question asks what is the personality or character that is appropriate to participation in democratic institutions, the second one asks how would such democratic forms of political and economic life contribute to the development of individual character.

I should remark here, parenthetically, that although there may be some distinction in usage between the terms *character* and *personality*, such that *character* (as used in the Aristotelian tradition) refers to virtues, vices, and other features that mark certain kinds of people, while *personality* suggests an individual and unique manner or style, I shall employ the terms interchangeably in what follows.

One additional qualification may be made at the outset. I do not suppose that the existence of traits of democratic character would in and of themselves produce institutional forms of democracy. Rather, the prevalence of some such traits may be a necessary but not a sufficient condition for democratic institutions. Similarly, the converse holds, namely, the existence of democratic institutional forms does not necessarily produce any particular set of character traits among individuals. Nonetheless, although personality is not determined by social institutions, it requires certain institutions and opportunities as conditions for its full elaboration.

In this chapter, I will focus on two general features of personality that may be seen as conditions for participative forms of democracy in political and economic life. These are democratic agency and the disposition to reciprocity. It is through the analysis of these basic categories of action and interaction that I propose to develop a conception of the democratic character.

DEMOCRATIC AGENCY AND THE DISPOSITION TO RECIPROCITY

One of the principal requirements for a fully developed form of democracy is that the participants must be active in the process of decision-making as well as in the execution of such decisions. This conception of agency as a fundamental feature of the democratic personality has been elaborated recently by C.B. Macpherson and Carole Pateman. It may be useful to begin this analysis by considering Macpherson's view of such agency and its relation to democracy.

In his various writings, Macpherson reconstructs liberal democratic theory as resting on two conflicting claims about liberal democracy, which in turn imply conflicting conceptions of human nature. The first is the claim that liberal democracy maximizes individual satisfactions or utilities. It thus sees the human being as essentially a consumer of goods or an appropriator. In this first conception, there is a right of unlimited appropriation or accumulation, which leads to the concentration of power in the hands of a few and thus to control by them over the powers of others. The second claim of liberal democracy, according to Macpherson, is that it maximizes human powers and not only utilities. This claim implies an alternative conception of human beings as active exercisers and developers of their own powers.[1] In contrast to the first conception of individuals as consumers which Macpherson identifies with the development of liberal theory from Locke to James Mill, this second conception, associated with John Stuart Mill, T.H. Green, and others, introduces into democratic theory a traditional Aristotelian conception of human beings as purposeful, self-developing agents.[2] Thus, according to Macpherson, liberal democratic theory is comprised of two claims about the nature of human beings and the ends of society, which are in conflict with each other.

The distinction that Macpherson draws between the individual as developer of his or her powers and the individual as consumer suggests the related traditional distinction between action and passion, which I would like to develop further here. In the traditional view, for example in Aristotle, Descartes, or Spinoza, *action* is understood as self-activity and *passion* as that reaction or response which is the result of being acted on by another. This distinction of activity and passivity is also manifest in Kant's contrast of autonomy and heteronomy. Along these lines, consumption as the satisfaction of desire is a response to a need for something external to oneself and in this sense is a passion or a dependency. The individual is passive in the sense of being driven by desires and dependent on the external things that would satisfy them. In liberal theory, as Macpherson suggests, human beings are characterized as infinite desirers and therefore infinite appropriators in order to satisfy these unlimited desires. This in turn leads, on his view, to the appropriation of the powers of others, that is, to control over others, as a means of satisfying one's own unlimited desires. But this, I would observe, has an apparently paradoxical result: namely, that infinite desire and thus passivity is transformed into an active power over others that is required for its satisfaction. But this power or control over the activity of others or its utilization for one's own ends leads at the same time to the dependency of these others and thus to their passivity in another sense, that is, with respect to the power that others hold over them or with respect to the lack of control over their own powers.

By contrast, the emphasis on the development of one's powers presupposes self-activity, that is, the initiation of purposes and projects of one's own, for the reason that one's own powers or capacities cannot be developed by someone else's activity. And, as I argued earlier, this entails that self-development cannot take place if one's activity is controlled by others. Moreover, such self-developing activity cannot be subordinated to the mere activity of meeting needs that are determined externally. Rather, if consumption is to contribute to the development of one's power, it is only to the degree that it is subject to the purposes and rational choices of agents, with respect to *which* needs or wants are to be met and also *how* they are to be met.

The priority of activity to passivity and of self-development to the simple satisfaction of needs follows from the centrality of the value of self-development as the meaning of human freedom. This is the fundamental value in the theory that I am proposing. Macpherson also holds that self-development is the fundamental value that a democratic form of society should serve to realize. However, in what follows, I use this concept, which I have discussed at length earlier, in a way somewhat different from Macpherson. Perhaps the main difference is that his concept of self-development is based on an essentialistic interpretation of human capacities and powers, whereas I regard the capacities to be developed not as given in the nature of things but as fundamentally open to the choices of agents.

Before considering the implications of the active–passive distinction for democratic participation, I want to suggest a qualification of the sharp dichotomy between these two polarities. If consumption is regarded as passive in the sense of being subject to external needs, consumption is nonetheless also a kind of activity. Moreover, a sharp separation between self-development and consumption disregards the fact that self-development requires consumption as a condition, both in the sense of the meeting of basic needs and in the sense of the utilities required for the development of specific capacities. More abstractly, one might say that passivity is a kind of activity, as Leibniz says, insofar as the way in which the passive individual receives an action or an exercise of power upon that individual is reactive or responsive and not simply passive reception. Thus for example, listening might originally be considered as passive in relation to speaking as active. But as Collingwood points out, listening to music or to a scientific lecture is not simply hearing the sounds but rather actively reconstructing the meaning.[3] Conversely, one may say that self-activity requires a kind of passivity, in the form of receptivity. For example, artistic creation requires not just activity, but simultaneously a receptivity to experiences, to the qualities of the medium and the requirements of form, or responsiveness to an audience. Likewise, in contexts of social interaction, self-activity requires at the same time an awareness of the actions and reactions of others, as these may serve to modify one's own actions. Thus, although it seems correct to give priority to activity over passivity, or to self-development over consumption, it is wrong to conceive of them as mutually exclusive.

How is this emphasis on activity or self-development relevant to democracy and thus to what we have called democratic character? We have seen that Macpherson ascribes to liberal democracy two alternative and conflicting views concerning human nature. His claim is that the first conception, which regards individuals as essentially consumers and as having a right to unlimited appropriation, is incompatible with democracy in the full sense, since it leads to the power of some over others (what Macpherson calls extractive power) and thus denies these others the opportunity for self-development. The second conception of human beings – as active exercisers and developers of their own powers – is, on

Macpherson's view, one that is compatible with full democracy and which it is the function of democratic society to enhance. I agree with Macpherson concerning the priority of the value of self-development as the foundation of democratic theory, though, as I have indicated, I interpret it somewhat differently. I also agree with his further claim made in a later work that participatory democracy is that form of democratic structure that provides the most suitable conditions for the self-development of individuals. Here I want to focus on an issue that Macpherson does not deal with in his theory, namely, what are the ways in which agency or self-activity as against passivity is articulated in the processes of participation and democratic decision-making or, in effect, what are the characteristics of the democratic personality in this context.

The first thing to note concerning the features of democratic agency is that it is not the agency of an isolated individual considered outside of any social context, but is rather the exercise of this power in free association with the agency of others. Further, the purpose of this association is to arrive at joint decisions and joint actions concerning matters of common interests and needs. The presupposition of such an association of agents is that they are equally agential; that is, as human beings they each have an equal basic capacity for free choice and decision. On the basis of this equal agency, as I have argued, they all have an equal right to participate in the codetermination of those actions in which they are jointly engaged. Such joint activities in institutional contexts or organizations clearly extend beyond the domain of political democracy where such joint decision-making is customarily recognized. It also pertains to contexts of economic, cultural, and social organizations as well, where, I have argued, there is a similar right of codetermination. An important context here is that of economic production where the firm becomes the locus of such codetermination or self-management by all those who work on it.

The first trait of character that is needed in such contexts is initiative. This trait emphasizes the quality of activity as against passivity which we noted earlier. Initiative is a complex trait and its significance here in part depends on the social context of democratic participation. Since participation in democratic decision-making cannot in principle be coerced or forced upon one, the forming of any structure of participation and its continuing function depend on the free act of association upon the initiative of agents. Moreover, to initiate such an action requires an understanding of the function of the organization one is joining and therefore an awareness of the relation of one's own interests or needs to the common interests of the group. Thus one may say that participation requires what one might call rational initiative and not merely initiative as willfulness or as simply a feature of one's temperament. It is rational in that it typically requires reasons for acting as well as self-understanding. The reasons have reference to considerations that would hold for anyone with certain purposes or in a certain circumstance (say, as co-workers in a given firm), and the self-understanding would be a determination that these reasons apply to one's own situation.

A second basic character trait of the democratic personality is what one may call a disposition to reciprocity. This is a relational character trait, expressible only in a situation of social interaction, which involves an ability to understand the perspective of the other as equivalent to one's own, and a readiness to act with respect to the other in ways that are equivalent to the other's actions with respect to oneself, as well as to have an expectation that the other will understand and act similarly. Thus, epistemologically, the structure involves a shared understanding by the participants that their actions are reciprocal. That is, reciprocity is an intentional relation constituted by the shared understanding by the agents that their relation is a reciprocal one. A number of sociologists, anthropologists, and political theorists regard reciprocity as the fundamental structure or as a tacit presupposition of human association.[4] I shall discuss various contemporary interpretations of reciprocity as a social relation – by Kohlberg, Rawls, and Habermas – later in this chapter. Here, however, the focus is on certain features of it as a character trait.

One of the essential features of this relation is a reciprocity of perspectives, which goes beyond the limits of one's own view and makes possible the establishment of a shared point of view, as well as an explicit understanding of differences in point of view. This requires receptivity to others' views as a character trait. Thus, for example, in the negotiation of nuclear disarmament, it is necessary for each side to understand the other's need for security and fear of attack in order to establish the common ground for a moratorium on testing or for deescalation. In the absence of such receptivity to the other's perspective there is little hope for resolution of differences by any means other than coercion or military force. In a context of democratic participation, two opposed positions, for example, on the plan of production in a firm, may be mediated by a recognition by the different sides of the need to compromise. Or it may be that good arguments on one side may persuade the others to agree. Receptivity therefore connotes an openness to alternative arguments and views.

A fundamental feature of the disposition to reciprocity is the recognition by an individual of the others with whom he or she is associated as equally agents. Such a recognition would include respect for others as individuals with purposes of their own and respect for their rights, where these rights include their basic equal rights as human beings and their specific rights within a given institutional structure. Such respect for others and a recognition of their rights is related to fairness and to what Rawls calls the sense of justice. Without this recognition of the equal rights of others and an appreciation of their interests and needs, democracy can become simply a contest of wills and powers, and tends toward tyranny of the majority.

The disposition to reciprocity expresses itself in the agreement on procedures which is necessary to forming an association and to its ongoing functioning. Any agreement, of course, is a reciprocal relationship: If A agrees with B, then B agrees with A. An agreement on procedures is therefore a reciprocal action in which different agents agree on how decisions will be made among themselves and also agree to abide by and carry out such decisions. Within the context of such procedural agreement on modes of making decisions, there may also be a procedure for agreeing to disagree, that is, where decisions are bracketed.

Perhaps the most prominent trait that has been traditionally ascribed to the democratic character is that of tolerance. This trait is related to the disposition to reciprocity in the sense that it suggests that each agent should reciprocally accept differences in the other and not require conformity by the other to any given set of beliefs or modes of behavior. Such an attitude of tolerance is clearly required in any democratic form of association, whether representative or participatory. However, such tolerance is limited to the recognition that individuals have the right to do whatever is not harmful to others. It is thus an expression of negative liberty as a freedom from interference. Such toleration does not yet include the relationship of respect, or what I have called social reciprocity, which would be required for democracy in the sense that I have proposed. This goes beyond tolerance (taken as an external relation to the freedom of others) to include also an understanding of the aims and interests of the other as worthy of consideration and possibly also of support.

The relation of mutuality was characterized (in Chapter 1) as that form of reciprocity in which each individual considers the other's needs and actively attempts to enhance the other's undertakings and self-development and, moreover, where each of the agents takes such mutual enhancement as a conscious aim. Such mutuality is not taken here to be a political or social condition for democracy. It entails an altruism that is supererogatory in these contexts. Yet, in democratic institutions, the joint activity of the members in the realization of a common aim may have the character of mutuality if the participants each consciously act at least in part with a view to benefiting the others. For example, in a trade union, the relations would be those of mutuality if each member consciously undertook his or her actions so as to contribute to the realization of the purposes of the others, for example, for job security or adequate wages, as well as to his or her own. Such a relation of mutuality obviously goes beyond tolerance in the active concern of each agent for the other's self-development or welfare, as against the mere refraining from interference with the activity of the other, which is required by tolerance.

Another character trait that is a corollary to several of those discussed above is flexibility and open-mindedness. This is clearly related to receptivity and to the disposition to reciprocity, since it requires taking the views and interests of others seriously. Flexibility and open-mindedness with respect to the opinions and arguments of others requires rationality, since it presupposes the comprehension of alternative views and frameworks. Only on the basis of such a comprehension of the reasons that others have for their views can one then attain to a critical or appreciative attitude toward such alternatives. This flexibility and open-mindedness has long been regarded as a mark of scientific character, that is, as the quality of mind that ensures objectivity and disinterestedness in science. Its role in democratic decision-making is likewise evident.

Commitment and responsibility are character traits that may also be noted here as relevant to the democratic personality. The specific relevance of these traits in the context of democratic association is that no such association can survive unless the commitment to continue within its framework and according to the rules that have been adopted is maintained. Responsibility to abide by the decisions in which one has participated and to act in accordance with such decisions is likewise a precondition for the viability of any democratic institution. However, because commitment here is understood as a free act, it is subject to being revoked if in the judgment of the agent it is not reasonable.

Finally, we may consider certain character traits that have been traditionally associated primarily with women, for example, supportiveness, sharing, communicativeness. I would argue that these traits are not feminine by nature but are rather historically contingent traits that have developed out of women's experience.[5] Moreover, they are clearly not exclusively women's traits. These characteristics, which are manifested in cooperativeness and a concern for community, while not strictly necessary for democratic decision-making, would clearly be relevant to the democratic personality. Yet, the expression of these traits has most often been relegated to the domain of personal life, while public life in the political and economic domains has largely been marked by the egoistic pursuit of self-interest in competition with others, and by authoritarian or hierarchical models of social relations in which the emphasis is on individual power or control over others. These features have been historically associated with male-dominant forms of action and organization (though these are no more gender-based by nature than are the "feminine" traits discussed earlier). It is in view of the model of conflicting individual interests that the traditional form of political democracy has often been understood as a means for mediating such conflict. If, however, the alternative character traits historically with women were to play a fuller role in political life, this could effect a change in the very procedures and structures of democratic decision-making as they are now practiced. For example, in place of the typical hierarchies of leadership that mark even the most advanced liberal individualist democracies, there could develop more egalitarian and participatory decision-making procedures; and in place of the competition of individual self-interests, there could emerge more cooperative and communal ways of pursuing common interest. This would introduce what one might characterize as political androgyny, that is, an opening up of the options for democratic decision-making to modes derived from the experience and character formation historically associated with women, as well as those typically identified with men.[6]

OBJECTIONS

Having sketched some leading traits of the democratic personality in their functioning in the context of participation, I want now to consider a serious objection that has been raised against such a view. This objection is directed against the general view that I have been espousing here, namely, that activity and self-development are the foundations of democratic character and are also values that a democratic society should serve to enhance. The argument offered in such criticism has two aspects: First, the account I have offered of human agency is empirically false in its description of human beings and unrealistic in its expectations of what they would be willing to undertake. It is argued that, in general, people do not tend to act as autonomous agents, but rather seek to follow, or subordinate themselves to, authority and on the whole prefer to have decisions made for them. Therefore, the expectation of self-activity and the norm of self-development through such activity are unrealistic and only rarely apply to actual cases, for example, to leaders but not to the mass of people. Second (the argument continues), because this view of agency is empirically false and unrealistic, wide participation in democratic decision-making, which moreover is proposed to extend even beyond the realm of politics, is simply not feasible.

The evidence offered in support of these objections is that historically people have most often tended to accept or even support forms of authority in which decision-making was in the hands of others. And even in the present, when opportunities for participation in decisions – for example, in U.S. elections – are available, only a minority of those who are eligible in fact actively participate. And even this degree of activity exhibits itself only in the occasional practice of voting; in forms of ongoing participation it is even less evident. The conclusion therefore is that the account of agency and participation that I have given is erroneous in fact and irrelevant as an ideal. In place of such a view, some critics who have advanced such objections have offered alternative models of democracy better suited to their views of human behavior, for example, as primarily a method of choosing among elites who then exercise their authority to make policies.[7]

The first objection – that the account given of human agency is empirically false – may be met by the following argument.

Historically it is not in fact the case that people have generally accepted or supported external authority over them, but rather that such authority was imposed upon them by coercion and very often by force. Thus the history of conquests, that of military police states, and the suppression of protests and rebellions is a long one. Furthermore, where people have seemed to passively accede to or willingly support external authority, this can very often be understood in terms of strong socialization and ideological persuasion which taught attitudes of subordination to authority as a virtue and insubordination as a punishable vice. Thus the historical evidence does not support the premise of the objectors concerning the facts of human nature.

The contemporary evidence drawn from the analysis of political behavior in democratic states is likewise vulnerable to criticism. Thus one may argue that the fact that people fail to vote or to participate in democratic processes is not the result of their unwillingness to be active or to exercise their powers but rather is because they believe their activity in these instances would be futile, that is, that they would not be exercising any real power. They regard such procedures as a sham or merely ritual. The claim can be made that if such participation in voting or in other decision procedures were regarded as really effective, then greater numbers would participate. And in fact, studies of participation in relation to beliefs concerning efficacy have shown that this is the case, namely, that where people believe their participation is effective, they are more likely to participate.[8]

Thus neither the historical nor the contemporary evidence would seem to support the claim that human beings prefer to accept authority rather than to exercise their agency and thus prefer to be passive rather than active. Yet the objection further maintains that because human beings are not in general disposed to act as autonomous agents, it is not reasonable to expect that they would take an active role in democratic associations and that therefore participatory forms of democracy are not feasible.

One counterargument that I would offer is that judgments

of feasibility cannot be based on the factual evidence that in the past people have not in general exhibited the requisite activity or commitment. For it may be the case that the necessary conditions for such activity were lacking. In this case, such necessary conditions would be the existence of democratic structures that would permit such participation. Of course, it may be the case that even where such possibilities for participation exist, they would not necessarily be utilized. Such democratic structures are necessary but not sufficient conditions for active participation.

A further argument may begin by granting the point that people often do not evidence a willingness to participate actively in political contexts even where the structures exist. But this does not show that they would not or cannot. We may recall the earlier point that people tend not to participate if they doubt that their participation would have any real effect, but that if they believe it will, then their participation is forthcoming. It is therefore plausible to suppose that if people had the opportunity to make effective choices about what really mattered to them, the degree of their participation in such contexts would increase. Thus for example, if workers could participate in important decisions concerning their work process and concerning the economic policies of their firms, or again, if people perceived their voting decisions as making an important difference in political policies, then they could be expected to participate actively. Further, one may argue as Pateman does (following Rousseau and Mill) that the initial experience of participation would reinforce this activity of participation itself and thus would lead to increasingly greater degrees of participation.[9] Thus as J.S. Mill has argued persuasively, participation in democratic processes is itself educative, not only with respect to the content of what one learns in the course of participation but also with respect to one's capacities for participation.[10]

However, against my view that participation is feasible given the appropriate conditions, it may be argued that such a claim is unfalsifiable and vacuous. For it seems that in any possible case where people fail to participate, one may revert to the ad hoc assertion that in that particular case some appropriate or necessary conditions were lacking. This seems to render my claim circular or question-begging, for it can then be cast in the form that when the appropriate conditions for participation exist, then necessarily participation will take place, where appropriate conditions for participation are defined as those conditions in which participation takes place. Thus even where the structures exist but people fail to utilize them because they doubt their efficacy, then it might be claimed that these existing structures are not yet the appropriate ones for participation. Therefore, the argument would conclude that my claim about feasibility is an empty one.

The answer to this criticism is that it is possible to give a reasonable account of what are the necessary or appropriate conditions for participation, an account which is independent of whether people would choose to participate under these conditions or not. Thus there is no claim here that the necessary conditions are themselves sufficient. Rather, they are only enabling conditions. The further requirement is that people do in fact make the choice to participate within these structures. And because this is an act of free choice there are no conditions that would guarantee it. The argument is therefore not one which seeks to assert that people will necessarily participate where the appropriate structures are available, but only that they can do so if they choose. Thus the argument does not involve the circularity that was alleged against it since it does not claim that the appropriate conditions in themselves necessarily elicit the act of participation. Therefore, the argument is falsifiable in the case where the appropriate conditions as plausibly described do exist and people choose not to participate.

I should add, however, that I do not believe that it is a toss-up as to whether people will or will not choose to participate given appropriate conditions. While it is possible that they may choose not to, I think it is very likely that they will choose positively to participate, given what I take to be their general interest in freedom and in expressing their autonomy.

There is one sense in which the objection that argues that

people prefer to put themselves under authority rather than to seek opportunities for participation seems to be plausible. That is, it seems evident that people need some order or rules that will govern their joint or common actions. This requirement is in effect one of knowing what to expect or what one can rely on. However, it is incorrect to infer from this that the rules or the order which may be required here must be derived from some external authority. Rather, I would hold that they may be jointly instituted through the common consent of the members of the relevant group so that the authority that is exercised is the self-authority of the members of the group and thus an authority in which they all share equally. This is therefore not a case of subordination to the agency of another but rather it involves reflexive agency and shared authority (as discussed in the previous chapter). Therefore, it does not follow from the need for rules or order in social life that such rules or order must be imposed on people by an external authority to which they subordinate themselves.

RECIPROCITY AND MORAL DEVELOPMENT: A CRITIQUE OF KOHLBERG, RAWLS, AND HABERMAS

In the final section of this chapter I want to return to the concept of reciprocity in its relation to character and to democratic participation. I would like to elaborate my own view somewhat further by remarking critically on a number of recent views about reciprocity, all of which consider it in its role in the development of moral character. Though I am not primarily concerned in this chapter with this latter question, nevertheless my focus on democratic personality and on the importance of the disposition to reciprocity makes these other views of interest here. The three theorists whose views I will consider very briefly are Lawrence Kohlberg, John Rawls, and Jürgen Habermas. Both Rawls and Habermas discuss the concept of reciprocity in connection with the development of moral character, largely in terms of the well-known schema that Kohlberg has proposed.

Kohlberg's original schema of moral development, modeled on Piaget's theory of stages of cognitive development, proposes that there are six distinct stages through which the child passes in attaining to full moral character ("stage six morality").[11] An ethical principle of reciprocity emerges and develops through these stages, though it expresses itself initially only in the child's orientation in its external actions to a simple exchange of equals for equals. Such elementary reciprocity is a mark of stage two, which Kohlberg characterizes as instrumental hedonism, in which actions are undertaken instrumentally in exchange for expected gratifications. This disposition to reciprocity develops through later stages to its final culmination as the character of an abstract and universal ethical principle of a Kantian sort, what Kohlberg also calls a justice orientation, namely, respect for the dignity of other human beings as ends, not as means only. The reciprocity entailed by this universal ethical principle is the reciprocal recognition by each rational agent of every other as equally free and rational, and therefore as possessing certain fundamental rights that must not be violated. The reasoning involved in the ethical orientation at this level also presupposes a reciprocity of perspectives, in the sense that the individual must be able to put him- or herself in the place of any other.

Several difficulties have been noted with Kohlberg's schema, but the problem that I want to pose is this: The concept of reciprocity in its fully developed form as a feature of the universal ethical orientation remains purely formal and abstract. That is, Kohlberg's interpretation of reciprocity in its finally developed form is an essentialist one which is indifferent to variations in context or to differences in individual, social, or cultural situations. Whereas I would agree that universalist ethical principles of the sort Kohlberg describes are of the greatest importance as features of moral character, yet they also need to be interpreted in relation to concrete differences among individuals and among situations. A related critique has been made by Carol Gilligan and Owen Flanagan, among others.[12] It seems to me, however, that Gilligan's critique swings too far in the direction of a purely contextual or situational morality, one which denigrates the importance of formal universal principles.

In response to Flanagan's criticism, Kohlberg acknowledges that moral principles have to be interpreted situationally or contextually. But against the charge that his own formulation remains purely formal and abstract, he invokes R.M. Hare's distinction between moral rules and moral principles, where rules include particular prescriptions (e.g., "Thou shalt not steal") whereas principles specify ways of deciding what features of a situation are morally relevant and what attitude to take in making moral decisions (e.g., Kant's Categorical Imperative or Rawls's Original Position). Therefore Kohlberg argues that such principles are sensitive to the particular features of different situations and contexts and permit these to be taken into account, whereas moral rules are more absolutistic and do not have this flexibility.

I believe that Kohlberg's response here makes a sound point. However, it does not fully meet my objection concerning the conception of reciprocity as a moral social relation and not simply as a formal principle. As such a social relation, I have argued that in its forms of social reciprocity and of mutuality, it necessarily requires not merely the recognition of universal and common qualities of persons as human beings (as Kohlberg proposes), but also the recognition of their individual differences and their specific purposes that define their unique mode of self-development. It seems to me therefore that Kohlberg's schema cannot give a systematic or adequate account of this relation of reciprocity as a moral social relation.

Further, it may be pointed out that neither Kohlberg's schema nor his discussion of its practical contexts is embedded in any relation to specific political or social structures. Thus Kohlberg's conception of reciprocity remains unrelated to any form of democratic institution, either in what would support such moral character or in relation to what such moral character would be best suited for in terms of social and political life. Of course, Kohlberg is not attempting to write political philosophy; yet any theory of the development of moral character that proceeds in abstraction from such contexts must surely be incomplete.

Rawls, on the other hand, is a political philosopher who discusses the development of moral character in relation to the concept of justice. Rawls draws on Kohlberg's theory in his own consideration of the growth of moral character. He understands the moral psychology of the development of this character in terms of three stages, namely the morality of authority, the morality of association, and the morality of principles. Rawls holds that at each of these stages reciprocity functions as a motivation for the appropriate moral response. Thus at the first stage, the love which the parents bestow upon the child eventually evokes a loving response in kind from the child, which leads it to follow the moral precepts that the parents set out. Here reciprocity motivates the child's obedience to parental authority and thereby to moral precepts. In the second stage of taking roles in associations, the experience of seeing others in the association fulfilling their duties and obligations with goodwill and the recognition that such activity is to the mutual benefit of the members of the association including oneself elicits a desire to reciprocate in one's own actions. That is, it elicits a comparable attachment to the association and recognition of one's own duties and obligations within the association. In the third stage, the recognition of the benefits that are derived from living under enduring just institutions tends to evoke an attachment to the principles of justice or a sense of justice. Thus in reciprocation for the benefits of a system of just institutions, the person comes to uphold principles of social cooperation and to support institutions that embody them.

In this account, Rawls uses the concept of reciprocity in a specific and traditional sense, namely, as a disposition to return benefit for benefit done. In each case, it requires first an action of others benefiting the individual in order to evoke the reciprocal response by the individual. Thus Rawls writes that the psychological laws of moral development in the three stages

> . . . are not merely principles of association or reinforcement. While they have a certain resemblance to these learning principles, they assert that the active sentiments of love and friendship, and even the sense of justice, arise from the manifest intention of other persons to act for our good. Because we recognize that they wish us well, we care for their well-being in return. Thus we acquire attachments to persons and institutions according to how we perceive our good to be affected by them. The basic idea is one of reciprocity, a tendency to answer in kind.[13]

The exception that I would take to Rawls's account of reciprocity is that in his understanding of it as a primitive psychological tendency to answer in kind, it undergoes no development in the three stages. Rather, this disposition to reciprocity simply attaches itself to different objects or situations and elicits different modes of behavior. Yet throughout it remains what I would characterize as a simple kind of instrumental reciprocity, namely, "tit for tat." It is instrumental in that it proceeds from the perception of one's own advantage, however this response may thereafter be elaborated.

By contrast, on my view, the original disposition to reciprocity does not simply have different applications over time, but itself undergoes a development or transformation. I have characterized these stages of the development of reciprocity earlier as proceeding from customary to formal and instrumental reciprocity to its fuller realization in social reciprocity and finally, in mutuality.[14] Though I cannot offer the full analysis of this development here, I would argue that Rawls, like Kohlberg, does not see the development of reciprocity to mutuality. While reciprocity at the level of mutuality does not require self-sacrifice and is compatible with one's own advantage, it cannot remain within the confines of instrumental actions. Rather, it involves a social relation in which each acts so as to enhance the self-development of the other and does so in terms of a shared understanding that their actions are equivalent in this way. Such mutuality is thus not merely responsive to the actions of others but is jointly constituted by the participants. Moreover, it sees the enhancement of another as itself a noninstrumental motive for one's own action. It is true that Rawls does discuss questions of mutuality in other contexts, but he does not articulate its relation to reciprocity. It is the case that Rawls considers reciprocity as a component of the principles of justice and this may be considered a higher development of it. Yet this articulation of reciprocity sees it as a formal principle which is therefore subject to the same criticisms I addressed to Kohlberg's version of it.

Moreover, as in the case of Kohlberg, Rawls also leaves vague or unspecified what political or social institutions would serve to embody such a disposition to reciprocity. He does of course discuss what principles should govern political and social associations, namely those of justice, and he also holds that these principles require forms of democratic representation in the political domain, as well as certain basic democratic rights. Yet he does not extend the requirement of such democratic forms to the social and economic realms, nor does he see that the full development of reciprocal social relations would require the introduction of more participatory forms of democracy in all of these realms.

Jürgen Habermas also advances a theory of moral development in terms of Kohlberg's schema, though he suggests some changes and additions. In Habermas's view, as in those of Kohlberg and Rawls, the relation of reciprocity is centrally involved in this development. For Habermas, reciprocity is not a moral norm, but is rather a necessary feature of any structure of social interaction. Thus, beginning with the level of concrete actions, through the level of social roles and systems of norms to the level of principles, each stage is seen to involve a requirement of reciprocity. According to Habermas, this reciprocal social relation is either incomplete, in which one person does or expects x only to the extent that the other does or expects y (as in a teacher–pupil or parent–

child relationship) or it is complete reciprocity, in which both do or expect the same thing $-x-$ (as in norms of civil law).[15] In addition to this interpretation of Kohlberg's stages, which is framed in terms of Habermas's theory of communicative action, Habermas proposes a seventh stage beyond that of universalistic ethics which is the final stage recognized by Kohlberg and Rawls. This additional stage is characterized as one of the universal ethics of speech. Here the justification of norms is no longer a matter of reflective conscience but is the object of practical discourse in what Habermas characterizes as the ideal speech situation. On his view, this constitutes a "communally followed procedure of redeeming normative validity claims discursively."[16] The precondition for the possibility of consensus in this context is reciprocity as the interchangeability of perspectives which is implied in the very possibility of discourse.

The criticism that I would offer here is first, that as in the case of Rawls, so for Habermas the relationship of reciprocity does not itself change or develop in the course of moral development but is rather seen as a basic structural feature presupposed in all the levels of social interaction. It varies only with respect to whether it is complete or incomplete, but this difference does not connote any development. By contrast, as I have indicated, though there are basic structural features common to all reciprocal relations, the concrete character of reciprocity as well as the form of this relation changes and develops. Second, I would argue that Habermas's interpretation of a proposed seventh stage of moral development, namely, of the consensual speech community, places too high a premium on agreement, even if only as counterfactual norm or ideal, and not sufficient emphasis on the recognition and encouragement of individual differences, that is, on the value of freedom as self-development. Now I would agree with Habermas's move in going beyond the purely formal universality of both Kohlberg and Rawls, and in proposing a concrete form of social interaction and communication for the development and validation of these norms. However, it seems to me that Habermas's proposal of consensus as the goal of communication hides an element of possible constraint or coercion on the individuals who disagree, in that such a goal might serve to exert the pressure of the community on those who dissent. In this way, it might lead to the denial of individual rights and to the delimitation of individual freedom.

Finally, as in the case of Kohlberg and Rawls, Habermas also fails to develop the norm of reciprocity in the ideal speech situation in terms of concrete democratic decision-making institutions. Moreover, he is explicitly skeptical not only about the viability of participatory forms of democracy, but even about their desirability.[17] Thus he permits the conception of the ideal speech situation and that of so-called discursive will-formation to remain somewhat vague and therefore also abstract.

By contrast, I have emphasized the need for a concrete institutional interpretation of reciprocity as a formal structure of social interaction. I have also characterized the disposition to reciprocity as a fundamental aspect of democratic personality. The moving force behind all this, however, is the self-active engaged individual, whose participation in democratic life is an expression of his or her freedom.

Chapter 12

Cosmopolitical democracy: moral principles among nations

Democratic theory with its joint requirements of self-determination, on the one hand, and human rights and justice, on the other, seems to break down when extended to the domain of international relations. For here, the principle of self-determination as the self-determination of nations would appear to require the recognition of state sovereignty and thus the principle of nonintervention in the internal affairs of any state by another. By contrast, the principles of human rights and of justice would seem to require intervention in the affairs of other states when such rights are violated, and such intervention would seem to violate the right of self-determination of nations and the sovereignty of states. Thus, whereas in the context of a single state, the democratic principles of self-determination and human rights are compatible – that is, self-determination in accordance with the decision of a majority of the people is bounded by the requirement not to infringe on the basic rights of any individual – in international relations, this compatibility does not appear to obtain and a different theory seems to be required.

This problem has given rise to two conflicting positions in the philosophy of international relations, each emphasizing one of these fundamental principles of democracy. The first, which emphasizes the right of self-determination of nations, has been called the "autonomy of states" view[1] and is associated with the work of Michael Walzer.[2] The second view, which emphasizes the priority of human rights or justice in international relations, has been called the cosmopolitan view and is associated with the work of Beitz, Shue, Goldman, Luban, and Wasserstrom, among others.[3] In this chapter I will argue that democratic theory, properly interpreted, can apply to the international domain as well as to the domestic domain. On such an interpretation, the requirements of self-determination and human rights are seen to be compatible.

I will begin with a brief presentation and criticism of each of the two conflicting views. One may note first the older framework in which both of these views arose. It is that of the traditional political philosophy, associated most clearly with Hobbes, that held that relations among nations are not subject to moral principles. The ground for this position is that nations stand to each other in a state of nature, in which each nation is sovereign and subject to no higher law. At most, morality among nations was held to consist in the upholding of international agreements or treaties and the observance of the rules of war. This view has come to be questioned in recent political philosophy. Recognizing the growing interdependence of nations and the development of a world economy, theorists have rejected the state of nature doctrine in international relations and have suggested that nations must be understood as more than separately sovereign entities and that relations among them ought to be bound by moral principles.

However, as I have suggested, there are conflicting views concerning what moral principles apply in this domain and concerning the moral status of states. The first major alternative in the recent literature is that of Walzer, which asserts the right of nations to self-determination as the primary value governing relations among states. It accepts the legitimacy of the nation-state and sees it as an entity having rights by analogy (though only rough analogy) to the case of individuals. Such rights are derived from the state's function in preserving and protecting the rights to life and liberty of its inhabitants and their forms of communal association, embodied in its historical continuity and integrity as a nation. The existence of the state and its rights is thus understood as founded on the consent of its members, where this consent is expressed in their mutual association. Such a collectivity, however it is organized (whether democratically or not), is thought to have a political right to self-determination or autonomy. The recognition of this right therefore prohibits intervention by other states in the internal affairs of a state and requires above all refraining from aggression across its borders. Although Walzer recognizes some exceptions to the principle of nonintervention, they are minor ones and leave the general principle essentially intact.

The second view concerning moral principles in international relations–the cosmopolitan view–emphasizes either international distributive justice or the enforcement of human rights across national borders. By contrast to the autonomy of states view, this cosmopolitan perspective denies the moral significance of national boundaries. Instead, it regards moral principles as holding universally among individuals, who are the bearers of human rights or who merit just treatment without regard to their membership in particular nations. Thus in one version of this view, namely that of Charles Beitz, a principle of global distributive justice requires the redistribution of natural resources, on the grounds that their original natural distribution is arbitrary. Further, because of worldwide economic interdependence and cooperation, he holds that it is not legitimate to limit the application of the principle of distributive justice within the confines of national boundaries. Beitz thus holds that economic and political intervention is legitimate in order to effect a just distribution and that only just states may be said to fall under the principle of nonintervention.

Another version of this approach, that of Henry Shue, also proposes economic redistribution across national boundaries on the grounds of a basic and universal human right to subsistence. He argues that it is morally necessary to transfer resources and goods from those who are more affluent to those who are impoverished. Yet another version of a cosmopolitan view has been presented by Alan Goldman. He maintains that the rights of states to self-determination should sometimes be subordinated to the moral requirement to uphold human rights universally. Thus Goldman argues that it is sometimes legitimate to intervene in the internal affairs of another state (sometimes including military intervention) where the ruling majority systematically denies the fundamental human rights of a minority and where the minority requests such protection of its rights from abroad. Thus these cosmopolitan views generally countenance intervention in certain circumstances on behalf of universal moral principles, though they qualify the occasions in which intervention would be justified.

Other views, which may be called cosmopolitan in emphasis, are those of David Luban, Richard Wasserstrom, and Gerald Doppelt,[4] who develop their ideas in the context of a critique of Walzer's view on the autonomy of states. Like Beitz, Shue, and Goldman, these authors raise the question of the state's legitimacy, rather than its mere sovereignty, as the condition for its moral right against intervention by external powers. Thus they argue that intervention in an illegitimate state, including military intervention, may sometimes be permissible in order to help enforce basic human rights or to protect minorities against severe repression. Luban is especially clear in advancing the argument for military intervention to enforce "socially basic human rights" in other countries and sees the need for such enforcement as a ground for just war (subject to the doctrine of proportionality).[5]

It seems to me that both of the major positions I have sketched, namely, the autonomy of states view and the cosmopolitan view, are open to serious criticisms, though each grasps some important features of moral principles in international relations. What is right in each of these two major approaches at the same time points to what is wrong in each of them. That is, it is the value of self-determination of peoples which is stressed on the first view that leads to its emphasis on state sovereignty and to the consequent subordination of human rights and justice. Similarly, it is the second view's stress on these values of human rights and justice, which leads it to diminish the importance of the principle of nonintervention in international affairs and of the self-determination of nations, to the possible detriment of peace and security.

The autonomy of states view recognizes the value of self-determination, conceiving it as a right of nation-states. Thus it takes the state to be the bearer of this right on behalf of its members. Indeed, I would agree that the value of self-determination is important in that it signifies the right of people in political or cultural associations to decide on the course of their own actions without external constraint or interference. Thus a right of self-determination of this sort implies a right against intervention. However, the view under consideration takes the political state, whatever its form, as the locus of such a right of self-determination. It presupposes that the existence of states is grounded in consent as a historical process of association and common cultural life. The problem with this, as has been noted by many critics of Walzer's view, is that it implies that even tyrannical governments are based on such consent. But this is implausible, for in a tyrannical or oppressive state, the oppressed minority (or even majority) may hardly be said to consent even in the most tacit or customary sense. As Goldman and Doppelt, among others, have pointed out, even where an oppressed population takes part in the economic or social life of the community, this cannot be taken as a sign of their consent, since they may be coerced by economic need or by the rulers to take part in such a way.[6] Thus Walzer has been criticized, for example, by Wasserstrom, for confusing consent with control, as the mere ability by the state to maintain order or to keep the populace under constraint.[7] Therefore, the right of self-determination, which belongs to people in their common association, cannot be said to have its locus in the state, where such a state is unrepresentative and violates the rights and disregards the interests of its citizens.

Yet, it would be too stringent to require that a state have the explicit consent of all its citizens in order to be recognized as legitimately claiming the right to self-determination. For, as states are presently constituted, no state would qualify.

Such a requirement for explicit consent, and the correlative opportunity for the people to give it, may be an ideal to be striven for. But at present, it may be more plausible to require of states minimally that they have some form of democratic political process, by which the state can be said to represent the self-determination of the people. It is only in such cases that one can speak of self-determination in a normative sense as involving self-rule. For, where the people of a state do not rule themselves or determine their own course, one cannot speak of self-determination by the state, since the state as such has no faculty of will, except as an instrument or representative of the people's will. The alternative view, which sees the state as such as the locus of self-determination, thus ascribes to the state a right that properly belongs only to the people.

Therefore, whereas the right of self-determination is a right against intervention, it applies to states only where such states are representative or legitimate. Thus the principle of self-determination interpreted as the autonomy of states does not provide a general ground for nonintervention by any state in the internal affairs of another, as Walzer takes it to. If nonintervention is to be justified on the basis of self-determination as a general principle for all states, including those that are not democratic, then such self-determination would have to be understood as the right of the people of a state and not of the state itself. In a sense still to be clarified, intervention even against a nonrepresentative and oppressive state infringes upon the right of self-determination of the people of that state.

Walzer in fact offers another ground for nonintervention (although he seems to regard it as part of the principle of self-determination). This is the function of the state in protecting the life and security of its individual members. This, I would agree, is a proper ground for a principle of nonaggression or nonintervention by military means. Here the state serves to enforce and protect the rights of its individual members.

Yet it would be a mistake to infer from this point concerning the rights of individuals that Walzer's general approach to the issues of state sovereignty and nonintervention is in fact based on a human rights perspective. As we have seen, his basic argument concerns the right of the state to self-determination insofar as it protects and gives expression to the common association of the people. Accordingly, Walzer has been criticized by several commentators for subordinating the protection of human rights to the requirements of the sovereignty of states and the principle of nonintervention. Walzer's argument here is that while states may rightfully be criticized internally or even overthrown by their own people in the name of basic rights, other states have no right to intervene on these grounds.

By contrast to the autonomy of states view, the cosmopolitan perspective takes as a fundamental moral imperative the protection and realization of human rights across national boundaries or the establishment of international or global distributive justice. To these ends, cosmopolitanism sees intervention across national borders, including military intervention in some views, as necessary in certain cases.

This perspective has the strength that it recognizes the existence of human rights as inherently residing in every individual simply by virtue of his or her humanity and thus holds that these rights are properly international. Another version of this cosmopolitanism (associated most clearly with Beitz), which stresses global justice, has the virtue of recognizing the need to reallocate economic resources more equitably in order to correct their initially arbitrary distribution.[8] Cosmopolitanism in both of these versions also has the strength of adopting a universalist ethical perspective, in that it sees certain moral obligations, not only of noninterference, but of positive aid, as holding equally for all humans regardless of their national affiliations. Further, this view correctly regards national borders and the nation-state as historically contingent and thus as not playing an essential role in defining moral relations.

Cosmopolitanism, in its recent formulations, is however subject to several criticisms. On one version at least, namely that of Beitz, the proposed criterion for the legitimacy of states is whether they accord with the requirements of justice, interpreted primarily in terms of the equitable economic distribution of resources and goods. Self-determination is seen as merely instrumental to social justice and may even be dispensable if social justice can be realized through other means.[9] But such an approach undervalues the process of collective self-determination and fails to see that such self-determination is required by the important value of freedom. On the other hand, the alternative version of cosmopolitanism that emphasizes the enforcement and internationalization of human rights also tends to undervalue the process of social self-determination because its criterion for the legitimacy of states is primarily that of individual human rights. Though genuine self-determination is appealed to as a warrant for nonintervention, its role on the level of principle and its relation to the preeminent individual human rights is not made clear.[10] Furthermore, this version of cosmopolitanism does not give explicit consideration to the values of cultural diversity and pluralism in its account of the bases for the legitimacy of states; and the relation of the plurality of cultures to individual human rights remains unclear in this view.[11]

An even more serious criticism of the cosmopolitan view generally, as it has been developed recently, is that it tends to countenance military intervention for the sake of human rights and social justice, and given the contemporary international situation, such intervention would pose a grave threat to world peace. Thus any military intervention against one nation by any others immediately poses the threat of escalation and possible engagement by major nuclear powers, who might regard their interest or balance of power as threatened. Against the risk of such global nuclear war and destruction, it seems thoughtless to advocate military intervention. Moreover, military intervention under any circumstances would most likely involve major loss of life and thus it seems to be justified only in such cases as that in which it is needed to stop large-scale destruction of life. Those who would endorse military intervention for the enforcement of human rights or social justice generally tend not to put sufficient weight on the value of life by contrast with these other values.[12]

Thus both the autonomy of states view and the cosmopolitan view of international relations are problematic: the first, in seeming to accommodate violations of individual human rights in deference to the sovereignty of whatever state happens to be in power; and the second, in failing to give due weight to the process of social self-determination or the fact of cultural diversity, out of a concern for the enforcement of individual human rights and distributive justice. Yet, the two values of self-determination and human rights stressed by one or the other of these two views would both seem to be fundamental democratic values and that they should come into conflict in the context of international relations seems an odd result. These two values are compatible within domestic contexts of democracy, but seem incompatible in application to international relations. Is there a way in which these two values may be understood as coherent in the international domain?

The resolution of this problem seems to me to lie in part in an understanding of the proper relation between the values of individual human rights and collective self-determination; and this in turn depends on a theory of the derivation and ordering of these values. In the perspective that I have developed in this book, the fundamental value is taken to be freedom understood as the activity of self-development and as grounded in the capacity for choice or agency that characterizes every human. The recognition and protection of this freedom as the characteristic mode of the life activity of every human being gives rise to a doctrine of human rights. These human rights include the basic rights of life and liberty, which are necessary for any action whatever, as well as other rights that are necessary for human action in the fuller sense as a process of self-development or of freedom.

In order to understand the place of social or political self-determination in this theory, it is necessary to consider how it is derived from the value of freedom. To recapitulate briefly: On the grounds that agency or the capacity for free choice is characteristic of each human simply by virtue of his or her being human, they may all be said to possess the bare capacity equally in this respect. As equally possessing this capacity, no agent has more of a right to the exercise of this agency or to the conditions necessary for its exercise than any other. Therefore, there is an equal right to such exercise and as we have seen, a *prima facie* equal right to the conditions necessary for it. Further, since social or joint activity by agents is a fundamental way in which they attain their common, as well as individual, purposes and through which they develop their capacities, all those engaged in such an activity for common purposes may be said to have a right to participate in decisions about it or to codetermine it. Such a right of codetermination is typically recognized as democracy in its political form. I have argued that such democracy should be extended to economic and social activities as in models of self-management and communal organizations. Such a process by which a group together decides on the course of its activities may be characterized as self-determination by that group. In the present international context, this norm of self-determination by nations would therefore require full democratic participation in decisions.

It may be seen from this analysis of the derivation of human rights and of self-determination that the human rights have priority over the right to self-determination by groups or nations. The reason is that the process of self-determination by a group as normatively understood within the theory presupposes the freedom of the individuals who participate in the process, including their freedom to participate. The freedom of individuals is therefore ontologically and ethically prior to the constitution of a self-determining collectivity. This freedom, as we have seen, is protected by the human rights which make its exercise possible, including centrally the rights of life and liberty, and also the right of each individual to participate in decision-making concerning those common activities in which he or she is engaged. Therefore these rights have a higher standing in the order of values than the collective's right to self-determination which depends on them. One may make a similar argument concerning the priority of considerations of justice over rights of social self-determination and also of sovereignty, but I shall not develop this parallel argument here.

This ordering of rights may be further clarified in terms of the classical distinction within democratic theory between rights against majorities and majority rights. The first concerns rights that are inviolable and therefore are protected against any incursion or diminution by majority decisions.[13] The second – majority rights – consists in the rights that a group has to make decisions that are binding upon its members by a procedure to which they all agree in advance. Typically, such a procedure is that of majority rule, though a group may choose to bind itself by some other decision procedure which must nevertheless be democratic, for example, decision by plurality or consensus. This distinction between rights against majorities and majority rights is essentially the same as that between human rights and the right of self-determination by groups or polities. Thus the human rights are rights against majorities in that they protect against interference and lay claim to basic conditions that are required for human action. By contrast, the right of self-determination by groups is the same as the right of majorities to make decisions binding upon the members of the group. It is thus a right of collective decision by the group in accordance with a procedure that its members have agreed to adopt. It should be clear from this analysis, then, that just as majority rights are restricted by the requirement not to infringe upon the rights held against majorities, so too rights of collective self-determination are restricted by the requirement not to infringe upon human rights.

We may use this theoretical framework to cast light on the issue of morality in international relations, which we have been considering in this chapter, namely, the conflicting claims of the two democratic values of human rights and self-determination. First, it is clear from this analysis that the cosmopolitan view is correct in its assertion of the priority of human rights across international borders. The analysis also suggests that human rights properly ought to be internationalized, that is, they ought to be guaranteed internationally and not simply be dependent on national enactment and enforcement. On some interpretations, this internationalization has already been accomplished in principle by virtue of the adoption of the UN Declarations on Human Rights in accordance with the UN charter.[14] However, this is a matter of some dispute, since on a common reading of the international agreements, these are agreements by the signatories to enact and enforce these rights nationally.[15]

Another conclusion from the foregoing analysis is that self-determination by groups or nations is not to be taken merely descriptively as an account of just any decision procedure that obtains at the level of sovereignty. Rather, such self-determination is to be understood normatively as a value of democracy in which agents exercise their human right to participate in decisions concerning matters of common purpose; and further, that such a process is legitimately self-determining when it is in accordance with democratic procedures. Some of the cosmopolitan theorists insist on this criterion of legitimation as the basis for recognizing a state as self-determining.

It also follows from the theory I have proposed that the process of social decision-making involved in self-determination itself represents an important value and should not be underestimated as it sometimes is by the cosmopolitan theorists. The importance of this domain of social decision-making is that it provides a major context in which human freedom is exercised and developed in the forms of social practice. Moreover, it is this domain in which the major modes of common action in social, political, and economic life are pursued and in which legitimation of social practices and their institutional forms is effected. The autonomy of states view recognizes the importance of this domain of self-determination, but tends to abstract the question of its legitimacy from the requirements for democratic process.

In proposing the extension of human rights and of democratic procedures of self-determination to the international domain, I do not want to be construed as advocating a narrowly or exclusively Western conception either of human rights or of democratic self-determination. As I proposed in Chapter 7, human rights should be understood to include not only the typical civil liberties and political rights that are identified with Western democracies, but also economic and social rights, such as rights to subsistence and health care, which have been stressed by presently existing socialist societies and by Third World societies. Beyond these, human rights include various rights to the conditions for self-development.

Similarly, there is no intention here of limiting the conception of democratic processes of self-determination exclusively to those that are most familiar in Western political democracies. Thus any decision procedure which all members of a group agree on, and which is compatible with human rights, may be considered democratic as being chosen freely by the participants (provided, of course, that they do not yield up their ultimate powers of decision without term). Thus this permits a diverse range of modes of self-determination and takes account of the pluralism of cultures and traditions. However, recognizing that most traditional forms of decision-making in the present world are far from democratic in this respect, it must be stressed that full and equal rights of participation by all the members of a group or polity is a sine qua non for any of the varieties of democratic self-determination.

A serious question arises at this point. Since I basically side with the cosmopolitan approach to international relations with respect to the priority of human rights and distributive justice across boundaries and the requirement of democratic forms of self-determination for the legitimation of states, it would seem that I should also agree with the cosmopolitan position that a state has no right against intervention, including military intervention, if it violates human rights or if it is not legitimately self-determining, or indeed that there may be a right to intervene in such cases. However, I part company with those cosmopolitan theorists who draw this conclusion. While agreeing with their premises, I come to the conclusion that military intervention is not justified in order to enforce human rights or democratic self-determination. (An exception here to which both Walzer and his opponents agree is intervention to stop a large-scale massacre.) However, on my view, military intervention in general is not barred primarily on the grounds that Walzer adduces, namely, that it is prohibited because of the claims of sovereignty on the basis of the self-determination of states. Such self-determination would function as a basis for nonintervention in those cases where the state is in fact democratically self-determining and where there is no systematic violation of human rights. But as we have seen, Walzer does not pose these requirements for legitimacy. Instead, he poses a much more lenient interpretation of self-determination such that all historical or common political associations of whatever degree of democracy or lack of it are nevertheless taken to be self-determining and therefore deserving nonintervention. However, if one advances the stricter criterion of legitimacy and human rights, as I would and as do the cosmopolitan theorists, most actual states would fail to meet the criterion and therefore would appropriately be subject to military intervention. This seems to me an insupportable conclusion, since it would make most nations vulnerable to presumptively justifiable military intervention and thus would pose a grave threat to world peace and security. It seems surprising that some cosmopolitan theorists, for example, Luban, Doppelt, Wasserstrom, and even Goldman, who explicitly take up this problem, do not take this danger seriously enough.

However, it seems to me that there is one sense in which self-determination may be said to be a legitimate ground against military intervention, and that is the sense in which what is at issue is the self-determination of the people of a nation rather than the autonomy of the state. For even in a tyrannical or a nondemocratic state, the right to self-determination is retained by the people. Military intervention against such a tyrannical state on behalf of the people of that state in order to secure them against the violations of their human rights by their government nevertheless is an infringement upon their rights of self-determination. For it purports to replace the agency of that people in overcoming their oppression with the military forces of an external power. It is in the first instance the people's own right to change their government, which would be the expression of their right to self-determination in this case. Thus even if such a military intervention were well-intentioned and not, as it most often has been, simply in the interests of the intervening power, it would in effect preempt the freedom of an oppressed people to determine their own destinies. This is similar to the argument that John Stuart Mill puts forth against intervention in such cases and which Walzer cites.[16] However, an exception where military intervention might be justified would be the case (cited earlier) of large-scale massacre if there were no other recourse to preventing it or stopping it.

It may be objected to this conclusion that it reverses the order of priority that I argued for previously between the human rights of individuals and the derivative right of self-determination of a people. For if human rights are indeed prior then it would seem that military intervention to protect or restore them should supersede even the right of the people as a whole to self-determination. But this objection is based on a misconception. For though it is true that the right of self-determination by the people of a nation as a whole derives from the more basic right of individuals to participate in joint decision-making, the preemption of a people's right to self-determination by military intervention necessarily denies to the individuals who constitute the people of a nation their fundamental human right as agents to participate in the collective decision concerning their own destinies. Therefore, the presumptive protection of human rights by the intervening power in fact denies one of these fundamental rights and therefore entails a practical contradiction of its own aims.

The only way in which the right to self-determination of a people could be exercised in the case of military intervention by a foreign power to protect their human rights is if the people as a whole decided to invite such intervention by

a procedure that involved their participation in this decision. Unless it were invited by a majority of the people
exercising their agency distributively, such intervention
would violate this agency. The intervention would then be a
paternalistic act, presuming the incompetence of the people
to be agents on their own behalf. Moreover, military intervention entails a violent state of war. Those whose human
rights have been violated and who have in the hypothetical
case invited military intervention by their own decision
must already be in a state of war with their own authorities,
that is, in a revolution, in order to justify such an invitation.
(This does not necessarily mean that the people in such a
revolution are in military confrontation with the existing government, since this may be beyond their means; but
it does mean that they have actively rejected the authority
of the existing government. They cannot depend upon the
intervention to bring this war about on their behalf.) But
even in such a case, an invitation of military action by a foreign power raises serious additional problems which we
will consider.

There are other major grounds, perhaps even more basic
than that of self-determination, which would require nonintervention in military terms, even in the face of violations of
human rights and lack of democracy. These grounds are the
values of life, peace, and security, which may themselves be
seen to be human rights. It should be clear that military
intervention by one state upon the territory of another entails
the exercise of force or an act of war, which is likely to produce major loss of life. Moreover, this risk has never been
strictly confined to military personnel and in modern warfare
is even less so. Thus such military intervention may be said
to violate the right of life and may be criticized from within
the theory of human rights. This right of life is a basic human
right, inasmuch as it is a condition for any human action
whatever and for any other rights, and thus has priority over
other rights. Though Walzer himself and some of his critics
among the cosmopolitan theorists, for example, Doppelt, recognize that one of the functions of a state is the protection of

the lives of its inhabitants, they do not develop this as an independent criterion for nonintervention.

Further, in the present world situation, any military intervention by one state against another poses an enormous risk of escalation because of the relations among the great powers. It thus poses at least a potential danger of nuclear war. In this circumstance, any act of military intervention poses a global threat to the fundamental human right of life. In addition to this, one may argue that there is a right to peace as a human right, derived from the rights to life and liberty, which would be violated by military intervention. For all these reasons, it seems to me that military intervention in another state is not justified as a means of rectifying violations of human rights, effecting global distributive justice, or establishing democratic self-determination.

These arguments against military intervention do not, however, rule out other forms of intervention short of military, in order to accomplish such purposes. Specifically, economic and political intervention would be justified in support of human rights or the relief of oppression when the violations are systematic and when a significant constituency of the nation requests this help. Such economic or political intervention must not of course have as its intention or as its consequence the imposition of foreign rule or of client regimes or puppet governments, and must not be undertaken on behalf of economic advantage of imperialist control. Yet another constraint upon such intervention is that it must not have as its intention or consequence more serious or equally serious violations of human rights than those it is intended to correct.

The account I have offered of the grounds of morality in international relations may be clarified by considering the social ontology that underlies it. What I argued for earlier in this book as the ontological primacy of individuals and the recognition of their equal freedom gives rise to the correlative primacy of human rights, as rights belonging to every human being simply in virtue of being human. This gives rise to a cosmopolitan perspective, which asserts the universal equality of all humans as agents and as bearers of human rights. Such universality therefore transcends national borders and all custom-ary and historical forms of association. However, the individu-als of this ontology are not abstract individuals, but rather socially related ones. That is to say, they are concretely differ-entiated personalities by virtue of a variety of cultural, histori-cal, and social contexts in which they live. In addition, these individuals enter into various relations and associations in which they pursue common purposes through the exercise of their freedom. The centrality in human life of such forms of common association and mutual activity underlies the value of the social process of self-determination. Likewise, the di-verse social contexts necessary for, and typical of, human ac-tivity point to cultural pluralism as a characteristic feature of social reality. These features of self-determination and cul-tural pluralism were seen to be central values in the autonomy of states view described earlier. Thus the particular form of cosmopolitanism that I am proposing here may be seen to take these values centrally into account as well.

There is another implication of the social relatedness of individuals that leads to a distinctive feature of the form of cosmopolitanism that I am proposing. This is the potential extendability of the social relatedness of individuals, which is a function of their ability to choose to enter into new social relations beyond the boundaries of their present particular associations. Thus cosmopolitanism in this interpretation comes to mean the recognition not only of the universal fea-tures of all agents as individuals, but also the possibility of extending forms of common association worldwide and of developing sociality and reciprocity globally.

A final implication of the social ontology for a cosmopoli-tan view concerns its conception of social and political institu-tions as constituted entities. Such entities are not to be taken as given in the nature of things, but rather as historically constructed by the actions of agents. In terms of international relations, this has the import that nation-states are not taken as fixed or necessary forms of institutional life, but are histori-cally contingent and transformable entities. Their present sta-tus depends on a certain consensus of intention and acquiescence with their rules and modes of functioning. This is not to say that because nation-states are contingent they ought necessarily to be disestablished, but it does question any essentialist view of their autonomy.

The consideration of the various features of this social ontology suggest the respect in which the view I am presenting here may be characterized as a cosmopolitical one. It is a cosmopolitan view, like the others I have considered, in that it regards the grounds of morality in international affairs as universal and as transcending national boundaries. Thus it emphasizes the priority of human rights and justice over considerations of state sovereignty. However, by contrast to some of these cosmopolitan theories, my view is also political in that it stresses the value and the function of self-determination at the level of social or political processes. In addition, it stresses what may be called the political aspects of human rights, namely the equal right to participate in joint decisions concerning one's social, political, and economic activities. Thus this approach may be properly called cosmopolitical in the particular sense that I am suggesting here.

I have previously noted that a cosmopolitan approach to international relations is founded not only on principles of human rights but also on a principle of distributive justice. But I have discussed this latter principle only in passing. Yet, as is well known, the question of global distributive justice is a central one in the discussion of morality in international relations. Its centrality arises from the enormous disparities between the have and have-not nations, so that redistribution of world resources and goods seems called for. However, this poses the conceptual difficulty of whether theories of distributive justice, which have been formulated solely in terms of national or domestic contexts, can be applied to international ones. I cannot treat this question within the compass of this chapter, but I want to make a few brief remarks concerning the principles that are at issue here.

The principle of justice on my view affirms the equal right of all individuals as agents to the conditions of their self-development. I have previously called this the principle of equal positive freedom. Like several other principles of justice that have been advanced, this one requires some major redistribution of resources. The question arises whether such a just distribution is to be conceived of on a world scale without regard to national boundaries or national economies, or instead whether it should be limited to the confines of a given nation-state, taken as a supposedly self-sufficient whole. Several commentators, while recognizing some international moral obligations in this respect, have proposed that there are considerations that properly concentrate our obligations within the national context. The considerations offered include the principle of individual entitlement, that is, the individual's right to the products or benefits of his or her labor;[17] the obligations acquired by participation in a scheme of social cooperation;[18] and finally, the principle of simple proximity, that is, that one's moral obligations decrease with distance or unfamiliarity.[19] Without evaluating the merit of these views, one may note an additional consideration that is relevant here. This is what I have called social entitlement, which I regard as an element of a theory of justice. Like the principle of individual entitlement, this principle asserts the right of individuals to the products or benefits of their labor. But it recognizes that much of this labor is fundamentally social, that is, it is the result of the cooperative activity of groups of individuals. The right to the product or the benefit of the activity is to this degree shared by the group. Such social entitlement therefore introduces a limiting consideration on any simple principle of equal distribution. That is, it localizes and differentiates the distribution of benefits by recognizing such social entitlements and thus introduces an element of proportionality in their distribution. In international terms, such a principle would qualify the requirement for completely equal distribution globally. However, this same principle may also in fact have an equalizing effect upon the present global distribution of goods and benefits since it would recognize the proportionate contribution made to the social product of labor by workers in underdeveloped or have-not nations, where such contribution is presently radically undervalued. Beyond these considerations of entitlement, there is an additional requirement of justice, namely, for some reallocation of natural resources, to compensate for the initially arbitrary distribution of them by nature.

Finally, I would like to make a few remarks on the relation between democratic forms of political and social life and the cosmopolitan principles that I discussed earlier. It might be thought that the recognition of cosmopolitan principles in international relations would lead to the view that national sovereignty should be replaced by some form of world government, which would ensure peace, enforce human rights, and effect global justice. But this is not, in fact, a conclusion that I would support. Such a world government would have to have power and authority concentrated in some centralized way and would possess the coercive capacities presently associated with nation-states. The concentration of power and authority on such a scale, even if limited by democratic controls, would pose a grave risk of unmatched global tyranny. There would be no effective alternative power to counter such totalistic authority. Therefore, it seems to me that proposals for improvement of the present international system would have to take a different direction if they are to be compatible with the principles of human rights and democracy discussed earlier. Indeed, these proposals for alternative forms of world organization would have to be judged in terms of the extent to which they serve to realize these principles, or more generally, the value of freedom. As to positive proposals for what such forms of international organization should be–whether in terms of nation-states or some new alternative–I will not discuss these here.

One last consideration: It is not only the case that cosmopolitical principles require the establishment of democracy, but in addition, the introduction and development of democratic forms wherever possible could be expected to contribute to the acceptance and further support the cosmopolitical principles and thereby to the improvement of international relations. For one thing, people who would benefit from the protection and enforcement of human rights, distributive justice, and democratic procedures would tend to support such principles more generally, on the basis of their own experience. Moreover, the further development of democratic participation at the local level, and not only in political but also in social and economic contexts, would engender cosmopolitan attitudes by virtue of the emphasis on qualities of reciprocity and social cooperation in this context, which entail the recognition of the equal freedom of others and thus tend toward universalism. Cases of democratic participation at these levels can also provide models to be emulated in international contexts. In these ways, the development of democratic forms locally may be said to contribute to the improvement of international relations.

Notes

1. It may be interesting to note how the connotations of the term "liberal" have shifted historically in popular usage. "Liberal individualism," as I am using it here and as it is generally used in the literature of political theory, is a term of art which preserves the original early 19th century connotations that identify "liberal" with freedom of the individual, in particular in market relations but also in political life, from regulation or interference by the state. The term has more recently come to be popularly associated with notions of social welfare, in which government agencies are taken to share responsibility for the well-being of the individual as well as for the protection of civil and political liberties. In this sense, the modern liberal is no longer an outright proponent of a free market economy but rather regards it as necessary to regulate the market to some degree for the sake of social justice. This shift in popular usage is paralleled by the theoretical attempts (considered in this chapter) to revise traditional liberal individualism in the direction of considerations of social welfare.

2. The liberal individualism in the form that is subject to this criticism has been modified in order to meet this objection, most notably by John Stuart Mill. He is concerned to develop the theory so that it can take into account social welfare and the requirements of sociality. But without giving the argument here, I would propose that Mill fails to resolve the antithesis between individuality and sociality or between liberty and welfare.

3. For my own reading of Marx's view from which it may be seen

329

how far he differs from most standard interpretations of social-ism, see C. Gould, *Marx's Social Ontology: Individuality and Community in Marx's Theory of Social Reality* (Cambridge, MA: The MIT Press, 1978).

4. See, for example, Joseph A. Schumpeter, *Capitalism, Socialism and Democracy* (London: George Allen & Unwin, 1943); and Robert A. Dahl, *A Preface to Democratic Theory* (Chicago: University of Chicago Press, 1956), and *Who Governs?* (New Haven: Yale University Press, 1961).

5. Robert A. Dahl, *Dilemmas of Pluralist Democracy: Autonomy vs. Control* (New Haven: Yale University Press, 1982).

6. Robert A. Dahl, *A Preface to Economic Democracy* (Berkeley, CA: University of California Press, 1985).

7. See, for example, C.B. Macpherson, *The Life and Times of Liberal Democracy* (Oxford: Oxford University Press, 1977), chapter IV; and Carole Pateman, *Participation and Democratic Theory* (Cambridge: Cambridge University Press, 1970), chapter 1.

8. John Rawls, *A Theory of Justice* (Cambridge, MA: Harvard University Press, 1971), and "Kantian Constructivism in Moral Theory: The Dewey Lectures 1980," *The Journal of Philosophy*, Vol. LXXVII, no. 9 (September, 1980), pp. 515–72.

9. This criticism has been made by Norman Daniels with respect to Rawls's distinction between equal liberty and the unequal worth of liberty. See Daniels's "Equal Liberty and the Unequal Worth of Liberty," in N. Daniels, ed., *Reading Rawls* (New York: Basic Books, 1975).

10. Robert Nozick, *Anarchy, State, and Utopia* (New York: Basic Books, 1974).

11. The "Praxis" group of philosophers and social theorists is so named because they originally were grouped around the Yugoslav journal *Praxis*, which was published from 1964 to 1975. The group included Mihailo Marković, Gajo Petrović, Svetozar Stojanović, Zagorka Golubović, Ljubomir Tadić, and Rudi Supek, among others. A one-volume collection of essays by members of the group is *Praxis: Yugoslav Essays in the Philosophy and Methodology of the Social Sciences*, edited by M. Marković and G. Petrović, *Boston Studies in the Philosophy of Science*, Vol. XXXVI (Boston and Dordrecht: D. Reidel, 1979).

12. Needless to say, the conclusion that workplace democracy is required as a realization of some more general democratic principles does not only follow from premises of a socialist

sort. There are nonsocialist authors who have also argued normatively for the introduction of worker self-management on grounds of democratic principle. See, for example, Dahl, *A Preface to Economic Democracy*.

13. See Mihailo Marković, "New Forms of Democracy in Socialism," *Praxis International*, Vol. I, no. 1 (April, 1981), p. 24. See a related discussion in Svetozar Stojanović, *Between Ideals and Reality*, translated by Gerson S. Sher (New York: Oxford University Press, 1973), esp. pp. 42–6.

14. See Mihailo Marković, "New Forms of Democracy in Socialism," pp. 36–8.

15. For Habermas's most recent major work setting forth these views, see his *The Theory of Communicative Action*, Volume I, tr. by T. McCarthy (Boston: Beacon Press, 1984).

16. See Angelo Bolaffi, "The Crisis of Late Capitalism and the Future of Democracy: An Interview with Habermas," *Telos*, no. 39 (Spring, 1979), p. 169.

17. C.B. Macpherson, *Democratic Theory: Essays in Retrieval* (Oxford: Oxford University Press, 1973), and *The Life and Times of Liberal Democracy*.

18. Carole Pateman, *Participation and Democratic Theory*; and *The Problem of Political Obligation: A Critical Analysis of Liberal Theory* (Chichester: John Wiley & Sons, 1979).

19. C.B. Macpherson, *Democratic Theory: Essays in Retrieval*, p. 56.

20. A number of recent works treat the economic questions of worker self-managed or worker controlled systems in detail. See especially David Schweickart, *Capitalism or Worker Control* (New York: Praeger, 1980); Jaroslav Vanek, *The General Theory of Labor-Managed Market Economies* (Ithaca: Cornell University Press, 1970); Jaroslav Vanek, ed., *Self-Management: Economic Liberation of Man* (Baltimore, MD: Penguin Books, 1975); and Alec Nove, *The Economics of Feasible Socialism* (London: George Allen & Unwin, 1983). The model I present later in the book differs in various ways from each of these.

CHAPTER 1

1. C.B. Macpherson, *Democratic Theory: Essays in Retrieval* (Oxford: Oxford University Press, 1973), and *The Life and Times of*

Liberal Democracy (Oxford: Oxford University Press, 1977); Carole Pateman, *Participation and Democratic Theory* (Cambridge: Cambridge University Press, 1970); Steven Lukes, "Socialism and Equality," in *Essays in Social Theory* (London: Macmillan, 1977); Mihailo Marković, *From Affluence to Praxis* (Ann Arbor, MI: University of Michigan Press, 1974); and "Philosophical Foundations of the Idea of Self-Management," in Branko Horvat et al., eds., *Self-Managing Socialism* (New York: International Arts and Sciences Press, 1975); David Schweickart, *Capitalism or Worker Control?* (New York: Praeger Publishers, 1980); Lawrence Crocker, *Positive Liberty* (The Hague: Martinus Nijhoff, 1980); and Kai Nielsen, *Equality and Liberty: A Defense of Radical Egalitarianism* (Totowa, NJ: Rowman and Allanheld, 1984).

2. Isaiah Berlin, "Introduction," *Four Essays on Liberty* (Oxford: Oxford University Press, 1970).

3. Thomas Hobbes, *Leviathan* (New York: Collier Books, 1962), p. 159.

4. Ibid.

5. Berlin, "Two Concepts of Liberty," in *Four Essays on Liberty*, p. 122.

6. S.I. Benn and R.S. Peters, *The Principles of Political Thought* (New York: The Free Press, 1965), p. 230. However, they also write that such an interpretation of freedom is too vague and needs to be qualified.

7. The distinction between negative and positive liberty is explicitly drawn by Isaiah Berlin in his "Two Concepts of Liberty." This distinction is also discussed by Benn and Peters in *The Principles of Political Thought;* Gerald MacCallum in "Negative and Positive Freedom," *The Philosophical Review*, Vol. LXXVI, no. 3 (July, 1967); and Joel Feinberg, *Social Philosophy* (Englewood Cliffs, N J: Prentice-Hall, 1973). These treatments are for the most part critical of the concept of positive liberty. A criticism of these views is given in Gene James, "Freedom: An Analysis" (unpublished manuscript). Virginia Held's *Rights and Goods* (New York: The Free Press, 1984), pp. 124–38, also contains an interesting discussion of this distinction. L. Crocker's *Positive Liberty* contains a full consideration of the distinction and a defense of the concept of positive liberty. The classical criticism of Berlin's view and a development of the concept of positive liberty is in C.B. Macpherson's *Democratic Theory*.

My own view is similar to his in several respects, for example, in the emphasis on positive freedom and its interpretation as self-development, the importance of equal access to the means of labor, and the interpretation of democracy as not merely a form of political governance but as a form of social life as well. However, my view differs from Macpherson's in important ways. For one thing, I do not hold an essentialist view of human nature as he does. That is, Macpherson interprets self-development as the elaboration of a set of "essentially human capacities" (p. 53), which he attempts to enumerate and which he takes to be a basic postulate of democratic theory. By contrast, I take these human capacities not as essential or fixed, but as products of free and self-transforming human activity. A further difference is that I emphasize more than Macpherson does the centrality of social relations as conditions for an individual's self-development. Macpherson sees society as either a "hindrance" or a "help" to an individual's self-development and thus as an external condition. However, I take individuals as social individuals and thus see their social relations as internal to them and to their self-development. Yet another difference is that whereas Macpherson is primarily critical of consumption as the criterion of individual good and emphasizes instead production or the development of powers, I would shift the context of the main critique to that of domination and exploitation and would see the development of powers primarily in contrast to this domination. Other differences between my view and Macpherson's are discussed in later chapters.

8. Berlin, "Two Concepts of Liberty," p. 131.
9. Ibid., p. 132.
10. MacCallum, "Negative and Positive Liberty," p. 314.
11. Macpherson, "Berlin's Division of Liberty," in *Democratic Theory*; Crocker, *Positive Liberty*. A similar interpretation has been offered more recently by David Miller, "Constraints on Freedom," *Ethics*, Vol. 94, no. 1 (October 1983), pp. 66–86.
12. Macpherson, *Democratic Theory*, p. 101.
13. Berlin, "Introduction," *Four Essays on Liberty*, p. LIII.
14. Macpherson, *Democratic Theory*, pp. 101–4 and p. 102, n 10.
15. For criticisms of the biological or genetic view of a fixed human nature, see Stephen Jay Gould, *The Mismeasure of Man* (New York: W.W. Norton, 1981); and Arthur L. Caplan, *The*

Sociobiology Debate: Readings on Ethical and Scientific Issues, New York: Harper & Row, 1978, and *Sociobiology: The Debate Evolves*, A Special Double Issue, *The Philosophical Forum*, Vol. XIII, nos. 2–3 (1981–2). Against the rationalist essentialist view, see John Dewey, *Human Nature and Conduct* (New York: Modern Library, 1930), and *Reconstruction in Philosophy* (Boston: Beacon Press, 1957); and Richard Rorty, *Philosophy and the Mirror of Nature* (Princeton: Princeton University Press, 1980). Against phenomenological essentialism, see Martin Heidegger, *Being and Time* (New York: Harper & Row, 1962); Jean-Paul Sartre, *Being and Nothingness* (New York: Philosophical Library, 1956); Maurice Merleau-Ponty, *Phenomenology of Perception* (London: Routledge & Kegan Paul, 1962); and Hans-Georg Gadamer, *Truth and Method* (New York: Crossroad Publishing, 1962). For another criticism of essentialism, see also my own argument in "The Woman Question: Philosophy of Liberation and the Liberation of Philosophy," in *Women and Philosophy: Toward a Theory of Liberation*, ed. by C. Gould and M.W. Wartofsky (New York: G.P. Putnam's Sons, 1976).

16. Macpherson, "Berlin's Division of Liberty," *Democratic Theory*.

17. I say "in part" here because the claim that an individual has to the conditions of his or her own self-development also derives in part from the social role that each individual plays with respect to the others, in constituting an aspect of the social conditions that are required for each one's self-development. An individual's claim thus derives in part from the recognition by other individuals of their need for this individual, i.e., from their mutual recognition of their interdependence.

18. Cf., for example, Joel Feinberg, "The Nature and Value of Rights," *The Journal of Value Inquiry*, Vol. 4 (Winter, 1970), reprinted in David Lyons, ed., *Rights* (Belmont, CA: Wadsworth, 1979), pp. 78–91; and Gregory Vlastos, "Justice and Equality," in Richard B. Brandt, ed., *Social Justice* (Englewood Cliffs, NJ: Prentice-Hall, 1962), pp. 31–72.

19. Feinberg, "The Nature and Value of Rights," in *Rights*, p. 90.

20. Ibid., p. 91.

21. Theodore M. Benditt, *Rights* (Totowa, NJ: Rowman and Littlefield, 1982), p. 17.

22. Richard B. Brandt, *Ethical Theory* (Englewood Cliffs, NJ: Prentice-Hall, 1959), pp. 410 and 446; William Frankena, "Are There Natural Rights?" *Philosophical Review* Vol. 64

(1955), pp. 10ff; and Gregory Vlastos, "Justice and Equality," in Brandt, ed. *Social Justice*, p. 40. See also Benditt's discussion of this in *Rights*, pp. 36–39. Cf. also Ronald Dworkin, *Taking Rights Seriously* (Cambridge, MA: Harvard University Press, 1978), pp. 191–4, who argues that an individual's fundamental rights against the government cannot be overridden for simply utilitarian reasons, though he allows cases, e.g., of competing fundamental rights, where such overriding may be necessary.

23. Cf. J.S. Mill, *Utilitarianism*, ed. by George Sher (Indianapolis, IN: Hackett Publishing, 1979); and H.J. McCloskey, "Rights," *Philosophical Quarterly*, Vol. 15 (1965), p. 24, and "Human Needs, Rights, and Political Values," *American Philosophical Quarterly*, 13 (1976), pp. 9–10.

24. Thomas Jefferson's language in the *Declaration of Independence* strikingly represents this view, associated more generally with much of natural rights theory, as well as with moral intuitionism in the conception of rights and duties.

25. Cf. Gregory Vlastos, "Justice and Equality"; Richard Wasserstrom, "Rights, Human Rights, and Racial Discrimination," *Journal of Philosophy*, Vol. LXI (October 29, 1964), pp. 628–41; and Ronald Dworkin, *Taking Rights Seriously*, though he bases these rights on the postulate of the equal concern and respect that is due to citizens in a state because of their human dignity.

26. Cf. Immanuel Kant, *Foundations of the Metaphysics of Morals*, tr. by Lewis W. Peck (Indianapolis, IN: Bobbs-Merrill, 1959), and *The Metaphysical Elements of Justice: Part I of The Metaphysics of Morals*, tr. by John Ladd (Indianapolis, IN: Bobbs-Merrill, 1965).

27. Cf. Alan Gewirth, *Reason and Morality* (Chicago, IL: University of Chicago Press, 1978).

28. Cf. H.L.A. Hart, "Are There Any Natural Rights?" *Philosophical Review*, Vol. 64 (1955), pp. 175–88; John Rawls, *A Theory of Justice* (Cambridge, MA: Harvard University Press, 1971); Thomas M. Scanlon, "Contractualism and Utilitarianism," in A. Sen and B. Williams, eds., *Utilitarianism and Beyond* (New York: Cambridge University Press, 1982), though there are significant differences among these views.

29. Ronald Dworkin, *Taking Rights Seriously*, p. 273.

30. Robert Nozick, *Anarchy, State, and Utopia* (New York: Basic

Books, 1974), pp. 30–3, 167–74, 228–35; and John Charvet, "A Critique of Human Rights," in J.R. Pennock and J. Chapman, eds., *Human Rights*, Nomos XXIII (New York and London: New York University Press, 1981), pp. 35–40.

31. Alan Gewirth, *Reason and Morality* (Chicago: University of Chicago Press, 1978), and *Human Rights* (Chicago: University of Chicago Press, 1982).

32. For Gewirth's summary of this argument, see his "The Basis and Content of Human Rights," in Pennock and Chapman, eds., *Human Rights*, pp. 124–34.

33. Cf. Richard B. Friedman, "The Basis of Human Rights: A Criticism of Gewirth's Theory," and Martin P. Golding, "From Prudence to Rights: A Critique," both in Pennock and Chapman, eds., *Human Rights*, pp. 148–57 and 165–74; and Bernard Williams, *Ethics and the Limits of Philosophy* (Cambridge, MA: Harvard University Press, 1985), chapter 4.

CHAPTER 2

1. S.I. Benn and R.S. Peters, *The Principles of Political Thought* (New York: The Free Press, 1965); J. Roland Pennock, *Democratic Political Theory* (Princeton: Princeton University Press, 1979); and Carl Cohen, *Democracy* (New York: The Free Press, 1971).

2. James Madison, *The Federalist Papers*, no. 10 (New York: New American Library, 1981); John Dewey, *Individualism Old and New* (New York: G.P. Putnam's Sons, 1962), and *The Public and Its Problems* (New York: Henry Holt and Company, 1927); Joseph A. Schumpeter, *Capitalism, Socialism and Democracy* (London: George Allen & Unwin, 1943); Robert A. Dahl, *Preface to Democratic Theory* (Chicago: University of Chicago Press, 1956); and Bernard Berelson, "*Democratic Theory and Democratic Practice*," in B.R. Berelson, P.F. Lazarsfeld, and W.N. McPhee, eds., *Voting* (Chicago: The University of Chicago Press, 1954).

3. F.H. Bradley, *Appearance and Reality* (Oxford: Oxford University Press, 1930), pp. 27–8.

4. C. Gould, "Beyond Causality in the Social Sciences: Reciprocity as a Model of Non-Exploitative Social Relations," in R.S.

Cohen and M.W. Wartofsky, eds., *Epistemology, Methodology, and the Social Sciences* (Boston and Dordrecht: D. Reidel, 1983).
5. F.H. Bradley, *Appearance and Reality*, pp. 513–21.
6. G.E. Moore, "External and Internal Relations," in *Philosophical Studies* (Paterson, NJ: Littlefield, Adams and Co., 1959).
7. Charles A. Baylis, "Internality and Interdependence," *The Journal of Philosophy*, Vol. XXVI (1929), pp. 373–9.
8. Aristotle, *Categories*, 6ᵃ 36–8, 6ᵇ 28–30.
9. Ibid., 6ᵇ 37.

CHAPTER 3

1. I do not mean to imply here that relativist theories in ethics are entirely recent phenomena. Indeed, they were already present in ancient Greek thought, e.g., in Xenophanes and Protagoras. I am speaking here of contemporary formulations of relativism.
2. For an argument against such essentialism, see my "The Woman Question: Philosophy of Liberation and the Liberation of Philosophy," in C. Gould and M. Wartofsky, eds., *Women and Philosophy: Toward a Theory of Liberation* (New York: G.P. Putnam's Sons, 1976), pp. 5–44.
3. Cf. C.B. Macpherson, *The Political Theory of Possessive Individualism: Hobbes to Locke* (Oxford: Oxford University Press, 1962).
4. This argument would seem to hold, however, only against those forms of moral relativism that endorse the relativity of values and see these values as having equal normative force.
5. John Stuart Mill, *Utilitarianism*, ed. by G. Sher (Indianapolis: Hackett Publishing Co., 1979), pp. 8–9.
6. John Rawls, *A Theory of Justice* (Cambridge, MA.: Harvard University Press, 1971), p. 261.
7. See, for example, ibid., pp. 578–79.
8. Rawls, *A Theory of Justice*, p. 51.
9. Norman Daniels, "Wide Reflective Equilibrium and Theory Acceptance in Ethics," *The Journal of Philosophy*, Vol. LXXVI (1979), pp. 256–82, and "Reflective Equilibrium and Archimedean Points," *Canadian Journal of Philosophy*, Vol. X, no. 1 (March, 1980), pp. 83–103.

337

10. For example, Rawls says in his "Remarks on Justification" in *A Theory of Justice*, "The aim throughout was to show that the theory proposed matches the fixed points of our considered convictions better than other familiar doctrines. . . ." (pp. 579–80). Or again, "There is a definite if limited class of facts against which conjectured principles can be checked, namely our considered judgments in reflective equilibrium." (p. 51) It is not the case that Rawls claims that such facts are immediate intuitions or self-evident or epistemologically privileged givens. They are, after all, "considered judgments." Nevertheless, they provide what one may call the "basic statements" which test our moral theory and in this sense retain the foundationalist appeal. The debate over Rawls's foundationalism is discussed by N. Daniels (see note 9), who defends a nonfoundationalist interpretation of Rawls.
11. John Rawls, "Kantian Constructivism in Moral Theory: The Dewey Lectures 1980," *The Journal of Philosophy*, Vol. LXXVII, no. 9 (September 1980), p. 518.
12. Ibid., p. 519.
13. Rawls, *A Theory of Justice*, p. 49.
14. For the most recent formulation of this view, see J. Habermas, *The Theory of Communicative Action*, Volume I, tr. by T. McCarthy (Boston: Beacon Press, 1984), pp. 301–9.
15. There are, of course, many other differences between Habermas and Rawls, not the least of which is that the Habermasian project unfolds against the background of the historical approach of a Hegelian and Marxist philosophy. Indeed, part of his project is what he calls "the reconstruction of historical materialism" as a corrective for what remained one-sided or incomplete in Marx.
16. Immanuel Kant, *Critique of Practical Reason*, tr. Lewis White Beck (Indianapolis, IN: Bobbs-Merrill, 1956), p. 13.
17. It would be wrong to take this analysis to imply that a person incapable of exercising agency – e.g. in a comatose state – should be regarded as no longer living. This is so for several interrelated reasons. Such an individual has an identity as a person based on his or her past activity and social relations. This identity as a living person should be presumed to continue as long as the person has any biological existence, since human biology is individuated by personality, and this would be true also of the biologically existing individual. Further,

since agency is a generic characteristic of human life, the fact of this class character of human beings should be an overriding consideration in an individual case where agency may be absent but the individual's biological existence persists. Beyond this, since it is not always possible to determine that the biological conditions for agency are irremediably lost, there is a prudential argument for presuming a future possibility of agency.

CHAPTER 4

1. See John Rawls, *A Theory of Justice* (Cambridge, MA: Harvard University Press, 1971).
2. See Robert Nozick, *Anarchy, State, and Utopia* (New York: Basic Books, 1974).
3. Cf. Adina Schwartz, "Autonomy in the Workplace," in T. Regan, ed., *Just Business: Introductory Essays in Business Ethics* (New York: Random House, 1983); David Ellerman, "Capitalism and Workers' Self-Management," in J. Vanek, ed., *Self-Management* (Baltimore: Penguin, 1975); David Schweickart, *Capitalism or Worker Control?* (New York: Praeger, 1980); Samuel Bowles, David Gordon, and Thomas Weisskopf, *Beyond the Waste Land* (New York: Anchor Press/Doubleday, 1983); and Robert A. Dahl, *A Preface to Economic Democracy* (Berkeley, CA: University of California Press, 1985). I have discussed the views of C. Pateman and M. Marković (in the Introduction), which are in some ways related to my own. However, they also do not adduce justice as a ground for self-management.
4. Rawls briefly discusses exploitation in *A Theory of Justice*, pp. 309–10, but does not interpret it in this sense but only as a market phenomenon of imperfect competition. His position on the injustice of exploitation in the way I define it in this chapter is not pursued there.
5. See, for example, *A Theory of Justice*, pp. 78 and 309.
6. In *A Theory of Justice*, Rawls formulates these principles as follows:

> First: each person is to have an equal right to the most extensive basic liberty compatible with a similar liberty for oth-

ers . . . (p. 60) Social and economic inequalities are to be arranged so that they are both (a) to the greatest benefit of the least advantaged and (b) attached to offices and positions open to all under conditions of fair equality of opportunity." (p. 83)

7. Norman Daniels, "Equal Liberty and Unequal Worth of Liberty," in N. Daniels, ed., *Reading Rawls* (New York: Basic Books, 1975).
8. Rawls, *A Theory of Justice*, p. 204.
9. Rawls seems to qualify his view by asserting that the principles of justice are meant to apply only when conditions of no worse than moderate scarcity pertain. But this qualification does not seem adequate to meet the criticism inasmuch as the conditions of moderate scarcity are not defined in such a way as to exclude all instances of life-threatening or debilitating and submarginal poverty. See Rawls, *A Theory of Justice*, pp. 542–3, and "Kantian Constructivism in Moral Theory," *The Journal of Philosophy*, Vol. LXXVII, no. 9 (September 1980), p. 536.
10. Henry Shue, *Basic Rights* (Princeton, NJ: Princeton University Press, 1980), pp. 127–9.
11. Nozick, *Anarchy, State, and Utopia*, p. 160.
12. See Bronislaw Malinowski, *Argonauts of the Western Pacific* (New York: Dutton, 1961) and *Crime and Custom in Savage Society* (Atlantic Highlands, NJ: Humanities Press, 1970); William H. R. Rivers, *History of Melanesian Society* (Atlantic Highlands, NJ: Humanities Press, 1968) and *Social Organization* (London, 1924); Marshall Sahlins, *Stone Age Economics* (Hawthorne, NY: De Gruyter, 1972).
13. Nozick, *Anarchy, State, and Utopia*, p. 186.
14. G.A. Cohen, "Robert Nozick and Wilt Chamberlain: How Patterns Preserve Liberty," in J. Arthur and W.H. Shaw, eds., *Justice and Economic Distribution* (Englewood Cliffs, NJ: Prentice-Hall, 1978).
15. See Daniel Zwerdling, *Workplace Democracy* (New York: Harper & Row, 1980).
16. It may be argued that those outside the firm have an indirect voice in production decisions insofar as they constitute the market for the firm's products and thus set the conditions for the profitability of the firm. However, the market does not make decisions about production but only provides some of

the information on the basis of which those engaged in the firm would make their decisions.

17. One possible objection to the idea of workers' self-management is that it substitutes a mere show of participation in decision-making for a real change in the economic power structure, since it leaves ownership and hence ultimate control over the conditions of activity in the hands of others. This objection has been raised with respect to worker participation in schemes at lower levels of management decision-making or in "quality-of-life" circles in industry, and also with respect to collaboration between labor and business in such institutionalized contexts as "codetermination" (*Mitbestimmung*) in some West European cases. Clearly, my view is not subject to this criticism, for as indicated, I take workers' self-management to include worker control. At the same time, the argument I develop here is not incompatible with degrees of worker self-management short of worker control, insofar as these represent increases in democratic participation. For a discussion of the details of my model of self-management, see Chapter 9.

18. Cf. Adina Schwartz, "Autonomy in the Workplace."

19. See, for example, David Ellerman, "Capitalism and Workers' Self-Management."

20. See, for example, the argument in Samuel Bowles et al., *Beyond the Waste Land*, chapter 13. Although Robert Dahl does not argue for workers' self-management principally on the grounds of productive efficiency but rather on the normative grounds of the value of democracy itself, as will be seen, he does argue, on the basis of an analysis of contemporary actual cases, that it is no less efficient and is probably more efficient than actual cases of capitalist corporate management. See R. Dahl, *Democracy, Liberty, and Equality* (Oslo: Norwegian University Press, 1986), pp. 106–13. This is a slightly revised version of chapter 4 of his *A Preface to Economic Democracy* (1985).

21. Dahl, *A Preface to Economic Democracy*, pp. 134–5.

22. Ibid., p. 82.

23. Lawrence Becker, *Property Rights: Philosophic Foundations* (London: Routledge & Kegan Paul, 1977).

24. Dahl, *A Preface to Economic Democracy*, pp. 82–3. A similar line of argument is developed in my discussion of property right in Chapter 6.

25. Dahl, *A Preface to Economic Democracy*, p. 57.

26. True, Dahl argues that such a free contract between a worker and an employer is something less than free, since the worker cannot easily leave one employment for another in the job market. Yet I am suggesting that the assumptions about liberty with which Dahl operates in the book could support an alternative interpretation of this employment situation which satisfies the requirements of liberty and which therefore leaves Dahl's objection concerning the constraints on the worker's freedom of exit as ad hoc.
27. Dahl, *A Preface to Economic Democracy*, p. 88.
28. Ibid., p. 57.
29. Ibid., pp. 113–6.
30. The discussion of this right is in Chapter 6.
31. It might be argued that the requirements for equal rights to the basic conditions for self-development in fact preempt democratic decision-making procedures in the economy or in the firm in that they establish standards that limit the scope of the decision-making. This objection may be addressed in two ways. First of all, such a limitation on the scope of democratic decision-making is in fact intended in my account, since I take these equal rights to be among the human rights which, as such, are rights against majorities. They therefore ought to be inviolable and protected against any incursion or diminution by majority decisions. Second, in a different sense, the equal right to the basic conditions for self-development may itself be seen as a precondition for democracy, since the equal right to participate in decision-making is undercut if people lack the resources – for example, subsistence, health, education – which permit them to be agents in such a process. A further discussion of these points is included in Chapters 7 and 12.
32. Rawls, *A Theory of Justice*, pp. 102ff and 462–504.
33. Ibid., p. 494.

CHAPTER 5

1. Ronald Dworkin, *Taking Rights Seriously* (Cambridge, MA: Harvard University Press, 1977), p. 273.
2. Gregory Vlastos, "Justice and Equality," in Richard B. Brandt,

ed., *Social Justice* (Englewood Cliffs, NJ: Prentice-Hall, 1962), p. 40.
3. Ibid., pp. 42–3.
4. Cf. Virginia Held, *Rights and Goods* (New York: The Free Press, 1984), pp. 129–30, 137–8, 184–5, 189, for a discussion of how a principle of equal liberty requires, as a matter of right, not only civil and political liberties but also economic and social means.

CHAPTER 6

1. I use the term "personal possessions" interchangeably with the terms "personal property" and "individual property." The term "possession" has the advantage of being colloquial. However, by this usage I do not intend to suggest a traditional distinction between possession as *factual* and property as *legal* right. Rather, I use both terms – "possession" and "property" – to connote legal rights.
2. A.M. Honoré, "Ownership," in A.G. Guest, ed., *Oxford Essays in Jurisprudence* (Oxford: Clarendon Press, 1961), pp. 107–47.
3. Lawrence Becker, *Property Rights: Philosophic Foundations* (London: Routledge & Kegan Paul, 1977), pp. 42–3.
4. Ibid., p. 54.
5. Although there are alternative versions of socialist theories of property, I am focusing here on the Soviet and East European conceptions as those that play the major role in contemporary discussions and in actual practice. I would argue that Marx's views on these matters are decidedly different from those developed in this socialist model. Cf. C. Gould, *Marx's Social Ontology: Individuality and Community in Marx's Theory of Social Reality* (Cambridge, MA: The MIT Press, 1978), pp. 87–8, 139–42.
6. In some of the socialist economies in Eastern Europe (e.g., in Poland), private enterprises hiring up to a certain number of workers and individually owned farms up to a certain size are permitted.
7. Thus, for example, V.V. Laptev writes, "In establishing the norms of economic legislation, the socialist state acts not only as the bearer of political power, but as the owner of the means of production. The management and planning of economic

activities are implemented within the framework of economic legislation. In this way the legal regulation of national economy becomes the most important form of managing socialist economy." See "Social Property and Economic Development," in Carl Wellman, ed., *Equality and Freedom: Past, Present and Future, Archiv für Rechts- und Sozialphilosophie* (Wiesbaden: Franz Steiner Verlag, 1977), p. 133.

8. Robert Dahl addresses this question of social property as state property in *A Preface to Economic Democracy* (Berkeley, CA: University of California Press, 1985) in a way similar to mine. He considers both direct state ownership in the case of what he calls "bureaucratic socialism" (referring to the British Labor Party policies of 1944–5) and also "social ownership" as in the Yugoslav case (pp. 142–4).

9. The right to control one's activity is often treated as a property right and as one that is alienable. That is to say, one may regard it as a commodity that one may sell or lease at a time-rate, that is, a wage. On my view, this right may be regarded as a property right in the sense that one's activity is one's own or belongs to one, but it would not be alienable property, since such alienation would entail control of one's activity by others, or domination, and thus is normatively excluded on the principles I have advanced. .

10. C.B. Macpherson, "A Political Theory of Property," in *Democratic Theory: Essays in Retrieval* (New York: Oxford University Press, 1973), p. 136.

11. Ibid., p. 137.

12. C.B. Macpherson, "On the Concept of Property," in Carl Wellman, ed., *Equality and Freedom: Past, Present and Future*, p. 84.

13. C.B. Macpherson, "A Political Theory of Property," p. 140.

14. It should be noted that in his book *The Life and Times of Liberal Democracy* (Oxford: Oxford University Press, 1977), Macpherson places considerably greater emphasis on participatory democracy, though not yet on workers' self-management.

15. Robert Dahl, *A Preface to Economic Democracy*, p. 145.

CHAPTER 7

1. Maurice Cranston, *What Are Human Rights?* (London: The Bodley Head, 1973), and "Human Rights, Real and Sup-

posed," in R.R. Raphael, ed., *Political Theory and the Rights of Man* (Bloomington: Indiana University Press, 1967); R.S. Downie, *Roles and Values* (London: Methuen).

2. Alan Gewirth, "The Basis and Content of Human Rights," in J. Roland Pennock and John W. Chapman, eds., *Human Rights*, Nomos XXIII (New York and London: New York University Press, 1981); Richard Wasserstrom, "Rights, Human Rights and Racial Discrimination," *The Journal of Philosophy*, Vol. LXI (October 29, 1964), pp. 628–41.

3. Henry Shue, *Basic Rights* (Princeton: Princeton University Press, 1980); Raymond Plant, Harry Lesser, and Peter Taylor-Gooby, *Political Philosophy and Social Welfare* (London: Routledge & Kegan Paul, 1980).

4. Cranston, *What Are Human Rights?*, p. 27.

5. Plant, Lesser, and Taylor-Gooby, *Political Philosophy and Social Welfare*, p. 76.

6. Shue, *Basic Rights*, pp. 37–8.

7. Susan Moller Okin, "Liberty and Welfare: Some Issues in Human Rights Theory," in Pennock and Chapman, eds., *Human Rights*.

8. Stanley Hoffman, *Duties Beyond Borders* (Syracuse: Syracuse University Press, 1981), p. 103.

9. Shue, *Basic Rights*, p. 19.

10. Ibid., p. 18.

11. Gewirth, "The Basis and Content of Human Rights"; Shue, *Basic Rights*, chapter 1; Plant, Lesser, and Taylor-Gooby, *Political Philosophy and Social Welfare*, esp. chapters 3 and 4.

12. Robert Nozick, *Anarchy, State, and Utopia* (New York: Basic Books, 1974), pp. 30–3, 167–74, 228–35.

13. John Charvet, "A Critique of Human Rights," in Pennock and Chapman, eds., *Human Rights*, p. 40.

CHAPTER 8

1. Cf. Carole Pateman, *The Problem of Political Obligation: A Critical Analysis of Liberal Theory* (Chichester: John Wiley & Sons, 1979); Robert Paul Wolff, *In Defense of Anarchism* (New York: Harper & Row, 1970); Richard Flathman, *The Practice of Political Authority: Authority and the Authoritative* (Chicago: University of Chicago Press, 1980), chapter 5, 10, and 13.

2. Wolff, pp. 19, 40, 71.
3. Talcott Parsons, "On the Concept of Political Power," in *Political Power*, ed. by Roderick Bell, David Edwards, and R. Harrison Wagner (New York: Free Press, 1969), pp. 263ff., cited in Flathman, p. 126.
4. Robert Dahl and Charles Lindblom, *Politics, Economics and Welfare* (New York: Harper & Brothers, 1953), p. 106.
5. Flathman, p. 35.
6. R. Friedman, "On the Concept of Authority in Political Philosophy," in *Concepts in Social and Political Philosophy*, ed. by Richard Flathman (New York: Macmillan, 1973), p. 126, cited in Flathman, *The Practice of Political Authority*, p. 35.
7. Cf. Flathman, *The Practice of Political Authority*, chapter 5.
8. Joseph Raz, "On Legitimate Authority," in *Philosophical Law*, ed. by Richard Bronaugh (Westport, Conn.: Greenwood Press, 1978), p. 27, cited in Flathman, *The Practice of Political Authority*, p. 110.
9. Cf. Pateman, chapter 5; A. John Simmons, *Moral Principles and Political Obligation* (Princeton: Princeton University Press, 1979), chapters 3 and 4; S.I. Benn and R.S. Peters, *The Principles of Political Thought* (New York: Free Press, 1965), pp. 385–91.
10. Thomas Hobbes, *Leviathan*, ed. by M. Oakeshott (New York: Collier, 1962), chapter 16, p. 125.
11. Cf. Hannah Pitkin's critical discussion of this point in Hobbes in *The Concept of Representation* (Berkeley: University of California Press, 1967), chapter 2.
12. Pateman, chapters 7 and 8.
13. Several theorists have noted that rules have to be recognized as a condition for following them. Cf., for example, Flathman, *The Practice of Political Authority*, chapters 5 and 6; Peter Winch, "Authority," in *Political Philosophy*, ed. by A. Quinton (Oxford: Oxford University Press, 1967), pp. 97–111.
14. Cf. the discussion of the mandate-independence issue in Pitkin, chapter 7.
15. Wolff, p. 3.
16. Ibid., p. 14.
17. Ibid., p. 9.
18. Ibid., p. 40.
19. Ibid., p. 19.
20. Ibid., p. 88. In response to Jeffrey H. Reiman's criticism, Wolff

says, in regard to what he had called "the special case of unanimous direct democracy," that, "It may be that men are bound by the collective commitments they make, but such commitments do not create the sort of political authority I was attempting to analyze. I stand corrected."

21. Cf. J. H. Reiman, *In Defense of Political Philosophy* (New York: Harper & Row, 1972); S. Bates, "Authority and Autonomy," *Journal of Philosophy*, Vol. 69 (1972), pp. 175–9; M. S. Pritchard, "Wolff's Anarchism," *Journal of Value Inquiry*, Vol. 7 (1973), pp. 296–302.

22. Cf. J. H. Reiman, *In Defense of Political Philosophy*.

23. Cf. Ronald Dworkin, "Review of R. P. Wolff: *In Defense of Anarchism*," *Journal of Philosophy*, Vol. 68 (1971), pp. 561–7, and *Taking Rights Seriously* (Cambridge, MA: Harvard University Press, 1978).

24. Flathman, *The Practice of Political Authority*, p. 89.

25. Keith Graham, "Democracy and the Autonomous Moral Agent," in Keith Graham, ed., *Contemporary Political Philosophy: Radical Studies* (Cambridge: Cambridge University Press, 1982), pp. 113–37.

26. Ibid., p. 129.

27. Ibid., p. 133.

28. Wolff, p. 23.

29. Ibid.

30. Ibid., p. 88. Cf. footnote 20 above.

31. Ibid., p. 8.

32. Graham, "Democracy and the Autonomous Agent," p. 132.

33. I am not considering here Rawls's view of a "natural duty of justice" (*A Theory of Justice*, Cambridge, MA: Harvard University Press, 1971, chapter VI), because I am taking up only those views that see political authority as based on obligation, which I take to involve a voluntary action in which it is freely assumed. On the other hand, I do consider Rawls's account of political obligation under the heading of the fair play argument. On this distinction in Rawls's conception, see Simmons, *Moral Principles and Political Obligation*, chapter VI.

34. Cf. Pateman, chapter 6.

35. Cf. Simmons, pp. 185–7.

36. Pateman, pp. 83–91.

37. Ibid., pp. 122–3.

38. Simmons, chapter V.

39. Ibid., p. 192.
40. Pateman, chapters 7 and 8.

CHAPTER 9

1. Similar proposals for workers' self-management have been made by a number of other authors, among them Mihailo Marković, "New Legal Relations for New Social Institutions," in *Proceedings of the IVR World Congress, 1975*, and "Philosophical Foundations of the Idea of Self-Management," in Branko Horvat et al., ed., *Self-Managing Socialism* (New York: International Arts and Sciences Press, 1975), pp. 327–50; Carole Pateman, *Participation and Democratic Theory* (Cambridge, England: Cambridge University Press, 1970); Radoslav Selucký, *Marxism, Socialism, Freedom* (New York, 1979); David Schweickart, *Capitalism or Worker Control? An Ethical and Economic Appraisal* (New York: Praeger Publishers, 1980); Jaroslav Vanek, *The General Theory of Labor-Managed Market Economies* (Ithaca, NY: Cornell University Press, 1977); Pierre Rosanvallon, *L'age de l'autogestion?* (Paris: Editions du Seuil, 1978); Robert Dahl, *A Preface to Economic Democracy* (Berkeley, CA: University of California Press, 1985).
   My proposal is similar in many respects to these, yet it differs from each of them in important ways. Thus, for example, although my proposal shares with Marković's an emphasis on participatory democracy in all spheres of social life, it differs from his (as noted later in the text) in keeping the political and economic spheres separate from each other. Again, my proposal has in common with Selucký's an emphasis on the role of the market, on political democracy, and on the importance of the protection of individual rights. Yet my view, while holding that the market is important, does not regard it as the most decisive factor, as his does. Moreover, unlike him, I stress the need for the further democratization of the political sphere in addition to the economic sphere. Although my proposals are similar to Schweickart's in basic features of worker control, market, and democracy, my differences with him concern what seems to me his overextension of the planning function of the state, inas-

much as on his view it controls virtually all new investment, and dispenses it though a general plan. Furthermore, my proposal differs from views like those of Marković and Schweickart in that it regards the social means of production as the common property of the workers in each firm rather than as belonging to society as a whole. However, some large-scale social means of production, for example, utilities and railroads, and some natural resources should be owned by society as a whole.

2. If social class is defined in the traditional Marxist way in terms of relations to the means of production, and if on this model all participants in economic life are members of worker self-managed and -owned firms, then effectively this would seem to be a classless society. If alternative definitions of social class are adopted, or alternative analyses of social stratification are made, then differences, for example, between those who work and those who do not or between highly skilled or semiskilled, or differences in merit or talent, may figure as characteristic social differences. But we may suppose that whatever difficulties such social differences may present, they can be mitigated by the egalitarian and democratic structure proposed here.

3. On the import and usefulness of the market, cf. Selucký, esp. chapter 5; Schweickart, pp. 50–1, 216–18.

4. This would provide an answer to objections which some Marxists have posed to the introduction (or reintroduction) of a market under any circumstances (even under socialism), objections ostensibly based on Marx's political economy. These objections seem to me to be based on a misunderstanding of Marx's critique. Marx's argument is not that the market as such, or more generally, any system of exchange as such, necessarily leads to exploitation and class domination. Rather, his argument is that the way use-value and exchange-value combine in the commodity form "mystifies" the capitalist system of economic exploitation precisely because there is a separation between ownership of the means of production and the producers of exchange-values (and a fortiori of use values) in that system. Thus, for Marx, exploitation arises in the sphere of production rather than exchange and is merely masked in the system of capitalist exchange, where, as Marx says, equivalents are exchanged for equivalents in what to all appearances is a fair trade.

However, it may be further objected along these lines that the market among self-managed firms would retain the commodification of social relations that Marx criticized in capitalist society, namely, the transformation of relations among people into relations among things or commodities. Here too, however, it may be seen that the fundamental forms of such "mystification" or of "commodity fetishism" do not persist in a market economy with worker self-managed firms. For here, there are no relations of exploitation between capitalists and workers to be masked by a system of market exchange in which both appear to be equals exchanging equivalent values, and in which the commodity labor-power is exchanged for a money-wage. For in this case, the producers are themselves the owners and the "employers" of their own labor and control the distribution of the revenue from the sale of their products. In addition, the relation between the producers and their products – namely, as the products of their own activity, which "belongs to them," as Marx puts it – is not masked by commodification since the producers in worker-owned and -managed firms determine the production of, and remain in control of the disposition of, the products of their labor. At the same time, since there is democratic control in the joint decision-making in the firm, the relations of the workers among themselves could be expected to be less alienated and more cooperative. In these ways, the classical forms of alienation that Marx described (both in his early writings and in his discussion of "the fetishism of commodities" in *Capital*) do not apply to the proposed model of workers' self-management.

Finally, there may be a related objection, again ostensibly based on Marx's political economy, to the effect that a market even of worker self-managed firms would nevertheless preserve the commodity form of labor. On Marx's analysis of capitalism, since the market must involve an exchange of goods in terms of some abstract measure of value by which they may be compared, and since this measure is the abstact labor or "socially necessary labor time" embodied in the products, therefore if a capitalist firm is to stay in business and show a profit, then the cost of the reproduction of such labor power or ability to work, namely, the wage, must always be less than the value of the commodity produced by such labor.

This difference, or "surplus value," is, according to Marx, the sole source of profits in a capitalist economy and also defines the exploitation of workers, as the appropriation of this surplus value by their employers. The objection to a market even among worker self-managed firms might therefore be that the commodity form of labor would continue as a necessary feature of any market economy – capitalist or other – and thus would facilitate the extraction of surplus value under the cover of a "fair wage," that is, a wage that is equivalent in value to the cost of reproducing the labor power. This, the objection continues, would open up all the same opportunities for profit making and for exploitation that exist in a capitalist market. However, this objection does not apply to the model I have proposed. For there is no commodity form of labor in an economy in which labor power is neither bought nor sold, that is, where there is no market between capital and labor. In effect, the model I propose is not, strictly speaking, a model of wage labor at all, for the "wages" that the workers receive are in fact their share of the net revenue of the firm, after the deduction of nonlabor costs from the total income of the firm.

5. A similar point is made by Selucký, p. 182.

6. The determination of who would count as "members" of one or another cultural institution is not always simple, and therefore the question of such membership for purposes of participation would have to be approached keeping the variety of forms and purposes of such institutions in mind. We might say that "membership" here is an open concept, the exact scope of which could vary from one social or cultural institution to another.

7. See Marković, "Philosophical Foundations of the Idea of Self-Management," in Horvat, ed., *Self-Managing Socialism,* and "New Forms of Democracy in Socialism," *Praxis International,* Vol. I, no. 1 (April, 1981).

CHAPTER 10

1. See Herbert Marcuse, *One-Dimensional Man* (Boston: Beacon Press, 1964); Jacques Ellul, *The Technological Society* (New York:

Knopf, 1964); Langdon Winner, *Autonomous Technology* (Cambridge, MA: The MIT Press, 1977); Bernard Gendron, *Technology and the Human Condition* (New York: St. Martin's Press, 1977); Ian G. Barbour, *Technology, Environment, and Human Values* (New York: Praeger, 1980).

2. Cf. Gendron, chapter 9.
3. Quality control may also be analyzed as an aspect of technical control in the case where the exercise of technical skill or judgment is applied in the operation of technology that itself produces technology, for example, machine tools.

CHAPTER 11

1. C.B. Macpherson, *Democratic Theory: Essays in Retrieval* (Oxford: Oxford University Press, 1973), pp. 3–4.
2. Ibid., p. 5.
3. R.G. Collingwood, *Principles of Art* (Oxford: Oxford University Press, 1938).
4. Cf. Marcel Mauss, *The Gift*, tr. by I. Cunnison (Glencoe, IL: Free Press, 1954); Bronislaw Malinowski, *Crime and Custom in Savage Society* (London: Routledge & Kegan Paul, 1961); George Simmel, "Superordination and Subordination," in *The Sociology of George Simmel*, ed. and tr. by Kurt Wolff (Glencoe, IL: Free Press, 1950), Part III, pp. 181–303; Alfred Schutz, *On Phenomenology and Social Relations*, ed. by H.R. Wagner (Chicago: University of Chicago Press, 1970); Peter Blau, *Exchange and Power in Social Life* (New York: J. Wiley and Sons, 1964); George C. Homans, *Social Behavior: Its Elementary Forms* (New York: Harcourt, Brace and World, 1961). Also see my discussion of these views in "Beyond Causality in the Social Sciences: Reciprocity as a Model of Non-Exploitative Social Relations," in R.S. Cohen and M.W. Wartofsky, eds., *Epistemology, Methodology, and the Social Sciences* (Boston and Dordrecht: D. Reidel, 1983), pp. 53–88.
5. Cf. C. Gould, "The Woman Question: Philosophy of Liberation and the Liberation of Philosophy," in C. Gould and M.W. Wartofsky, eds., *Women and Philosophy: Toward a Theory of Liberation* (New York: G.P. Putnam's Sons, 1976), pp. 5–44.
6. Cf. C. Gould, "Private Rights and Public Virtues: Women, the

Family and Democracy," in C. Gould, ed., *Beyond Domination: New Perspectives on Women and Philosophy* (Totowa, NJ: Rowman and Allanheld, 1984), pp. 15–18.

7. See, for example, Joseph A. Schumpeter, *Capitalism, Socialism and Democracy* (London: George Allen & Unwin, 1943); Robert A. Dahl, *Preface to Democratic Theory* (Chicago: University of Chicago Press, 1956).

8. See the studies cited in C. Pateman, *Participation and Democratic Theory* (Cambridge: Cambridge University Press, 1970), chapter III.

9. Ibid.

10. J.S. Mill, *Considerations on Representative Government*, 3rd ed. (London, 1865), pp. 58–69.

11. Lawrence Kohlberg, "From Is to Ought: How to Commit the Naturalistic Fallacy and Get Away with It in the Study of Moral Development," in Theodore Mischel, ed., *Cognitive Development and Epistemology* (New York: Academic Press, 1971), pp. 151–235, and "Moral Stages and Moralization: The Cognitive Developmental Approach," in Thomas Lickona, ed., *Moral Development and Behavior: Research and Social Issues* (New York: Holt, Rinehart and Winston, 1976), pp. 31–53. In his more recent work, Kohlberg has somewhat revised the schema of stages by including stage six as a substage of stage five.

12. Carol Gilligan, *In a Different Voice* (Cambridge, MA: Harvard University Press, 1982); Owen Flanagan, Jr., "Virtue, Sex, and Gender: Some Philosophical Reflections on the Moral Psychology Debate," *Ethics*, Vol. 92, no. 3 (April, 1982), pp. 499–512.

13. John Rawls, *A Theory of Justice* (Cambridge, MA: Harvard University Press, 1971), p. 494.

14. See also the discussion in my "Beyond Causality in the Social Sciences: Reciprocity as a Model of Non-Exploitative Social Relations," in R.S. Cohen and M.W. Wartofsky, eds., *Epistemology, Methodology, and the Social Sciences* (Boston and Dordrecht: D. Reidel, 1983).

15. Jürgen Habermas, "Moral Development and Ego Identity," in *Communication and the Evolution of Society*, tr. by Thomas McCarthy (Boston: Beacon Press, 1979).

16. Ibid., p. 90.

17. See "An Interview with Jürgen Habermas," by Angelo Bolaffi, *Telos*, no. 39 (Spring, 1979), p. 169.

CHAPTER 12

1. I am here following the terminology used by Charles Beitz to describe this position. Cf. his *Political Theory and International Relations* (Princeton, NJ: Princeton University Press, 1979), part two.

2. Michael Walzer, *Just and Unjust Wars* (New York: Basic Books, 1977), and "The Moral Standing of States: A Response to Four Critics," *Philosophy and Public Affairs*, Vol. 9 no. 3 (1980), pp. 209–29. See also his "The Distribution of Membership," in Peter Brown and Henry Shue, eds., *Boundaries: National Autonomy and Its Limits* (Totawa, NJ: Rowman and Littlefield, 1981).

3. Beitz, particularly part three; Henry Shue, *Basic Rights: Subsistence, Affluence and U.S. Foreign Policy* (Princeton, NJ: Princeton University Press, 1980); Alan Goldman, "The Moral Significance of National Boundaries," in Peter French, Theodore Vehling Jr., and Howard Wettstein, eds., *Midwest Studies in Philosophy VII 1982: Social and Political Philosophy* (Minneapolis, MN: University of Minnesota Press, 1982), pp. 437–54; David Luban, "Just War and Human Rights," *Philosophy and Public Affairs*, Vol. 9, no. 2 (1980), pp. 106–181; Richard Wasserstrom, "Review of *Just and Unjust Wars*," *Harvard Law Review*, Vol. 92 (December 1978), pp. 536–45. Also relevant here is Gerald Doppelt, "Walzer's Theory of Morality in International Relations," *Philosophy and Public Affairs*, Vol. 8, no. 1 (1978), pp. 3–26. See also Judith Lichtenberg, "National Boundaries and Moral Boundaries: A Cosmopolitan View," in Brown and Shue, eds., *Boundaries*.

4. Doppelt's position should not be taken as a paradigm of the cosmopolitan, since he, like Walzer, places significant emphasis on the principle of nationhood (albeit not of state sovereignty) as the basis for self-determination.

5. Luban, pp. 174–6.

6. Goldman, p. 442; Doppelt, pp. 15–16.

7. Wasserstrom, p. 542.

8. Beitz, pp. 136–43.

9. Ibid., pp. 104–5.

10. See for example Luban.

11. A similar point is made by Goldman, p. 444.

12. This criticism seems to apply to the arguments of Luban, Wasserstrom, Doppelt, and Goldman.

13. Ronald Dworkin, in *Taking Rights Seriously* (Cambridge, MA: Harvard University Press, 1978), elaborates an argument in support of this view that there are inviolable rights of the individual against the government. He argues that no appeal to social utility or general benefit can justify an infringement of such individual rights, and that only conflicting rights of other individuals can weigh in the balance here. He makes the distinction between "majority rights" and "rights against majorities," but holds that the rights of majorities are not of the sort that can compete with the rights of individuals against the government. See chapter 7, and especially p. 194.

14. Thomas Buergerthal, "Domestic Jurisdiction, Intervention, and Human Rights: The International Law Perspective," in Peter G. Brown and Douglas McLean, eds., *Human Rights and U.S. Foreign Policy* (Lexington, MA: Lexington Books, 1979), pp. 111–20.

15. The conflicting interpretations are discussed in Louis Henkin, "International Human Rights as 'Rights'," in J. Roland Pennock and John W. Chapman, eds., *Human Rights*, New York: New York University Press, 1981.

16. John Stuart Mill, "A Few Words on Non-Intervention" in *Dissertations and Discussions*, New York, 1873, Volume III, pp. 238–63, cited in Walzer, *Just and Unjust Wars*, pp. 87–8. However, whereas Mill suggests that there is no right to intervene even where a people fails to free itself and is subject to bloody reprisal, I would hold that intervention might be justified where such reprisals take the form of the massacre of large numbers of people.

17. Robert Nozick, *Anarchy, State, and Utopia* (New York: Basic Books, 1974), chapter 7.

18. Beitz; cf. also Lichtenberg.

19. Goldman, p. 452.

Index

Index

Index

Merleau-Ponty, Maurice, 46, 334 *n*15
Mill, James, 92, 286
Mill, John Stuart, 92, 119, 284, 286, 297, 321, 329 *n*2, 335 *n*23, 355 *n*16
Miller, David, 333 *n*11
Mischel, Theodore, 353 *n*11
Moore, G. E., 110, 117
mutuality, 77, 124

natural law theory, 115–16, 117, 127
natural rights theory, 116–17, 127
Nielsen, Kai, 32
Nietzsche, Friedrich, 118
Nove, Alec, 331 *n*20
Nozick, Robert, 8, 12–13, 69, 134, 138–142, 156, 157, 193, 205, 339 *n*2, 355 *n*17

Oakeshott, Michael, 218
Okin, Susan Moller, 195
ontology, social, 19, 26–7, 91, 104–13, 127–32
 see also individualism, abstract; individuals; pluralism, ontology of; relations; socialism, holistic
Owen, Robert, 284

Parsons, Talcott, 218
participation, 20, 21, 81, 84–6, 87–8, 215
parties, political, 97
Pateman, Carole, 8, 18, 20–1, 32, 191, 222, 240–2, 284, 297, 330 *n*7, 339 *n*3, 345 *n*1, 348 *n*1, 352 *n*8
paternalism, 59
Pennock, J. Roland, 92, 336 *n*30, 345 *n*2,13, 355 *n*15
Peters, R. S., 35, 46, 92, 218, 332 *n*6,7, 346 *n*9
Piaget, Jean, 300

Pitkin, Hannah, 346 *n*11
planning, 3, 146, 253–4
 centralized, 6–7, 13–14, 101
Plant, Raymond, 190, 194–5, 202
pluralism, 8–10, 92, 97–100
 cultural, 324
 ontology of, 98–100
political obligation, 228, 239–46
 reflexive, 244
 see also authority, political; autonomy
Praxis philosophers, 14–16, 259, 330 *n*11
Pritchard, M. S., 347 *n*21
private sphere, 82, 89
production, 144–5
 in Nozick, 138–40
 in Rawls, 137–8
property, 133, 171
 individual, 177, 178, 343 *n*1
 labor theory of, 173, 176–7
 legal conception of, 172, 188–9
 personal, 181–3
 private, 4
 social, 14, 172, 177–8, 181–4, 187
 social ontology and, 172, 176, 177–8
 state, 187
purposes (or aims), 45–9, 56–7, 72, 107, 109, 112
 common, 50, 71, 74, 78, 95, 107–8, 180, 324

Quinton, A., 346 *n*13

Raphael, R. R., 345 *n*1
Rawls, John, 8, 10–11, 101, 115, 119–24, 126, 127, 129, 134–8, 142, 156, 158–9, 290, 299, 302–4, 305, 306, 330 *n*9, 335 *n*28, 338 *n*10, 339 *n*1,4, 340 *n*9, 347 *n*33
Raz, Joseph, 219
reasons for action, 45–6

Index